It Was a Rough Road!

. . . and other

Arizona Game & Fish Stories

for Cheri Klaut
Have some fun reading
Best Wishes
John N Carr

collected by

John N. Carr

Front Cover Photo: *Wildlife Managers Art Queenan and Tom Taylor used some poor "mud judgement" in the 1960s when traveling in the Los Buros area north of McNary. Lucky for them a pulpwood cutter and his one-ton Clydesdale horse pulled them out of the mud! It was a rough road for these two Wildlife Managers! (Photo by Tom Taylor, from September 1968 Quail Calls.)*

Back Cover Photo: *A group of Game and Fish and U. S. Forest Service employees telling stories in camp. They are at Holder Cabin on the Mogollon Rim getting ready for elk surveys. From left to right is the Director, John Hall, standing; with George Assby, Phil Cosper, and two unidentified Forest Service employees. (Photo from an old Game and Fish Department Federal Aid report dated 1957.)*

It Was a Rough Road! — and other Arizona Game & Fish Stories
collected by John N. Carr.
p. cm.
Includes bibliographical references.

ISBN 0-9643307-0-9: $10.00

1. Wildlife management — Arizona — Anecdotes. 2. Wildlife management — Arizona — Humor. I. Carr, John N.

SK369.I83 1994 94-41243
639.9'09791 — dc20 CIP

Printed in the United States of America
Copyright ©1994 by John N. Carr. All rights reserved. This book or any portion thereof, may not be reproduced in any form, except for review purposes, without the written permission of the author.

Information in this book is deemed to be authentic and accurate by author. However, author disclaims any liability incurred in connection with information appearing in this book.

Heart Track Publications
3801 W. Belmont
Phoenix, AZ 85051

Acknowledgements

I want to thank each Arizona Game and Fish Department employee, both past and present, who contributed the stories that made this book possible. It's easy to tell a story, but putting it in writing is something else. I now know how hard it is. Thank you, everyone for your time and trouble. I am sure all who read these stories will appreciate your effort and your willingness to share some of the times you and your friends experienced while with the Department.

I would also like to thank the officers of the Arizona Game and Fish Department Employees Association, the Arizona Game Rangers Association and the Game and Fish Alumni Association for their support in gathering stories and encouraging individuals to contribute.

Thanks to the Arizona Game and Fish Department for their support and for the use of old photographs and file information. A special thanks to Richard Beaudry for providing some old Game and Fish file photographs and to Ron Engle-Wilson for giving me access to four boxes of old Game Management files, the source of the historical stories. These old stories give a clear picture of "how it was" back then. Also thanks to Don Vance, first for keeping the old "Quail Calls" and second for letting me browse through them to look for stories and old photographs.

A special thanks goes to Jim Palmer, a retired game warden from Wisconsin, whose book *Game Wardens verses Poachers, Tickets Still Available* gave me the inspiration to tackle this project. I met Jim through a mutual friend at a horse endurance ride near Silver City, New Mexico. It was there I first heard some of his stories.

Thanks to my daughter, Susan, for the quail art seen throughout this book. And finally, I would like to thank my wife, Sally, and my daughter, Cathleen Cherry, for their time helping edit the writings of this old retired wildlife manager and his many friends.

Introduction

All of us who have worked for Arizona Game and Fish have stories to tell. When two or more of us get together we almost always tell stories about something that happened last week or last year. The best of these stories are told at camps where there are half a dozen folks to listen and respond. I know the written story is not quite the same as the spoken one and there is a difference between telling a great story to friends around a camp fire and when it is "told in writing" and transcribed into a book. The personal feelings and companionship are often lost.

Reading Jim Palmer's book reminded me of many stories I heard during my twenty-eight years with Arizona Game and Fish. I thought if I could gather these stories an entertaining book would be created. I wanted to provide an opportunity to share some of the adventures that happened to game rangers, wildlife managers, biologists and others in the Department. I also wanted to save these stories so some of the "old times" would not be forgotten.

Sending a letter to all retired and present employees, I explained what I wanted to do and asked if they had a story or two they would like to share. I was amazed at the response. Over fifty individuals contributed some great stories. Most are funny. A few are serious.

Unless noted, all the names in this book are real people. If you know any of the individuals mentioned, these stories will be more interesting and fun. Also, if you know anyone who has worked for a wildlife agency or if you hunt or fish you will appreciate these stories. All the stories in this book are based on real events. Some, however, may be enhanced just a little by poor memories or by poetic license of the story teller.

I was also able to browse through old Department records and photographs and from them I created some stories about the past. These old stories, while not as personal as those by individual contributors, indicate how the Department operated and a little about wildlife management in those days.

This book has only a few of the hundreds, maybe thousands of stories about experiences of Department people. I know of wildlife managers kidnapped at gunpoint; of biologists being lost or stranded, spending days alone in the desert or forest; of lives being saved by acts of heroism; of a Department vehicle being disabled by 20 mm cannon fire from an F-16 military jet; of wildlife managers being caught in the middle of a dope bust; of an undercover wildlife officer being invited to the wedding of a poacher's daughter; of a wildlife manager who had to shoot the lock off of his car's trunk to gain access to a jack; and many others. A book could be written just about the buffalo hunts. I also know a few stories that I absolutely and wisely will not print. These, and many other stories are not in this book. Maybe someday, someone will read this book and be inspired to write another chapter about the adventures of Arizona Game and Fish employees. I hope so.

For me, this project has been rewarding. Many retired friends I had not heard from for years responded with stories and personal notes. Some contacted me by phone to tell a story and we had nice visits. I visited a few old friends at their homes and heard their stories over a cup of coffee. I spent more time with this book than I thought I would, but it has been fun. I hope you enjoy reading these stories as I did.

Dedication

This book is dedicated to the following Arizona Game and Fish employees who lost their lives while performing their jobs:

Wildlife Manager Estevan O. Escobedo, 1994 helicopter crash

Wildlife Manager Allen Severson, 1980 helicopter crash

Wildlife Technician and Pilot Ross Moores, 1949 airplane crash

Wildlife Technician William "Bill" Smith, 1949 airplane crash

Contents

Story Contributors

ANDERSON, WAYNE 1962—1982, Wildlife Manager

BASSETT, BUD 1957—1979, Fisheries Manager, Chief of Fisheries, Chief of Regions

BEAUDRY, RICH 1968 to present, Wildlife Manager, Information Branch Chief

BICKEL, JIM 1967—1983, Airplane Pilot

CARR, JOHN N. 1961—1989, Wildlife Manager, Game Biologist, Planning and Evaluation Branch Supervisor

CARUFEL, LOUIS 1963—1968, River Basin Specialist, Aquatic Biologist

CONNEALLY, JOHN 1983 to present, Live Wildlife Permit Coordinator

COSPER, PHIL 1949—1983, Range Management Technician, Chief of Game Management and Administration, Assistant Director

DAUGHTRY, DAVE 1969 to present, Photographer, AV Specialist, Assistant Director Information & Education

DAY, JERRY 1953—1988, Assistant District Biologist, Research Biologist

DICKENS, GLEN 1977 to present, Wildlife Manager, Habitat Specialist, Funds and Planning Manager

ESSBACH, AL 1965—1982, Warm Water Fisheries Supervisor, Chief of Fisheries

FLEMING, WES 1950—1974, Waterfowl Biologist, Waterfowl Area and Buffalo Ranch Supervisor

GALLIZIOLI, STEVE 1950—1983, Research Biologist, Chief of Research, Chief Wildlife Management Division

HAUGHEY, RUSS 1985 to present, Fisheries Assistant, Wildlife Manager, Habitat Program Manager

HERNBRODE, BOB 1953—1979, Game Ranger, Wildlife Manager, Education Coordinator

HOREJSI, RON 1973 to present, Research Biologist, Wildlife Manager

HURLEY, TRUDY 1957—1976, Secretary Game Division, Secretary for the Director and Commission

KING, RANDY 1964—1989, Systems Comptroller, Finance and Accounting Branch Supervisor

KIRKPATRICK, BOB 1950—1974, Game Ranger, Wildlife Manager

KNIPE, TED 1940—1968, Game Technician, Federal Aid Project Leader, Region VI (Tucson) Supervisor

MCDONALD, HOWARD 1963—1977, Fisheries Assistant, Regional Wildlife Assistant

MONTGOMERY, LINN 1983—1986, Commissioner

NEFF, DON 1958—1985, Research Biologist

O'BRIEN, PAT 1966 to present, Wildlife Manager, Information & Education Specialist, Admin. Specialist for Director

O'CONNER, CHARLYNE 1975—1990, Clerk Typist, Front Counter Clerk in Information & Education

OCKENFELS, RICHARD 1981 to present, Research Assistant, Research Biologist

PACKARD, LEVI 1954—1984, Game Ranger, Region II (Flagstaff) Supervisor

POPPLETON, WARNER 1962—1989, Wildlife Manager, Project Specialist, Funds Coordination Branch Supervisor

POWELL, LAWRENCE E. 1954—1965 Game Biologist, Chief of Game Management

PRATT, HAROLD 1948—1982, Game Ranger, Wildlife Manager

QUEENAN, ART 1962—1985, Wildlife Manager, Fisheries Biologist, Law Enforcement Specialist

REED, MARY 1975—1983, Watercraft Clerk Typist

RILEY, LARRY 1983 to present, Fisheries Biologist, Planner, Wildlife Specialist Supervisor

SCHADLE, DAN 1952—1983, Biologist, Development and Maintenance Branch Supervisor

SCHANTZ, JOY 1970 to present, Information Education Division Secretary, Deputy Director's Secretary

SHAW, HARLEY 1963—1990, Research Biologist

SMITH, RON 1958—1988, Biostatistician, Game Research Supervisor

SORRELLS, CLIFF 1947—1972, Game Ranger, Game Ranger Captain, Chief of Law Enforcement

STOTTS, HENRY 1947—1972, Game Ranger, Ranger at Large

SWANK, WENDELL 1952—1968, Biologist, Chief of Research, Assistant Director, Director

THOMPSON, JACK 1954—1980, Print Shop Manager

VAN SICKLE, HAROLD 1953—1973, Game Ranger, Wildlife Manager

VANCE, DON 1961—1991, Fisheries Assistant, Wildlife Manager, Law Enforcement Specialist, Law Enforcement Branch Supervisor

WEBB, PAUL 1953—1984, Transplant Biologist, Big Game Supervisor, Game Branch Supervisor

WEGGE, JAMES R. 1961 to present, Management Assistant, Research Assistant, Wildlife Manager

WHITHAM, JIM 1968—1991, Wildlife Manager, Regional Law Specialist, Enforcement Coordinator

WOOLSEY, NORM 1957—1986, Wildlife Research Assistant

YATES, VIRGINIA 1952—1978, Administration Division Secretary, Secretary in Director's Office

Deputy Game Warden W. D. Hunt's Report

from the files

The following interesting and informative report of Deputy Game Warden W. D. Hunt was found in the old Game Management files. The report deals with the 1932 deer season in the Chiricahua Mountains. In those days the Commission often hired temporary wardens to patrol hunts. Dr. Hunt was one of the temporary wardens. His report follows:

Douglas, Arizona Nov. 18th, 1932

Report of W. D. Hunt, Deputy Game Warden

I began my duties as deputy warden on October 14, 1932 and served until November 16th, 1932, at the Old Hermitage Cabin in Rucker Canyon. I covered all of the Rucker Canyon territory; John Long, Sand Creek, Brushy Creek, Little Rucker, Rock Creek, Monte Vista, Box Springs and Fern Canyon. I would drive my car as far as possible then walk until about 4 o'clock pm, then return to the cabin where I could check the cars in and out at the gate entering Rucker Canyon.

I would inquire the number that had a license and the number of guns and the number of the auto license. Also examine the cars and wood trucks as they came out. The house is near the gate so I got most every one that came out day or night. They got the idea as they went in that they could not get by with anything going out.

My greatest trouble was people with guns and no license. I sent several women out without licenses and many Mexican and whites also who were wood haulers and would have guns with them. I would have them leave their guns at the house and get them as they went out. My wife looked after the gate mornings when I was out, but there was little going in and out mornings. Mostly evenings and nights.

I did not get my official commission card for two weeks after the season opened and had to get along without it. I sent two license stubs to Phoenix, two to Tucson, two I sent to Bisbee and one I turned in to Mr. Cooper at Douglas and one I asked to turn in to Mr. Lee at Paradise. I am enclosing seven more. There was a total of fifteen bucks that I had a check on. I found four dead does and one fawn. Three dead javelina or wild hogs. One large and two small ones. Two dead cows. One large cow shot through the head twice with different sized guns. She was shot while lying down. The other, a young cow shot in brush. I discovered a female black bear and two small cubs one mile and a half south of our cabin on Little Rucker. I did not bother her as I noticed she was a little peevish. No sign of turkeys was found. One pair of pheasants was located at Box Springs east of the junction about two miles.

The first few days there were thousands of blue back or bandtail pigeons and several hundred roosted just back of our cabin, but when the first heavy frost came they were all gone the next day.

Several people came to the house and reported that a large lion was seen up near Chiricahua Peak. I went up to see him and found his tracks and many signs of him, but did not see him. He had scared or frightened all the deer and cattle also that they left the north side and crossed the Creek to the south.

I noticed many does and fawns late in the evening going over to the south side.

Several men reported seeing bobcats but I found only one while there. Every time I turned around I could see a woods pussy or skunk and my dog brought some of their sweet scented perfume home with him.

Three people were lost while I was there. An old man from Bisbee was lost all night and I found him at nine next morning. A boy from Lowell, 17 years old, lost all day, I found him at 9:30 that night with a gas lantern. A boy, 14, lost from 4 pm until midnight, was found at a cattle corral near our house.

We had plenty of callers wanting matches, gasoline, coal oil, bread, butter, coffee, sugar, cigarettes and tobacco, ammunition and everything you can think of.

I find many of the wild hogs are moving from the Swisshelm's over to the Chiricahua Mountains.

I am enclosing a statement of one dollar per day and gas and oil bill. I hope to be of much service to the Game Association next year.

Respectfully,

Dr. W. D. Hunt, 1148 9th Street, Douglas, Arizona

Arizona Game Protective Association

THE ELEVENTH ANNUAL CONVENTION

from the files

The old files provide an interesting view of what it was like "in the good old days." How many times have we heard, "Oh, the good old days. I wish I could have been in Arizona when there weren't so many people and lots of game to hunt." The following excerpts come from the report of the eleventh annual convention of the Arizona Game Protective Association, November 18, 1933, at the Santa Rita Hotel in Tucson.

There was a report by Ben Foster of the U. S. Biological Survey in which he said " ... predatory animals kill more game each year than the hunters". He also stated, " that the coyote and the members of the cat family were the greatest enemies to our game life. The funds for Government hunters have been cut off almost completely, ... from $39,000 to $4,800." Remember, this was during the Great Depression.

Another report about hawks and owls was given by Walter P. Taylor, senior biologist for the Biological Investigation Field Office in Tucson. He had a display of 37 different species of hawks and owls found in Arizona. The display was grouped according to their being beneficial or enemies to our game birds. He spoke of the habits of hawks and owls from years of observation and study. He stated that the foremost enemies of our quail, doves, white wings and ducks were the hawks belonging to the darter family. This type of hawk is the hardest one of the whole hawk family for the hunter to kill.

The record shows the ... official report of the Fish and Game Department, by S. L. Lewis, State Game Warden.

Mr. Lewis gave in his report the following data:

YEAR	TOTAL INCOME TO DEPARTMENT
1929	$115,804.27
1930	117,829.02
1931	91,395.65
1932	66,182.25
1933	30,157.13

(This is for the first nine months and Lewis estimated the total for the year to run about $50,000.)

The following figures show the revenue from each County in the

State for the first nine months of 1933:

Maricopa	$10,478.10	Apache	$1,267.05
Yavapai	2,580.45	Pinal	1,200.45
Coconino	3,577.43	Cochise	1,430.42
Pima	2,744.39	Yuma	428.29
Santa Cruz	212.63	Navajo	1,453.97
Graham	797.68	Gila	3,637.34
Greenlee	96.51	Mohave	252.22

The total expenses for the first nine months of 1933 amounted to $31,622.35.

The following figures show an itemized account of the expenditures:

State Warden's Salary	$2,208.40
State Warden's Expenses	783.74
Commission Expenses	1,053.21
Office Employees	2,596.15
Fish Hatcheries and Ponds	8,599.04
Truck Expense	579.12
Office Supplies	123.09
Insurance	194.00
Printing	21.50
Recording	22.65
Express	61.62
Postage	123.85
Miscellaneous	807.40
Care of Buffalo Herd	216.55
Salary and Expense of all Deputy Wardens	$14,232.03

Mr. Lewis stated that the yearly payroll and expenses were about $45,000. This is about 90% of the total expenses. He mentioned the fact that 5% of all income was taken by the State for the General Fund.

Mr. Lewis has a staff of eleven Field Deputies, six in the Fish Department, and three in the office, making a total of twenty on the payroll.

There was a discussion about the Wild Turkey Situation. Mr. J. Q. Thomas of Flagstaff was the leader. It was the opinion of all of the turkey hunters present that if the season for turkey is not closed for a year or more, the birds would become extinct in our state. Roads into the turkey country, predatory animals and cold wet springs were the causes given for the killing off of the birds.

There was another discussion about stocking game in depleted or entirely lacking areas. M. E. Musgrave gave a short address on this subject. He pointed out that the only way to move deer, elk, mountain goats, mountain sheep and antelope is to trap the young and raise them by hand feeding. When old enough to care for themselves, then turn them loose on the depleted ranges.

A discussion was *How can our present Refuge System be improved?* The leader in this discussion was Prof. A. A. Nichols of Tucson. Mr. Nichols has a wall map of the State, showing the existing refuges as they are at this time. He has worked out a system of rotation in opening and closing these refuges from year to year, completing the cycle every seven years.

Should we have a regulated antelope and elk hunt next year? The leader in this discussion was State Game Warden S. L. Lewis. Mr. Lewis said that after surveying the feeding range of these animals that the range is not over stocked, and he is not in favor of having a regulated hunt. It was brought out that possibly in the future it might be wise to kill off a few of the old bull elk each year.

There were nine resolutions passed at this convention and three were rejected. Of those passed, three asked for more law enforcement, one supported more predator control work, one asked for wildlife research, one wanted the turkey season closed and one supported habitat work on the Santa Rita Experimental Station by the CCC. Of the three that were rejected, one wanted every peace officer in the state to enforce game laws, one asked the Forest Service to stop building more roads and one wanted all the regulations printed on the back of the license.

The "good old days" didn't sound all that great, at least as far as hunting was concerned. However, one part sounded OK. Wouldn't it be amazing if the Department was able to print all of today's regulations on the back of your hunting or fishing license!

Dud

by Bud Bassett

Alvin W. "Dud" Yoder was the undisputed senior veteran of the Game and Fish Department when he retired in 1963. Soft spoken and likeable, he knew how to survive in a long vanished Department where your ticket out could come at any time, for any reason, and from any direction. He first got on with the outfit in 1923, and stayed for forty years, which includes the two years he was "loaned out" to New Mexico. His primary work was in fisheries but he also served a couple of short stints as Director, a job he disliked. For many years he was the boss at Pinetop Hatchery, which went defunct in 1954. He also ran Tonto Hatchery for a few years. He was Chief of Fisheries when I worked for him, from 1957 to 1963.

Dud told some great stories of the early years. Here are a few, as I remember them.

"When I went to work for the State everybody was expected to provide for themselves, including a vehicle, gas, equipment and grub. If you wanted a new hatchery you'd better have a shovel. That's the way things were until the mid 1930s. This didn't pose a big problem until 1930, the year the State of Arizona went broke. As a result, nobody got paid a red cent for five months which was a difficulty for folks that didn't have any money to begin with. Nobody quit work though, because, during the Depression there was nothing else to do anyway. In the meantime we got gas, grub and supplies on the cuff because nobody else had any money either, and everyone figured that sooner or later the State would pay us. I wasn't too sure, but eventually the State did. After I paid everybody off I was as broke as before.

"The joy of seeing some coin flowing back my way didn't last forever. Not too long after, I think it was 1932, the Governor decided to reward a number of his cronies with jobs in the game and fish field. He forthwith canned everybody in the Department and replaced them with people more of his own persuasion. Everybody that is, except me. He was scared to fire me because I was the only guy who knew how to hatch and rear trout. The Department Director was fired along with the rest. He was replaced with the Capitol janitor, and that's the truth. He remained in that position until a subsequent administration attempted to put things back together. I was on pins and needles for quite a spell.

"Planting trout in the State's streams in the 1920s and 1930s involved mostly fingerlings and fry. There was no money for expensive stuff like catchable trout programs. Planting could get kind of sticky at times because there were still a lot of pretty salty characters out in the hills. Lots of them weren't real happy with the outsiders that fish planting attracted to their areas. One time, I think it was 1929, I loaded my Model T with milk cans filled with fish and iced them down. I'd decided to try a release at Bear Flat on Tonto Creek. There were a couple of homestead cabins on the way to the creek and those boys were making ends meet by turning out moonshine whiskey. I drove on by and emptied my cans of fish into the creek. I guess I looked a little too official because on the way out I was greeted by two fellows with shotguns who wanted to know just what I was up to. The upshot of it all was that in spite of the fact that I looked pretty suspicious to them, I could continue to drive through to plant fish. They told me, however, I was never to look at their cabins or to stop in the road if I valued my hide. I thought it was a workable arrangement. As it turned out, not reporting them was a great community relation move as well, because those boys were evidently turning out some mighty fine whiskey. I don't know how they treated the anglers, but nobody ever complained. Could be that folks went down to Bear Flat for the whiskey and not the fish."

Dud kept an old long barrel Colt automatic pistol, Model 1903 as I recall, in his dresser drawer at home. He showed it to me when I was over for a visit. He explained the reason for the pistol as follows. "One of my many chores when I was with the hatcheries involved going out to neighboring ranches to buy crowbait horses for use as fish feed. That was before there was any commercial dry feed. I was also expected to shoot those horses and this pistol was one more piece of equipment I needed to buy to do my job. I got real handy with it as I also had to buy my own shells. Each hatchery had a big meat grinder to turn horses into fingerling feed. This practice went on until fairly late. One was still at Page Springs Hatchery long after it was needed."

About 1938, Dud was having trouble with the local politicians who wanted "their" fish planted in "their" pet places. They were not happy with Dud and got together and decided he had to go. They accused Dud of stealing stuff from the Pinetop Hatchery and selling it. There was a pretty lengthy investigation conducted by a court in Phoenix. The outcome showed Dud to be straight as a string and the politicians to be about the same as they are today. Dud showed me the book of minutes of that investigation. Dud was pretty proud of that little book and he kept it in a place of honor behind his desk.

Dud retired as Chief of Fisheries in 1963, after forty years of service with the Department. The State gave him a pension of $87 a month. He crossed over the range about 1970.

My Father, the Poacher

by John Conneally

During the Great Depression, my father worked as a cowhand, first for Bill Spence at the Staple X Ranch near Springerville, and later for the Apache Indian Service at White River. When working for Bill Spence he earned one dollar per day, or as he put it, thirty dollars a day once a month. Dad and Mom followed the cattle from winter to summer range and lived in a variety of line cabins.

One fall Dad killed a legal buck. Having little money, they pretty much lived off what ever happened to be in Dad's rifle sights, but this deer was legal. In those days game meat had to be consumed within a short period of time, presumably because no one owned a refrigerator or freezer. Mother couldn't stand to waste any meat, so she put it up in Mason jars and put them outside in the hay stack. She tells me a hay stack in the winter is almost as good as a fridge.

The local Game Ranger was Al Wilson, but we called him Jackrabbit Al because he wrote the local kids tickets for shooting jackrabbits. Somehow, Jackrabbit Al found out about the venison in the hay stack. He drove miles out of his way to the line shack, seized the meat and arrested Dad.

In court, the judge gave Dad a choice, thirty dollars or thirty days in the county jail. Mom argued with him right there in the court, and told Dad he could not go to jail for a month. Dad told Mom to hush, knowing that the county didn't have any money and couldn't afford to feed him for a month. He chose the jail term and sure enough the judge suspended the sentence immediately.

The next winter, Jackrabbit Al rescued a trapper from freezing and the nearest place to warm him up was the line shack my parents were living in. Dad took in the trapper, but told Al he had to stay outside. Jackrabbit Al stayed outside in the snow waiting for several hours, while my parents warmed up the trapper.

Years later, during World War II, when Dad was in the Pacific, Mom was deer hunting with her two brothers. They were crammed into the cab of a 1936 pickup when they encountered Jackrabbit Al.

While the Game Warden checked the hunting licenses of her two brothers, Mom sat in the truck tapping her fingernails against the stock of her rifle, taunting Al to take his best shot. Jackrabbit Al never moved toward his gun and left Mom and her brothers alone after checking their hunting licenses. Mom never forgave Jackrabbit Al for arresting Dad and she told me she would have killed him if he had moved toward his gun. Now, how could you believe that about your own mother? But that's what she told me.

Beaver Trapping—1939

from the files

While not a real story, this is an interesting account of one Game Ranger's activities many years ago. Al Wilson was a Game Ranger in the 1930s and 40s and worked out of Springerville. He not only enforced the game and fish laws, but on occasion was assigned to trap problem beavers. His report, discovered in the old Game Management records, is a hand written, four page document, written on Department stationary. The letterhead indicates that at the time, George Wrench of Winslow, Lynn Lockhart of Phoenix, and Charles P. Beach of Vail, were the Commissioners. S. L. Lewis was the State Game Warden, and Wm. H. Sawtelle Jr. was the Chief Office Deputy. Following Al Wilson's report is a letter from Ralph Morrow, the Game Ranger from Hilltop in the Chiricahua Mountains, to Mr. Roy Gambrell in Phoenix, the Federal Aid Program Leader.

Springerville

Report of Beaver Trapping and Transplanting - Pittman Robertson Project D - 5

I received telegraphic instructions on December 15, 1939, to start trapping beaver in overpopulated areas on the Little Colorado River in farming areas where said beaver were doing damage.

On Dec. 16, 1939, I started a survey which covered approximately thirty miles of stream on the Little Colorado and Nutrioso: extending from Greer to Richville on the former and Springerville to Nutrioso on the latter.

The survey disclosed that farming land was being submerged in some instances from reservoir filling; ditches at Greer were dammed off; that bank beaver were burrowing back from the stream and digging out dens which were dangerous to grazing stock.

Enclosed pictures, so marked, are of one den, in which a cow caved in and died. The hole measured four to six feet deep, three to seven feet wide and ten feet long.

I also investigated the complaint from Showlow which beaver will have to be trapped as soon as possible now.

Actual trapping was started December 26, 1939, and continued until January 22, 1940, when I received instructions from Mr. Sawtelle to resume my regular duties.

During that time I caught eight beavers. Two were transferred by the Forest Service, three were transferred by Ralph Morrow to the southeastern part of Arizona and three were transferred by Mr. Wrench to the region south of Winslow.

The number of beaver caught is not indicative of the beaver population.

It was necessary to figure out the best way to set the traps for the best results and most of the time the traps would freeze over.

During the cold weather the beaver would not emerge from their dens for upwards to seven days at a time.

Nearly every warm night I would have from two to five of my traps clogged with trash that the beaver had put in them. On two occasions the traps were blocked open by sticks placed directly under the pan. Upon the occasion when my traps were clogged it was necessary to change the position of the set until I made a catch.

Beaver will gentle easily, as those I held a few days would soon loose their fear and eat quantities of willow and aspen bark.

From this survey and previous study I would recommend that any future trapping in this region be made in the fall - October - November and first of December or in the spring during

March and April.

In computing time, please be advised that I worked every day on the project, except one, from December 16, 1939 to January 22, 1940.

Respectfully submitted: Al Wilson

The following is a hand written letter from Ralph Morrow, dated August 28, 1940. It is written on Department stationary and the letterhead indicates that Thomas J. Imler of Phoenix, Charles P. Beach of Vail, and George Wrench of Winslow, are the Commissioners. Wm H. Sawtelle is the State Game Warden, and M. S. Mills is the Office Deputy and Auditor.

Hilltop, Arizona
August 28, 1940
Mr. Roy Gambrell,
Phoenix, Ariz.

Dear Roy,

In answer to your letter of August 24th regarding the beaver.

I got two beaver from Pima. Caught by William Carter. I turned them loose, February 27, 1940, in South Fork Cave Creek, East Chiricahua Mountains. One male and one female.

I also got three beaver from Springerville. Caught by Al Wilson. I turned them loose January 14, 1940, in South Fork Cave Creek, East Chiricahua Mountains. One male and two females.

I hope, Roy, you get this letter, this is the third time I have made a report on these beavers for you, but since you have started sending postage guess I haven't any kick.

With kindest personal regards, I am,

Sincerely,

Ralph Morrow

Two Hearts are Better than One

by W. R. "Bob" Hernbrode

On March 29, 1963, Game Ranger Ralph Morrow retired after 34 years of service with Arizona Game and Fish Department. He later served as a Commissioner, the only employee to do so. Ralph retired as a Wildlife Manager, but to his friends and everyone he met in the field he was a Game Ranger at heart. Most of Ralph's time with the Department was spent in and around the Chiricahua Mountains of southeastern Arizona.

At the farewell banquet given in his honor by the local sportsmen and fellow employees, the following story was told of Ralph's "bloodhound proclivities."

A small mining claim, deep in the Dragoon Mountains in the famous Cochise Stronghold area, became his focus of attention when Ralph learned that two well known poachers were to take over the mining operation. Waiting a few days for the poachers to settle in and practice their craft, Ralph made his plans to visit the mine. He knew every foot of this country, probably as well as the Apache Indians whose stronghold it once was. He knew the men would be living in a rough boarded, tin roofed shack, located in a grove of Mexican blue oaks. The shack was in a deep, narrow canyon near a spring, and not too far from the mine itself. The only approach was up the long canyon from the San Pedro Valley by horseback or on foot. Ralph was a product of the Old West, so there was only one way to travel, by horse. Ralph invited a Game Ranger recruit along to further his education. What the new Ranger learned that day, he clearly remembered as he told this story, even after twenty-five years had passed.

After a dry, dusty ride through the mesquite bosques of the San Pedro River Valley and across the greasewood flats, the two rangers entered the coolness of the sheltered canyon and approached the mine cabin through the oak grove and a few scattered pinon pines. Smoke from a crooked stove pipe, protruding from a boarded up window, indicated the poachers were home and were probably preparing their evening meal.

Tying the horses to nearby trees, Ralph and the recruit walked quietly toward the cabin door. The mutter of voices and an occasional laugh came through the screen door. As Ralph stepped forward and raised his hand to knock, his action was arrested by a loud laughing voice from inside. Ralph listened.

"By God, wouldn't that damned warden Morrow crap if he could see this!" the voice laughed.

The laughter inside was interrupted by a quiet authoritative voice from the doorway. "I'm looking right down your neck, Bill!" Ralph said.

As Ralph stepped through the doorway, the speaker was still frozen, open-mouthed and slackjawed. Both his arms were bent at the elbow, index fingers pointed toward the ceiling — and impaled upon each index finger was a fresh deer heart.

Jay Klaus' Daily Diary—1940

from the files

The following is a three month account of the activities of Jay Klaus, Game Ranger in charge of Wildlife Depredation. While there is no detail account of each day's activity, the entire record is an interesting account of this man's work for the Department. It is a graphic account of how work policies have changed over the years. These typewritten records are from the old 5-D Federal Aid Project, beaver trapping files, located in Game Management Branch.

July, 1940

1. Monday: Contacted Mr. Gambrell at the office, and turned in reports.

2. Tuesday: Made ready to leave on beaver survey and trapping trip to Prescott, Cottonwood, Camp Verde, Long Valley, Greer and Springerville.

3. Wednesday: Left Phoenix at 4:00 am, drove to Prescott via Black Canyon. Contacted Mr. Hover Wood and with him investigated the Old Sullivan Ranch, and found it unsuitable for beaver transplanting. Contacted Mr. Walter D. Armer, Secretary, County Land Use Planning Committee, regarding beaver and muskrat damage on lower Oak Creek, then drove to Clarkdale.

4. Thursday: Contacted Mr. Prospero Bignotti, at his small ranch at the mouth of Oak Creek regarding beaver damage to young willow shoots that he had planted for flood control.

5. Friday: Contacted Mr. A. E. Hancock and Mr. Jack Marston regarding beaver damage (see detailed report). Drove to Camp Verde

and contacted Mr. John W. Boggs regarding beaver damage at mouth of Beaver Creek (see detailed report).

6. Saturday: Left Camp Verde about 7:00 am and drove to Long Valley. Contacted Mr. Bill Brown, District Ranger, and looked over some contemplated locations to plant beaver. Drove to Lakeside via Rim Road.

7. Sunday: Spent the morning with Deputy McGaughey, showing him back roads and places I had found violations when I had worked this territory in 1937. Drove to Springerville via Greer, secured a cabin, stayed all night.

8. Monday: Contacted Deputy Al Wilson and with him looked over the beaver area where he had complaints of damage. Moved into the cabin at the old Squirrel Springs Hatchery.

9. Tuesday: Set two beaver traps. Found that the three traps that had been used at Yuma would not work on account of rust and being hammered out of shape. Worked on traps.

10. Wednesday: Caught one 45 pound female beaver at pond opposite store at Greer. Set other four traps, the three still not working so well. Held the beaver in carrying case at cabin.

11. Thursday: No activity among the beaver. The breaks I had made in the several dams showed no signs of any beaver coming near them or the traps. Found that the three traps above mentioned still would not work so pulled them and gave them another working over.

12. Friday: No activity among beaver. Got the three traps to working and set them. Lots of fisherman tramping up and down over beaver dams and along banks.

13. Saturday: No luck. Reset traps in new locations. Still more fishermen. No beaver activity.

14. Sunday: No luck. No activity among beaver. Almost drained one pond and still no activity. Reset traps.

15. Monday: No luck. Caught some orange peelings and other garbage thrown into stream by fishermen in one trap. Reset traps.

16. Tuesday: No luck. Moved traps and reset.

17. Wednesday: Caught two beaver, one 45 pound male and one 35 pound female. Transplanted these two, together with the one I had been holding, to Hall Creek at the request of George Crosby. Pulled the

other traps and I left for Phoenix about noon as I had broken my upper plate a few days before.

18. Thursday: Spent the morning in Dr. Morrison's office. Contacted Mr. Gambrell after lunch at his office, who instructed me to investigate beaver damage complaint on the Fort McDowell Indian Reservation. Called and made appointment to meet Mr. Willard Whipple the next morning at 9:30.

19. Friday: Contacted Mr. Whipple at Fort McDowell (see detailed report), returned to Phoenix, made out and turned in report to the office. Received my upper plate from Dr. Morrison at 4:00 pm. Packed up and left for Greer at 6:00 pm, arriving here at 1:30 am Saturday.

20. Saturday: Set three traps at Greer. Gave the other three a real working over as they had not been working. Reset them.

21. Sunday: No luck. No activity on the part of the beaver.

22. Monday: No luck. Reset traps below box on Little Colorado, using bait and musk scent. Set one trap at pond below mouth of south fork. Found three old beaver ponds that were used last year now dry and abandoned, the beaver having been trapped entirely out during the winter by cooperative trappers with steel traps. Found no fresh beaver sign between the mouth of south fork and Campbell's ranch. Set two traps in pond quarter mile below intake of big ditch. Set one trap in pond just above crossing of Springerville and St. Johns roads, and two at pond across from store at Greer.

23. Tuesday: Caught three beaver, one 30 pound male in pond below mouth of south fork, and two at Greer, one 45 pound male, one 35 pound female. These I turned loose on Hall Creek above Crosby's ranch. Reset traps in same location.

24. Wednesday: Caught one 31 pound female in pond below mouth of south fork. Caught one 55 pound male at Greer and one 35 pound male

in pond quarter mile below intake of big ditch. Held all three to transport. Reset in same location.

25. Thursday: Caught one 22 pound female in pond below mouth of south fork. This gave me two pair to fill order of Walter Mann at Williams for North Canyon on Kaibab North.

26. Friday: Arose at 5:00 am and ran traps. No luck, as we had a terrific storm during the night; high water. Pulled traps to keep them from washing away. Loaded the two pair of beaver in carrying cases and departed for Williams, arriving there about 4:30 pm. Contacted Mr. Mann who sent the beaver on to the Kaibab North that night.

27. Saturday: Returned to Greer via Long Valley and Rim Road.

28. Sunday: Reset all six traps. All are now working well for the first time.

29. Monday: No activity, still flooded.

30. Tuesday: Caught one 42 pound male in pond below mouth of south fork. Reset traps. Water going down.

31. Wednesday: Caught one 60 pound female at pond quarter mile below intake of big ditch, making one pair of beaver on hand ready to be transplanted. Contacted Mr. Gambrell at Springerville, who accompanied me while I reset four traps at Greer, the other two being set at the pond where I had caught the 60 pound female beaver.

August, 1940

1. Thursday: 74 miles. Caught one 35 pound male beaver at beaver pond below Crosby's Lodge at Greer. No activity at the other three sets. The beaver made no effort to repair the breaks in the several dams. Caught one 30 pound female beaver at beaver pond quarter mile below intake of big ditch, eight miles upstream from Springerville.

2. Friday: 339 miles. Arose 5:00 am, ran traps. No luck. Loaded the two pair of beaver on hand and drove to Long Valley, via Heber and Rim Road, assisted by Fire Guard Lloyd Bliss, released the large pair of beaver three quarter mile above Pinchot Ranger Station, and assisted by Fire Guard Eugene F. Pyle, released the smaller pair of beaver in Barbershop Canyon. Returned to Greer, arriving at 11:30 pm.

3. Saturday: 79 miles. Caught one 40 pound male beaver at beaver pond quarter mile below intake of big ditch. Set two more traps at same location, as no activity at Greer. Contacted Mr. Bob Ewing at

Springerville regarding beaver to be planted on head waters of San Francisco River.

4. Sunday: 48 miles. No activity around traps on ponds at Greer. Pulled all the traps and moved them to ponds quarter mile below intake of big ditch. Contacted Deputies Al Wilson and Mervin Smith who came by my cabin at Greer. Rained all day.

5. Monday: 51 miles. Caught one 55 pound female beaver at pond quarter mile below intake of big ditch. Explored river from this point to Udall's Ranch for new beaver ponds and found that most of the beaver in this locality had been trapped out last winter by the cooperative trapper with steel traps. Found several beaver ponds, the dams torn out and ponds dry.

6. Tuesday: 56 miles. Another storm, high water. No luck. Reset traps. Most were full of debris. Delivered one pair of beaver to Bob Ewing at Springerville to be planted on the head waters of the San Francisco River by the Forest Service.

7. Wednesday: 46 miles. No luck. High water. No activity among beaver reset traps. Got in a hard rain. Wet to the skin.

8. Thursday: 78 miles. No luck. Water going down. No activity among beaver. Reset traps. Took three traps back to Greer.

9. Friday: 54 miles. Caught one 40 pound male beaver at pond quarter mile below intake of big ditch. Moved two traps from Greer to Udall's Ranch about 6 miles above Springerville on Little Colorado River.

10. Saturday: 82 miles. Caught one 38 pound female beaver at beaver pond quarter mile below intake of big ditch. Released one pair beaver on head of East Fork of Little Colorado.

11. Sunday: 117 miles. Caught one 42 pound male beaver at Udall's Ranch. He fought trap so hard he broke the wire anchor, turned the trap over into deep water and was drowned when I arrived. At the suggestion of Mr. Ed Becker of Springerville, I took the dead beaver to Mr. Sherwood at Nutrioso, a taxidermist, to be mounted for the Game Department, charges to be paid by the White Mountain Game Protective Association.

12. Monday: 91 miles. Caught one 33 pound female and one 35 pound male beaver at Harry Udall's ranch. The female had been previously caught in a steel trap losing a right front foot. It had completely healed, however, and the animal was in perfect condition.

13. Tuesday: 52 miles. Accompanied by Vince Butler, I packed one pair

of beaver into the head of South Fork about seven miles above its mouth. Returned to Greer about noon, ran the traps in the afternoon. Caught one 30 pound male beaver. It had also been previously caught in a steel trap losing a left front foot. It had completely healed and the animal was in perfect condition. Noted that the four beaver caught at the Udall ranch were unusually wild, due I suppose, to the fact that Mr. Udall has torn out their dams as fast as they built them; and to extensive trapping with steel traps. Had a bad hail and rain storm leaving about 4 inches of hail stones all over the ground.

14. Wednesday: 275 miles. High water. No activity among beaver. Pulled traps and brought them into Greer. Accompanied by Vince Butler, I released the one male beaver with left front foot off at Crosby's ranch on Hall Creek, about half a mile above where the others were released. Packed up and drove to Phoenix, arriving about 10:00 pm.

15. Thursday: 55 miles. Reported to the office. Had a new set of Firestones put on State owned pickup # 1162.

16. Friday. 60 miles. Reported to the office. Had pickup # 1162 worked on.

17. Saturday. day off

18. Sunday. 282 miles. Left Phoenix for Greer, arriving there 10:30 pm in a bad rain storm.

19. Monday. 139 miles. Arose early, drove to Harry Udall's ranch and found that severe floods had washed out all the beaver dams while I was in Phoenix. No activity. Drove to Springerville, and picked up Al Wilson. Accompanied by him, I drove to Showlow and set two traps on Showlow Creek at Martin Ellsworth ranch. Mr. Ellsworth was to notify me at Springerville Forest Service in the event I caught any beaver. Returned to Greer.

20. Tuesday. 45 miles. Had another hard storm. High water. No activity. No call from Showlow.

21. Wednesday. 68 miles. Had a bad storm. High water. No activity among the beaver. No call from Showlow.

22. Thursday. 74 miles. Had a bigger storm last night. Water higher than ever. Contacted Bob Ewing about beaver on Black River at Diamond Rock Ranch. He was of the opinion that they were not doing any damage other than slowing up the water where Mr. Merrol Gee was trying to speed it up. He admitted the fishing was good, especially at the beginning of the season. I decided as the water was too high to

trap I had better move to the Verde Valley as was planned. Drove to Nutrioso and tried to contact Mr. Sherwood who was going to save the castor from the beaver that had drowned, but found that he was away on vacation. Returned to Greer.

23. Friday. 242 miles. Arose 6:00 am. Ran and pulled traps. Packed up and started for the Verde Valley. Stopped at Showlow and found that they had a terrible storm and flood on the previous Wednesday. Both traps were washed away. I found one, but the other was completely gone. I spent seven hours looking for it with no success. According to Mr. Martin Ellsworth, it was the highest water in 20 years. He promised to continue to look for the trap and notify Al Wilson at Springerville if he found it. I moved twenty feet of debris, eight feet deep trying to find the trap. Finally another storm struck and I was forced to leave for the Verde Valley. I drove in a down-pour all along the river road, arriving in Camp Verde at midnight. Still storming.

24. Saturday. 50 miles. Arose 6:00 am and found the Verde River at flood stage. Contacted Mr. Boggs at the mouth of Beaver Creek, who said the creosote I had told him to use was doing the job, and that the beaver had moved out.

25. Sunday. 21 miles. Another storm. Verde River higher than ever. Contacted Mr. Holder Zan Jero on the OK ditch. He said beaver were not doing any damage at present.

26. Monday. 35 miles. High water. Containing a heavy red silt deposit. No fresh beaver sign.

27. Tuesday. 81 miles. High water. Going down a little, still awfully red. No fresh beaver sign. Accompanied by Weaver Haydon and John W. Boggs, I examined Beaver Creek from one mile above mouth and Verde River three miles below, and found no fresh sign since the flood. Contacted Dave Murdock and Ralph Monroe at their ranches. Returned to Camp Verde, then drove to the Hancock Ranch above mouth of Oak Creek, and accompanied by the Hancock boys, examined the Verde River back of their ranch. No fresh beaver sign. Drove to Prospero Bignotti's ranch and found the same conditions. Returned to Camp Verde. River still muddy.

28. Wednesday. 62 miles. Water still high, but going down. Accompanied by Weaver Haydon examined Verde River from White Bridge at Camp Verde to Bridgeport. At several points I noted tracks of lone beaver emerging from the water while the River was a foot and half higher, crawled some two feet from waters edge and apparently sat

there some time. It was heavily covered with mud and silt, as little piles had formed where the mud and silt had dripped off his body. No real fresh sign.

29. Thursday. 31 miles. Accompanied by Jim Grimes, I set two traps at beaver dens on Marksburry ranch three miles above Camp Verde on Verde River. River still muddy. No activity among beaver.

30. Friday. 31 miles. No activity among beaver on Marksburry ranch. Left traps set. Accompanied by Jess Haydon I examined the head of Wood's ditch five miles above Camp Verde and found fresh sign of a large beaver. Set one trap.

31. Saturday. 83 miles. No activity at Marksburry ranch. Re-baited traps. No activity at head of Wood's ditch. Re-baited trap. Examined the Verde River at the Hancock Ranch one mile above the mouth of Oak Creek. Found fresh beaver sign. Set two traps, baiting with cottonwood and scenting with beaver castor.

September, 1940

1. Sunday. 29 miles. Ran traps, no activity, no fresh sign. Accompanied by Howard Wingfield of Camp Verde, made an intensive examination of the Verde River from the White Bridge at Camp Verde to Bridgeport and estimated 15 beaver inhabited this area. Owing to the scarcity of food, they keep on the move. Noted lots of muskrat and raccoon sign.

2. Monday. 72 miles. Ran traps, no activity, no fresh sign in vicinity of beaver traps. Re-baited with fresh cottonwood limbs and beaver castor. Another bad storm in the evening.

3. Tuesday. 35 miles. High water, traps covered by three feet of water and mud. Dug them out and brought them to Camp Verde.

4. Wednesday. 136 miles. Arose at 6:00 am. Drove to Prescott. Contacted Mr. Walter D. Armer and made arrangements to meet him at Cornville on Lower Oak Creek. Contacted Mr. Armer at 2:00 pm at store at Cornville, and with him made a thorough investigation of the muskrat damage complaint (see detailed report).

5. Thursday. 173 miles. Packed up and left Camp Verde about 1:00 pm. Stopped in Prescott and contacted Mr. Armer, then drove to Phoenix, arriving at 8:30 pm.

6. Friday. 21 miles. Reported to the office. Contacted Mr. K. C. Kartchner. Contacted Roy Gambrell and worked on reports.

7. Saturday. 80 miles. Made survey of Salt River at Lat. 19; found fresh beaver sign. Returned to Phoenix. Was instructed by phone by Roy Gambrell to contact Dave Gorsuch at the Hotel Adams, and to participate in the 1940 quail census survey. Contacted Mr. Gorsuch and Leon Lawson at the Adams Hotel, and mapped out plans for the survey.

8. Sunday. 47 miles. Prepared to leave on quail surveys.

9. Monday. 210 miles. Accompanied by Leon Lawson, I left Phoenix at 6:00 am, surveyed quail in Pinnacle Peak area to Cave Creek, Seven Springs, Lime Creek Game Refuge, Bloody Basin, Horseshoe Ranch to Cordes, then down the Black Canyon Highway to Phoenix, arriving at Phoenix at 10:30 pm.

10. Tuesday. 165 miles. Accompanied by Leon Lawson, left Phoenix at 6:00 am, surveyed quail from Lehi to Granite Reef Dam, Stewart Mountain Dam, Bush Highway to Los Verde Ranger Station and Dose S. Ranch. Returned to Phoenix in time to vote.

11. Wednesday. 258 miles. Accompanied by Leon Lawson, I left Phoenix at 6:00 am. Drove to Wickenberg and started survey along Hassayampa River to Congress Junction, to foot of Yarnell Hill; then to Hillside, Kirkland, Kirkland Junction, to Prescott, Mayer, Sycamore Ranger Station, across the Seneca to Yarba Wash and Cherry Creek-Dewey Road, to Altman and Camp Verde to Clarkdale. Camped near Clarkdale, about 8:30 pm. It rained on us almost all night.

12. Thursday. 116 miles. Accompanied by Leon Lawson, surveyed quail in the Verde Valley and Lower Oak Creek, Clear Creek, Fossil Creek. Camped near Payson.

13. Friday. 194 miles. Accompanied by Leon Lawson, I left Payson at 6:00 am. Surveyed quail down Oxbow Hill, Rye Creek, Tonto Basin, Roosevelt Lake, Apache Trail to Phoenix arriving about 8:30 pm.

14. Saturday. 32 miles. Reported to the office. Received instructions from Roy Gambrell to report to Harry Connolly on Monday morning as the beaver project ends September 15, 1940.

15. Sunday. No miles. Worked on beaver and quail reports.

This is the last entry in the Jay Klaus typed diary report as it was the end of the 5-D Beaver Trapping Project.

The Chocolate Milkshake Boys

by Ted Knipe

It is said, on good authority, that wildlife management came to Arizona in 1939, even though there was a state Game and Fish Department 27 years earlier and wildlife was fairing well, better than today, in some respects.

It was in 1939, that the Game and Fish Commission budgeted matching funds to acquire Arizona's pro-rated share of federal monies derived from an excise tax on firearms and ammunition. This federal money is known as Pittman-Robertson Act (P-R) and is named for the Senators who sponsored the bill, earmarking the funds for wildlife programs, such as research and habitat improvement. (The Dingell-Johnson Act in 1951, a tax on fishing tackle resulted in Federal monies for fisheries) None of these federal monies could be used for law enforcement, not even to increase the game warden's low salaries. This was a new program for Arizona and all the states.

The initial cadre hired by the Department under the P-R Act were a different sort from the politically appointed law enforcement oriented game wardens. With one exception, they were city dudes with a college degree in wildlife management. I was the exception. I was a rube ranch boy without a college degree of any kind. On the other hand, I had six years experience as the sole employee of a University of Arizona deer research project. Perhaps that qualified me to outrank a warden?

That is not to say wardens weren't capable of handling the affairs of wildlife management. Later, the degree was waived and many wardens were assigned wildlife management districts. They acquitted themselves well in all phases of the job.

At first P-R field personnel were officially called Game Technicians. Unofficially, the game wardens (or rabbit sheriffs) referred to them as "the chocolate milkshake boys," because they ordered chocolate milkshakes with their lunch instead of the customary coffee — hot as the front seat in hell and black as Satan's heart.

The milkshake gang was given the monumental task of managing certain species rather than districts, so they worked all parts of the State where "their" species were found or needed attention. Tom Kimball traded fish for quail. Gene McGuire was the antelope and elk expert. Lynn Griner was a waterfowl authority. Javelina, desert mule deer and whitetail deer were my concern. These assignments weren't

In this 1942 photograph taken on the west side of the State Capitol, are the Department's "Chocolate Milkshake Boys", the agencies first biologists. From left to right are, Roy Gambrell, Lee Arnold, O. N. Arrington, Ted Knipe, Tom Kimball, Ken Kartchner and Secretary Dorothy Sparks.
(Photo courtesy of Ted Knipe.)

given indiscriminately. They were based on experience to some extent, but personal preference carried a lot of weight. Norman Jacobson was our pathologist. Norene Pomeroy was the office secretary. Andrew Nichol was the Project Leader. Roy Gambrell was Chief of the Division, but his office was in Phoenix with the big boys. Dr. Ernest Tinkdan came on the crew two months later, but having a Ph.D. in botany, he didn't associate with the peons, and never came to the office. Whitewing dove and mourning dove were his charges. Until the later part of 1941, this Division of the Game and Fish Department was headquartered in a residential building acquired by the University of Arizona. The location was across the street from the northwest end of the football stadium, the address was: Arizona Game and Fish Dept., Federal Aid Division, 627 N. Vine Ave., Tucson, Ariz. Phone 3286.

There was a good reason why the Federal Aid Division was housed on the U of A campus. The University was planning to mass produce the wonder boys of wildlife — and a few girls. Having a division of the Game Department on campus would be an excellent complement to the

University's program.

The noble consideration was soon bushwhacked by a human frailty. Nobody in the Phoenix Office knew what was going on in the Tucson based Division; and in Tucson nobody cared about what was going on in Phoenix. Consequently, Federal Aid was moved to Phoenix, but still housed in a residential building across the street, east of the State Capitol. The staff was increased with the addition of Lee Arnold, a game bird specialist who did an in-depth study on whitewinged doves, and O. N. Arrington, who devoted most of his time to trapping and transplanting antelope, turkeys and Abert squirrels.

Eighteen years later, in 1960, Arizona Game and Fish wildlife administration returned to Tucson when the Department reorganized and created seven regional offices. The new Region VI headquarters were in the new State Building on West Congress Street.

I became the new Supervisor. As my cowboy friend would say, "I hit the trouble trail right down the middle." I traded the Department's best job for one of the worst!

O. N. "Pop" Arrington's Field Notes

Quail Trapping—1942

from the files

At the time these notes were made Mr. Arrington was the trapping and transplant biologist for the Department. He later became Chief of the Game Division and Chief of Special Services Division. He started with the Department in 1940 and retired in the 1960s.

Nov. 30, 1942, 6:30 pm Left for Yuma, clear. 1:30 am camped 6 miles from Yuma.

Dec. 1 Contacted Mr. Amundson at Fish and Wildlife Service office and talked about buying pheasants from Nebraska where an over population exists and releasing them along the Colorado River north of Yuma. Doesn't seem like a good idea, in my opinion, due to many predators. Letter in office. He said he would be glad to release chukars in the Kofa Refuge, if we shipped some for an experiment.

Met Mervin Smith, the Deputy Game Warden in Yuma and picked up quail traps the Yuma Game Protective Association had made several years ago.

Dec. 2 Left with Warden Smith for Roll to contact farmers about trapping depredating quail. Smith says pheasants are in the farmed valley south of Yuma for 30 miles. 45 birds were released in 1926, 10 in 1936. 100 on October 29, 1942, birds came from California, for which 300 quail are to be sent. Smith estimates there are 500 pheasants in the valley now and that they are steadily increasing. He says he can show anyone 30 pheasants any morning or evening in a 5 mile drive. Went to Hollenbeck Ranch and set 7 large traps. Set traps at A. Gibson farm. Went to Todd's for crates and Department traps. Took the 16 birds he had caught. Stayed at Wolley's all night, Smith returned to Yuma.

Dec. 3 Clear. Took 23 birds at Wolley's myself. Ran Pretzer's traps which he had baited the day before, got 5 birds. He has killed off most all his quail reqardless of his strenuous statements that he has many. Set traps at Western Farms and took 20 that evening.

Dec. 4 Slightly cloudy all day. Took quail from traps at Western Farms. A. Gibson took 63 birds from his traps.

Dec. 5 Pretzer had no more quail even though his traps were baited and set. Took his 32 quail. Owe him for 37 total. Left no traps or crates or bands. Has our traps. He refused to band birds. Took quail from Western Farms traps in brush near feed mill and corral, near hay stacks and along field farthest south. Left for Tacna, got permission to trap. Used 6 large traps and the 6 small Department traps. Owe for 25 quail. Ship crates to Welton and notify Yuma GPA. Left A. Gibson, owe for 110 quail. To Dateland, picked up quail. Owe for 173 quail. Left for Phoenix at 5:00 pm. Arrived Phoenix at 10:45. Birds OK.

Dec. 8 Shipped 12 pair Gambel quail to H.A. Prain, Corsecana, Texas. Received 30 birds from W. S. Wolley. All OK.

Dec. 9 Received 60 birds from W. S. Wolley via express. Birds OK.

Dec. 10 Received 90 birds from A. J. Croslin via express. 2 dead. Total birds trapped in Yuma area 839. Owe Pretzer, Gibson, Croslin, Todd and Wolley ten cents for each bird they trapped.

Dec. 11 Clear. To Prescott with Chas Nehuis to release quail. Released 105 birds at Contraris Study Plot. All OK. Released 90 birds at Mullen Tank. All OK. Released 121 birds at E. J. Polley house. All OK. Released 161 birds at Sipes, near barn. All OK. Released 101 at Tonto Ranger Station. All OK. Shipped 24 to Drane and 20 to Lamb. Holding 60 for Raymond Ranch. Arrived back in Phoenix at 1:00 a.m.

O. N. "Pop" Arrington's Field Notes

Chukars & Turkeys—1942

from the files

Nov. 19, 1942 9am. Talked with Mr. Mercer, Mr. Ligon and Mr. Merkle. Agreed to put castro (beaver) in Grahams.

1:30 pm. Left Phoenix for Maricopa to investigate chukars that Father Antonio has raised. In 1938 the Padre and a Mr. Blackburn paid $1.00 each for 100 eggs. 57 hatched and 49 were raised and released. Now, the Padre has reports of birds as far as Casa Grande, 22 miles away and of chukars scattered in every direction. He counted 450 on the roof of a building near the church the other night. Chukars were all over the place, 20 ran from under a mesquite tree when I drove in. They are hard on local gardens. Back to Phoenix at 2:30. At 4:15 left for San Carlos, Tucson, etc. to check turkey trapping areas, antelope release sites, masked bob white lands. Arrived in Globe at 8:30 for the night.

Nov. 20 8:15 am. Left Globe for San Carlos and Point of Pines. Met with San Carlos Supervisor Ernest McCrea and Earl Hobson, Extension Agent, to go look over possible pheasant release sites on the Reservation. There are 9 miles of cultivated land, 5 miles above and 4 miles below the village. Good spots to plant frequently. Recommended release of 30 in one spot near bridge, 2 miles below San Carlos.

Reached Point of Pines at 2:00 pm. Met Walter Williams there. He is a Reservation stockman, stayed with him all night waiting for Barney Borneman who is camped west of Pole Corral in Sawmill Canyon. Williams has lived in the vicinity for 40 years as a cowboy and cattleman and his statements about former wildlife populations are studied carefully and seem very authentic. He told me:

"Prior to the time the Indians had guns wildlife was plentiful. In 1900 antelope were numerous over antelope country extending for miles. By 1904 the last herd had disappeared. Both kinds of deer plentiful even later. The last grizzly under rim in 1908. The last grizzly in mountains north about 1920. The last grizzly Williams saw taken was by a Louisiana sportsman with many prized dogs and a big outfit. Grasses

have disappeared that used to be here. Have seen roundups when you couldn't see across the cows. Before the Indians took over control of grazing land there were 130,000 cattle on the Reservation. The CCC and Double Circle had 100,000, Cross S had 15,000, the Hat had 15,000. Indians now only have 40,000 cattle on the Reservation."

Williams saw 35 turkeys in a bunch at Double Circle Tank, north of road approximately 15 miles west of Point of Pines.

Nov. 21 Clear. Barney Borneman came in about 11 from across mountain. Saw many elk and several bulls around Malay Gap. Saw turkeys, 12 at Summit, 6 at Double Circle Tank, 8 at Ash Creek, and 3 at Pole Corral. Ligon, Barney and I saw an abundance of sign at OO Tank and a place where campers had cleaned one. Barney had 24 coyotes since arriving 20 days prior and a bad eye had prevented him from doing full time work.

Nov. 22 Clear. Returned to San Carlos about 5 pm. Saw Mr. Hobson, Reservation Agent who seems to have authority in most matters, directly under Supervisor McCrea. Ordered material from him to be taken to Barney. Material for turkey traps included: 28 pcs 1x4x16, 1x4x14, 3 sacks of oats, 5 # nails and some old motor oil. Lumber to come from White River, but San Carlos truck will bring it in about 10 days. Hobson very anxious to help. Gave us the oats. I am quite sure they can pay Barney for a couple of months when Ligon said we couldn't keep him out there for 4 or 5 months. Also asked for names of other trappers so they can put them on, 6 or 8 of them. Want some agreement of a minimum catch, but will be reasonable. On to Globe for the night.

Nov. 23 Clear. Left Globe for Tucson via Oracle. Gambel quail along road from Christmas to Oracle, several coveys. Arrived in Tucson, saw Vorhies. Talked with Alex Russell who has a ranch between Cottonwood Springs and the San Pedro River, who substantiates Jim Caldwell and Lumber Company Manager at Willcox that antelope range, or have recently ranged, from Hooker's southeasterly in typical antelope country. Ligon recommends plant here to save the herd. Saw Herbert Browns collection of birds at U of A. Masked bob white collected on mesa east of Baboquivari Mountain in 1887.

Nov. 24 Left Tucson for Arivaca. Met Deputy Game Warden George "Pete" Peterson from Nogales at Kinsleys Ranch Store. A woman working at Kingsleys reported Sal Rhea, foreman of Manning Ranch, with headquarters 5 miles west on Arivaca Road, found a dead antelope and was quite concerned. Rhea was not home but Peterson is to write of antelope Rhea has seen. Turned right and followed road 7 miles - through corral of a ranch house - into Manning range north of rugged Cerro Colorado Mountains and south of Sierrita Mountains. Valley extends into Altar Valley 15 miles west. Excellent antelope range east of Baboquivari Mountains by Altar lowlands, though antelope might cross. Peterson saw 22 antelope on north slope of Cerro Colorados and 2 herds of 3 each on south slope, making a total of 28 this year.

Abundance of coyote sign, 30 skulls and skeletons of trapped animals near road. Trapper Jones had trouble with Gil Ranch about trapping coyotes. Gil saying coyotes ate rabbits and rodents that ruined range. Ligon recommended a trapper in here 4 months prior to antelope kidding time to save herd rather than mix strain with transplant. Camped all night near Boise Arivaca Ranch. Peterson states pheasants reproducing in Nogales area. Of 12 birds left by Lawson at Nelson Brown's, 3 pair were left at Brown's and 3 pair taken to a release point back of Carmen's Store, 2 miles across railroad track on Castenalia Ranch. 2 pair of old still there in September 1942, one had 17 young. At Brown's 2 hens and 3 cocks remain. Brown's is on Washington Camp road.

Nov. 25 Clear. To Ted Clark's ranch to check masked bob white cover. 3.5 miles west of Arivaca. 1.5 miles south of house, cover begins at permanent water and extends thru fenced pastures. This type of cover described below extends with few breaks for a distance for 12 miles down Arivaca Valley. Cover is majority of sacaton with interspersion of pig weed, sunflower, Bermuda, careless weed, poppy and other weeds, with a mesquite border. This is excellent masked bob white quail cover and Peterson states it has been there in this fine condition for 7 years that he knows of. It is used as a horse pasture and is as permanent as any cover we saw. Ligon planned to return to see Clark who was not home. Worked cover but saw no masked quail. Few predator tracks.

Returned to Boise Arivaca Ranch, past it half mile, cut right 1.25 miles to right hand gate and went to Jalisco windmill and new Clifford windmill .75 mile south of Jalisco. This formerly was masked cover but now very thin. Very little sacaton in canyon valley and very dry. Saw 2 peccary sows, many tracks of peccary, coyote, coon and bobcat. This is area where Ligon turned 3 pair of masked loose, but no suitable cover could be found. Returned to Jalisco windmill and went 2.5 miles down canyon (north) to Papalote windmill. Went thru 1.5 miles of excellent masked cover of sacaton and weeds. 1 mile from Jalisco was spot were

Peterson saw masked bob white in 1936. Worked area but saw no birds, though some tracks were thought by Ligon to be masked bob white. Masked may still be in this area. There is an abundance of cover of the proper type, but near windmills cattle have worked it down. Very dry.

Clark's would be more suitable plant because of more permanent water and wider range. Returned to Boise's and went through Arivaca to Sasabe - Tucson road for the night.

Nov. 26 Clear. Peterson left, agreed to meet him at Sonoita if we plant turkeys at Peterson Park near Sunnyside. Or at Nogales for San Rafael Valley antelope plant south of Mowry Wash. Worked wash with Ligon .8 mile south of house on west side of road with scales, 2.5 miles south of cattleguard, 4 miles north of Arivaca cutoff. Benchmark on west side of road, south side of gulley, showing elevation 3441 feet. Very dry, but some weeds and good mesquite. Ligon thinks similar land might be fenced and made into masked cover.

Left Ligon. Recommended: Clark's as best masked cover. Plant turkeys in Huachuca Mountains at Peterson Park northeast of Sunnyside. Plant antelope south of Mowry Wash in north part of San Rafael where Marshall Ashburn knows of location. Plant antelope in R21E,T23S west of Willcox in area know by Russell and Jim Caldwell. Put trapper around Cerro Colorado Mountains for 4 months prior to antelope kidding time. See Mercer to get trappers for San Carlos. Get Barney more pay. Order 2 nets for turkey traps.

Stopped at Anvil Ranch, owned by Manuel King, whom I have known for 12 years. Located 8 miles from Sells Road, .25 miles off Sasabe Road on west. King has been in this location for 57 years, since 1885. He said:

"When I first came to this country grass extended from mountain slope to mountain slope. Here in the valley (from Baboquivari to Sierritas & Cerro Colorado) all the way down. Hay stacks were everywhere in winter time. I raised two crops a year including corn, maize, wheat and other grains. Duck ponds were all over. Sacaton grew in lower parts. There were no trees at all - no mesquites or shrubs - just grass. The mesquite has gradually come in.

"The old stage road ran where the channel now is and it was the road that started it. The people realized it in 1887 and I was one of the first to help have it moved to higher land. The channel grew, however, and drained off all the water instead of it setting as it formerly did and it is the drainage that has ruined the valley, not overgrazing. In 1901 and

1902 dry years and grass wasn't as good as formerly, but farming continued good until 1915 when a very wet year flooded valley badly and the wash ran for over a month cutting it quite deeply. After that we had difficulty farming and the grass decreased more rapidly.

"The last patch of sacaton was 300 acres at Palo Alto in 1915. Duck ponds left in 1916 and 1917. Farming practically stopped in 1915 and 1916. All the mesquite and shrubs have come in since 1900.

"Antelope were in droves up to 200 around Baboquivari from 1885 to 1900, but the Indians shot them. The last herd I remember was in 1900 when I got a fawn they ran on and left. He use to play with the children and knock them over. This herd had about 30 in it and was at the northeast point of Baboquivari. After that I saw small bands and then in groups of 2 or 3. In the summer of 1933 I saw one buck about halfway between point and house. I don't know where he came from or where he went. I have heard that there are a couple in front of Brown's Canyon below Baboquavari, but if there are any they are mighty scarce. I think the Indians will shoot them if you try to plant any.

"Seven or eight years ago I saw the last masked bob white. He was a different quail without the top-knot and not like the blue quail at the base of the mountains. I am sure he was the masked. They used to come up to the water trough in little bunches along with their young, but they have all been gone for 7 or 8 years. I don't think you could possibly bring them back and it would be foolish to fence up any land to try for your grass wouldn't stick. We sow Bermuda and Johnson grass every spring but it usually doesn't do so well."

The operator of the filling station at the Sasabe-Sells junction says an old time deer hunter said he saw some antelope on the west side of the Sierritas about a month ago. He returned the next Sunday to try to locate them but couldn't.

R. C. Locke has bought the old Robles Ranch. Drove to his patch of Johnson grass which can be seen from road junction. He says 500 acres runs down for 2 miles and that whether he gets rain or not drainage always brings up Johnson grass into high stands. It is heavily pastured, however, and leaves little cover in winter and spring.

Locke saw about 15 white wings 2 days ago, 1.5 miles north of the house in mesquite. Insists they weren't doves. Says he saw largest flight of white wings he has seen in years, the latter part of August, along Rillito Creek near the race track northeast of Tucson about 7 miles.

In Tucson all night and then on to Phoenix. On the way to Phoenix stopped at Sacaton and talked with Supervisor A. E. Robinson about chukars on the Maricopa Indian Reservation. He reported some complaints about birds damaging gardens around Maricopa. Has reports of chukars spreading from Maricopa to Hidden Valley, lower end of reservation 6 to 8 miles south of Maricopa and about 11 miles toward Casa Grande. He is interested in experimenting with birds in other areas.

The Willie Hole

by Ted Knipe

When A. A. Nichol made his survey in 1937, to determine the status of desert bighorn sheep in Arizona, he traveled in style. He had a Tucson carpenter rig up a superstructure for his Reo truck that turned out to be just short of being what is known today as a recreational vehicle. It had cubby holes galore for this and that, and a special compartment he called the "Willie Hole." Willie was an Irish setter, Nichol's devoted friend and fellow traveler. The Willie Hole was next to the cab. It had sliding glass panels to the compartment that measured four feet long, three and a half feet high and the same width. Under the compartment was an extra gas tank and a 50 gallon water tank with an outside faucet.

I had the use of this "home on wheels" when I made my 1942 antelope survey in northern Arizona, so my wife and four year old son, Ted Junior, were my traveling companions and the Willie Hole became my sons sleeping and resting quarters. My wife and I slept on the inlaid, canvas covered bed that topped the structure.

I did a lot of mapping during the two month sojourn, including one that showed roads traveled and locations of the 1,544 antelope seen. It was this map that intrigued my son Ted.

The project was an enjoyable, challenging experience in new country, learning the ways and requirements of a wildlife species I knew little about. It ended with an odd and mysterious happening.

I submitted my report before leaving to do my part in winning World War II. Upon returning two years later I was looking for something in the Phoenix Office files and came across a file titled, "Theodore Knipe." It consisted of one page with a note attached declaring, "This is Knipe's entire field notes." The one page was my sons hand drawn "map" done in black crayon, consisting of all sorts of lines and figures, but no words.

Field notes are the private property of the employee, cherished by the writer, useless to anybody else; some are undecipherable.

The mystery is this: hoax or not, how in the world did the crude map my son made on my antelope survey get into the Game and Fish Department files? I left it where I found it, without comment. Maybe the map is still there. Better yet, maybe it has been transferred to the State's Archives in the Capitol building where strange happenings are customary.

The Goose Hunter Lost His Hat

by Levi Packard

George "Pete" Peterson, the Game Ranger from Nogales, told me this story in the 1950s when I was a Game Ranger working out of Tucson. It happened during World War II.

Rube Neill, the Game Ranger from Winslow, and Pete Peterson were working in the Roosevelt Lake area looking for goose hunters. As they patrolled along the shore of the lake, they spotted a lone hunter on a Bermuda grass flat. The two rangers parked the car and walked a couple hundred yards through the mesquite and cactus to check his license and bag. The hunter was a great big man wearing a very large hat and carried an old ten gauge pump shotgun.

When the rangers approached, the hunter became irritated and threw down on them with the shotgun and told them to leave. With the hunter pointing the shotgun at them, the two rangers thought it best to do as he said and they walked back to the car. When they got to the car Rube reached into the back seat and pulled out his big .348 Winchester lever action rifle. He raised it up and shot at the hunter, knocking off his big hat. The hunter immediately dropped his shotgun and threw up his hands.

Pete looked at Rube and said, "Rube, that was one hell of a shot!"

Rube put his rifle down, shrugged his shoulders and said, "No Pete, I missed!"

* * * *

Another story about Rube Neill. At a Game and Fish meeting or training session Rube was in charge. In the morning, a new, young Game Ranger came up to Rube and said, "Rube, my wife is pregnant and I have to go home."

Rube looked at the young man and replied, "Well, who do you suspect?"

* * * *

Note: While working in the Winslow area in the 1940s as a Deputy Sheriff, Rube had to kill four men in self defense.

A Quirky Bear Story

by Ted Knipe

The strangest bear case I was ever involved with occurred in 1943. I happened to be in the Phoenix Office, when a call came from Falcon Army Air Force Field, north of Mesa. A bear, the caller said, was sitting in a nearby saguaro.

A bear in the desert in Arizona is not that unusual, but this one was different.

Binoculars are standard equipment at all military installations, but nobody at Falcon Field thought to use them. Had they done so, they would have seen that the combination of shadows and the arms of the saguaro made it look like a bear was sitting in the cactus, fast asleep.

After my inspection, I left the premises without any comment from the embarrassed military.

Oh well, they won the war and that is all that mattered.

Department Newsletters

July 16, 1945 and July 31, 1945

from the files

This old Department newsletter pre-dates the Quail Calls newsletters of the 1960s. The excerpts selected give a little bit of information about a few of the fellows working at that time.

July 16, 1945

Rangers' Ramblings: Orson Whipple, a Ranger we have written about so few times we can't remember, gets in by accident this time. Accident is the wrong word, it was all done on purpose. In May eight arrests, eight convictions, $10 per for fishing without licenses. In April, one arrest for possession of elk meat, $125.

We come upon Glenn Hunter with a very young buck mule deer in the back of his car. A rancher on top of Mingus Mountain had it in his illegal possession costing him $150. The young buck was so weak it could hardly stand up. The buck was turned over to A. G. Ericson, Prescott, who hopes he can care for it until it is grown and big enough to care for itself.

Kearney Moore came through with an unusual one. A man sold an illegal beaver skin. The individual was fined $100. Seems to the writer this is one of the first of its kind for a long, long time. Beaver are certainly picking up in public interest.

George Peterson caught some rather big game, an alien, and turned him over to U. S. authorities.

Mervin Smith slipped over on the California side of the Colorado and picked up a fisherman with set lines, hailed him into a California court and collected a $100 fine. Mervin has a tough problem there on the Colorado River.

Fur Clippings: We have snapped the whip of ridicule and friendly jest over Bud Fox so often we are beginning to feel ashamed of ourselves, so for this time we'll not do so, not because we haven't anything on him, no, we have plenty and some rather choice items, too! We had occasion to get on Bud's trail on our last trip. Beaver are establishing themselves in the Hassayampa where he turned them loose. They have trimmed up trees in Granite Greek in Granite Dells, another restoration project. Altogether, Bud and George Daniels have trapped and transplanted 47 beavers to date. Not only that, people in communities where he has been working are getting plenty 'beaver conscious.'

A Handful of Orchids: Ever since the abandonment of Upper Oak Creek Rearing Ponds as a rearing station, because of the war, shortage of manpower and centralization of fish rearing activities, the house has been used from time to time by various Rangers stationed on Special Duty in Oak Creek. First we throw an orchid at Dan Purtyman. His talent for making a place liveable, while stationed there gave it running water, a sink, breakfast nook and many other features. Then Glenn Hunter maintained and kept it clean for a period of years. He even supplied some beds. Now Vance White added new linoleum, another bed, some lanterns and paint for the kitchen. Thus, after all these years, this communal stopping place of various members of the AGFC, having business in that end of the country, furnishes certain comforts, all because of a cooperative spirit.

July 31, 1945

Wardens' Doings: George Peterson, on special patrol duty in Tonto Basin, reports there are more trout in the creek in that vicinity than he has ever seen. Pete should know. He has been in that section every trout season for the past three years. Some of Pete's old cronies, G. I.'s from the war, were camped near him. They dropped down to the Boy Scout Camp in the evening and saw motion pictures projected by the Department.

Vance White took vacation leave and slipped way down into Havasupai Canyon and fished Cataract Creek. Yes, it was planted a year ago last April with trout from Page. Vance caught several trout but one measured 19 inches long, which is some growth, considering they were only one inch fry when Gus Evers and Charlie Niehuis put them in.

Fur Clippings: Buddy Fox is looking around for a shoehorn and a button hook. He is beginning to get that middle age spread, and either he has to get the above named items or go to a 30 inch waistband in his Levis.

George Daniels and Buddy planted two new sections of water with beaver at the last report, and when last seen were on their way to a section of the Verde below Camp Verde to remove some nuisance beaver. These, if there were any, were to go into the section of the East Verde under the Tonto Rim.

Georgie Daniels is all of 17. He had a birthday this last month, but in spite of his tender years he is rapidly becoming a seasoned beaver man under the able tutelage of the old master. Last year he turned in some very well prepared beaver pelts that brought the admiration of hardened beaver buyers.

Federal Aid Division: Phil Welles announces his resignation with the end of the month. Phil is going down Mexico way and will go into the importing business, which he should do very well as he knows his border...

Pop Arrington is pretty well satisfied with himself, at least he was when we saw him last, because he is getting lots of improvement work done on the Raymond Ranch. Pop is always good for a laugh. Recently he had a hole in his pajamas (shoulder) and decided to patch them. Very carefully he trimmed the ragged edges, matched the material and lined up the stripes, even got the right colored thread because this was to be a work of art! Then he sewed and finished as neat a job as could have been done by a reweaver of textiles. And, when he had finished, the shirttail was sewed as neatly on the under side of the patch. We don't know whether he did it on purpose or not, but at least it will keep it from flapping when he steps out into the wind on a cold night up on the Raymond Ranch.

Here is a footnote in reference to the beaver released in the Hassayampa River. A news article in the ***Prescott Evening Courier*** *dated May 21, 1945 reads as follows:*

Three pairs of beaver have been successfully live trapped from the Colorado River and released on the Hassayampa River above Wickenburg, B. C. Fox of fur conservation of the Arizona Game and Fish Commission reported today. But, not without incident, he pointed out.

Three males and five females were caught and brought to the Hassayampa for release. Two of the females, attempting to orient themselves in their new home got up on the highway during their investigation, were promptly run over and killed by the first passing automobile. Another was found in the River by Sunday picnickers and immediately surrounded by a horde of stick and stone wielders who were abusing the animal when it was rescued by Fox. It was identified by the various picnickers as a porcupine, small bear, fox, in fact everything but a beaver.

"The beaver has been extinct from this area so long numerous people evidently did not recognize the animal," commented Fred Merkle, State Game and Fish Director.

Director H. L. Reid's 1946 Report to the Arizona Game Protective Association

from the files

The following excerpts from Director H. L. Reid's annual report to the Arizona Game Protective Association meeting on October 12, 1946, in Prescott gives a clear picture of what conditions were like for Game and Fish employees and for the hunters and fishermen of the State shortly after World War II.

A long and arduous war had just been successfully concluded. Arizona has had her share of the growth and development that most of the States have been contending with. This is continuing today. Tremendous development is going on all about us; towns and cities are pushing out into the desert and the forests - new lands are being cleared in every possible place for the planting and growing of crops. Each new Arizona resident must have a place in which to live - each old Arizona resident, returning from the wars, must have a home and means of livelihood. Our wildlife is being surely pushed back and back into a steadily smaller area each year. The number of hunters and fishermen has nearly doubled since Pearl Harbor. These things must be considered in our management plans. We cannot escape them.

At this time last year, as it had been during the war, the problem of personnel within the Department was difficult. This is gradually improving with the return of suitable men from the Armed Forces. The problems of material and equipment was, and still is critical. Much of our work is being hindered because of shortages. Transport is chief of these shortages.

Nevertheless, we have made much progress. We shall itemize each phase of our work during the past year:

First - **The Predators:** Realizing that an important factor in game management involves an active and constant pressure upon the predators, we went into this last winter with every possible energy directed at the coyote. We did not overlook the other predators, but the coyote felt the full brunt of one of the greatest cooperative programs ever directed upon him in this State.

Over $71,000 was spent on predatory animal control during the fiscal year ending June 30, 1946. The bulk of this money was spent on the coyote, bob-cat and mountain lion for salaries of predator hunters. The sportsmen contributed $19,100 of this money, $5,500 of which was Pittman-Robertson funds. They were well repaid for their investment.

Predator hunters of the U. S. Fish and Wildlife Service, Arizona Livestock Sanitary Board and the State Game Department destroyed 6,007 predatory animals during this period. Stockmen and other cooperators accounted for an additional 1,236 predators for a grand total of 7,234 major predators removed during the twelve month period.

A break down of this total is interesting: four of these predators were wolves, 35 mountain lions were hunted down and destroyed, 489 bob-cats which will no longer prey upon our game; the greatest results were seen in the use of chemical control methods upon the coyote, 6,647 coyotes were actually accounted for during this period and we know that this figure is only a conservative 40% of the coyotes killed by poison set out by the predator hunters.

These 7,234 predatory animals, and their off-spring, would have taken a tremendous toll of your game. They are no longer at large to do so.

...I would like to bring out here that some of the GPA locals have been against the use of poison. This has not helped materially in our work. Other groups have been more than cooperative, and their moral and physical support has been of great assistance.

The poison program is not a hit or miss proposition. Only men who are well trained or experienced in its use are permitted to handle the strychnine drop-baits and Cyanide Coyote-Getters. Every possible effort is made to safeguard everything but coyotes, bob-cats, lions and wolves. The poison is never used close to areas of population without complete cooperation of local residents. It is never used in turkey country or where bear are known to roam. It is never placed in areas where dogs are used to hunt lion. It is never placed along or near water courses. The poison dissipates rapidly when exposed to the elements, and it takes a great deal of it to harm domestic cattle. Properly understood and practiced, the chemical control method is the most selective, the safest, the cheapest and most effective answer to the coyote problem. We are proud of our twelve month's work. We intend to continue in this work.

Enforcement: Shortly after I became Director of the Commission, the 1945 deer season opened. More deer hunters than at any time in our history were in the field. There was, however, a noticeable tightening up all down the line in the enforcement field, and this aspect of the Game Department has continued to improve during the past year until both the Commissioners and I feel that we have the highest caliber of Rangers in the history of the Department.

During the calendar year 1945, nineteen full time Rangers checked 15,449 licenses. They made, during the same period, 475 arrests for game and fish law violations, losing only 6 cases and obtaining total fines of $11,100.50 and two jail sentences.

During the nine-month period from January first through September 30th, this year, twenty-three Rangers have checked 16,122 licenses, secured 635 convictions for fines totalling $11,392.75.

We recognize from experience that it takes several years before a maximum of efficiency can be expected of a Ranger after he has been employed. Early this year the Commission decreed that new men being employed as Rangers be young enough to do the work, with special emphasis on intelligence, ability, energy and personality. Our apprehensions and convictions have reached an all time high during the past year. We are demanding of these men, not only full enforcement of the game laws, but representation of the Department to the public and assistance to the field technicians in gathering data and information. The efficiency of the enforcement division is getting better all the time. It is going to continue to do so.

BIG GAME: I had not long been in the Director's chair until I had to admit that it took more than one man to supervise and oversee, <u>if</u> we were to accomplish anything. Therefore, I chose from men in the Department, various ones in whom the Commission and I had confidence, to administer the several Departments, *under our supervision.*

Since the big game of Arizona is the most valuable of our wildlife assets we organized a new and separate division for it. O. N. 'Pop' Arrington, P-R Technician, was given the job of supervision of big game. His is a big job.

The goal of this new division is to maintain and improve the big game herds of the State. Management practices will attempt to increase the numbers of big game where the range permits, and to remove the harvestable surplus to the greatest benefit of the most hunters - always carefully considering the necessity of healthy herds and ample brood stock.

Consequently, the first job of this new division was to set up the machinery for gathering the information necessary to any game management program...

As a result, we are working out simplified annual survey methods, to be used as a yardstick to measure trends of our antelope, elk, deer and turkey. Other big game species will follow. In addition, we have placed in operation this year, the new deer and turkey permit system which will give us invaluable information from over 40,000 hunters in the field, supplementing that information gathered by a few dozen game department employees. This permit system, checking station operations and continuing game surveys during both summer and winter, will give us a tremendous fund and store of knowledge concerning our big game herds which has never been available to us before.

DEER: First the Kaibab North. For years, the sportsmen and the public have been told that they have a nice, healthy and shootable herd north of the Grand Canyon Rim. For the past five years, the herd count estimates there have been held at between 12,000 in 1941 and 11,000 in 1945. The highest kill in any of these years was 694 deer. During two of the last five years, the kill fell below 400 animals. Mind you, this includes not only bucks, but does and fawns as well. Now, gentlemen, it did not take any so-called game expert to see that you were being taken for a ride — perhaps not by deliberate intent, — but, anyway, here's the picture as we saw it: If there were anywhere near 11 or 12 thousand deer on the Kaibab, why were the hunters not getting more deer?

Last fall and winter, we sent P-R men into this area with instructions to come out with facts. They were also instructed to work with the Forest Service and the stockmen. After all data had been collected and put together, it was quite clear that your Kaibab deer herds were neither as large nor shootable as had been reported. They were healthy - they were fat.

We did find, however, that the buck-doe ratio was such that we could hunt some bucks and do no harm to the herd. Five hundred buck permits have been issued for this year. The killing of does and fawns has been stopped. It is the duty of the Commission, as well as the Forest Service, to watch this herd and not let it increase beyond the carrying capacity of the range, but it is also the duty of both to build this herd back to that shootable deer herd we have heard so much about.

...You now have a deer and turkey hunting permit which will give us the number of hunters in the field after each species of game, coupled with a hunting report card which is pre-stamped and pre-addressed for your convenience. You also now have a metal, self-locking seal for your deer and turkey. In the past, many excuses have been presented for not using the paper coupon deer tags provided, with the result that untold numbers of deer were sacrificed to the game hog killer who got his own deer, and one for some member of his family and perhaps another for a sick friend. We in the Game Department know only too well, and so do you, the many leaks through which our game has been dribbling. The bottom of the barrel is near enough in sight so that the leaks had better be stopped.

... One of the biggest problems is not in game management, but in hunter management. Most of our hunters insist on concentrating, year after year, in the same hunting areas. There is a scarcity of deer in these traditional hunt spots. At the same time, we have some areas with an over-population of deer, such as Pine Mountain, where the hunters seldom go because it is difficult to get to, and where some of our so-called sportsmen cannot drive up and down fire roads and highways with gun barrels poking out of car windows - ready to shoot at anything which moves or makes a sound.

ELK: An elk hunt is being held this year because we believe we have elk to hunt, provided the hunting pressure can be controlled. We have set up a total of 490 permits and the Fort Apache Tribal Council has granted permits for 100 elk on limited parts of their Reservation. Four separate open areas have been set up, and the number of permits for each of these has been limited to what our field men, the Forest Service and the Indian Service have determined can be safely allowed. The elk hunting permits will be issued by drawing to ensure the fairest possible distribution... Some cow elk will be permitted because of elk damage complaints in certain regions. We must hold the number of elk down in farming areas. They can do considerable damage to the small farmer. This must be kept under control...

ANTELOPE: Here is where your predator control efforts show the best results. During the July survey of the antelope herds, at which time 1,685 antelope were classified, 30.7% were young. This is a better antelope kid survival success than has been obtained for years. The antelope cannot be hunted this year, but progress has been made toward restoring this valuable big game animal, and we are perfecting methods of getting a definite picture of the condition of antelope each year...

I must make mention of the Federal Aid Division of the Game Department, commonly known as the P.R. Roy Gambrell, who was instrumental in organizing this division, has returned from the Armed Forces to resume the supervision of this valuable work. We are using these trained men more than ever before to bring in field information and facts. They are reaching an all time high in cooperation with Federal Departments, and they are working together with the Rangers more closely than ever before to get the most possible utilization of our limited personnel. As a result, we know at all times, as much as is possible to know of field conditions so that each program can best be worked out.

P.R. projects continue to function, as witness the Raymond Ranch buffalo and antelope refuge which has carved out a 22,000 acre home and sanctuary for an additional buffalo herd and provides a refuge for antelope. This will soon be one of the show places of Arizona. Other projects include quail development work in Cochise and Yuma Counties, the quail watering devices being built by Tommy Kimball in the desert and the excellent work being done on our big game herds by Gambrell, Wright, Edwards and Knipe. These men are of the highest caliber and we in the Commission are proud of their abilities and their work...

Other well qualified men will be added to the P.R. Division. We have already put each of the present P.R. technicians in charge of a species, or have located him in a given area to work with the game in that region. Theodore Knipe, one of the most able of wildlife experts has been assigned to the southeastern part of the state. J. T. Wright has been instrumental in the Kaibab investigations and has few peers in knowledge of game and range. Mr. Edwards has been assigned to live, and work on wildlife, in the Williams region. Other technical experts will be located similarly throughout the state. Kimball spends all his efforts on quail.

There has been a noticeable growing interest in hunting the javelina. We have noted that this animal is changing his range and his habits. Since there is no regular mating season for this species, the hunting season may be set at any time. We have found through our P.R. technicians and Game Rangers that we have been hunting javelina during the mating season of desert mule deer. Hunting disturbance should not be permitted on any deer at such a time and the pig season has been slightly altered to avoid this conflict...

REFUGES: During the past year, only one new refuge has been established. This one, just outside of the city of Mesa, was well planned by the Mesa sportsmen and should, providing their interest does not wane, achieve a definite purpose...

We feel that many of our existing refuges have outlived their period of usefulness. Some refuges may have been established in the past for other purposes than to protect game. We had hoped to make a thorough survey of all refuges and do away with those which were not of value to the wildlife. We have not been able to get to this because of other more pressing affairs...

FUR CONSERVATION: This division, under B.C. "Buddy" Fox, continues to supervise the fur resources of the State. Mr. Fox has made good advantage of the State's beaver population by live trapping and transplanting the animals to streams and water courses for restoration purposes. Many fine things have come from introduction of beaver. Soil and erosion control have resulted, some waters have been made suitable for fish. We control entirely the taking of beaver. When, some years ago the legislature forgot to close the season on beaver, commercialization almost wiped the animal from the state. This is now averted by total protection. We do pelt some beaver where they are surplus and cannot be transported to other locations. This permits the Fur Division to pay for it's own operation...

FISHERIES: I carried on the immediate supervision of this Division until several months ago, when A. W. "Dud" Yoder was appointed as Director of Fisheries. Mr. Yoder is capable and thoroughly experienced to continue the past accomplishments and to improve upon them to meet the growing demand...

We are not particularly wealthy in fishing waters in Arizona, but I am sure that we can point with pride to the greatest possible utilization of available waters. Our production and planting of catchable size trout has been increasing annually. In 1941 we produced and planted 70,979 trout of six inch length or more; in 1942 our planting of six inch or better trout increased to 320,000. Note that these figures include trout which were one inch under the legal length limit. In 1943, we changed our records to show only legal length fish planted, and during that year planted 286,513. In 1944 we planted 231,069 and in 1945 the figure rose to 325,971...

We now produce 2.46 pounds of trout annually per fishing license holder... Arizona fishermen pay $1.75 for the license. Arizona is practically the only state entirely sustaining trout fishing artificially. You are getting your money's worth, and more...

QUAIL: Last year at the Tucson convention we presented to you our thoughts on the quail situation... The annual survey has been made on our quail population each year along the same lines since 1937. Tom Kimball, P.R. Technician, has conducted this survey personally since 1939 except for an interlude of military service... This year a representative of your organization accompanied Kimball on the quail surveys... We found this year an average of .39 young quail to each adult. We also found a serious reduction of adult quail. This was foreseen last year... Upon presentation of the findings of the surveys to various GPA locals, the majority of the sportsmen went along with the closed season...

About a year ago, we began to clear up and develop the property know as Cluff Ranch, located at the foot of the Graham Mountains, for the purpose of experimenting with a game bird farm. L. L. Lawson, P.R. Technician, and just returned from the Armed Forces, was transferred to the Game Department and put in charge of this project. Lawson was sent to other states to study methods of operation of their game bird farms. He has worked hard and accomplished what I thought was impossible. I was not at the start, convinced that a game bird farm was a sensible way to spend our money. We have proceeded cautiously in this, also, but I am now convinced that the game bird farm will prove its worth and may give the sportsmen something to shoot at...

Because we feel that the sportsman should know what we are doing, and why, we have made a special effort, during the past year to invite all persons who might be concerned to attend the meetings of the Commission... One point — I would like to suggest that AGPA representatives attending these Commission meetings do not come instructed. Our men are constantly in the field gathering information to present to the Commission. We feel that those attending the Commission meetings should come with an open mind, - not necessarily willing to accept anything without murmur, but at least to grant up the benefit of the full time and energies we are devoting to the job you have given us.

We have nothing to gain by concealing facts, or by distorting them. To the contrary, we have everything to lose... Every man in the Game Department is there because he has a natural and sincere interest in the wildlife. We are free of political interference, thanks to the sportsmen, and we have no axes to grind - except to serve you as best we can. Given the proper support and cooperation, we will do exactly that...

Department Newsletters

June 15, 1946 and June 29, 1946

from the files

June 15, 1946

Ranger Ramblings: We're going to give this week's fur lined thundermug for the Ramblingest Ranger to Al Wilson. We tried to catch up with Al for two days and finally had to give it up. We cut his sign, however, for Al had posted those "No Seining of Trout Streams" signs every place where a drop of rain could get through the tree leaves.

We ran into Orson Whipple up that way and bypassed an opportunity to ride with him in the Showlow Constable's new two-way radio equipped car. Darn good thing we did, too, since Orson and his fallen-arch friends got way out in the sticks, blew out two tires and then found out that the radio didn't work. We were toasting our tootsies before a gas-lighted fireplace in a nice comfy cabin, while Orson and Co. sweated out getting back to town. And should we mention that it was freezing outside.

George Daniels, who has no business in the Rangers column, sent in this one about Somerton's Mervin Smith, who took leave of Yuma County several weeks ago to sit out the opening of trout season along Oak Creek. He was swapping lies with one of the Forest Service boys when a couple of fishermen swaggered up to show off their nice catch of trout. Merv counted two more fish between them than he had fingers, and had no alternative but to haul them in for having an excess of the possession limit. As George says, the fishermen had no one to blame but themselves. You said it George!

This Gene Holder is getting to be somewhat of a publicity hound, seems to us. Now he's gone and started taking pot shots at mountain lions with a pistol. (We can't hit the side of a barn from the inside with one of them things.) Good thing ammunition is getting less scarce, 'cause Gene sure did load that lion down with lead. Next day, he brought his catamount dawgs around and caught another lion. Then the derned guy couldn't even take a rest but has to come back again the following day and get two more lions. Some of those guys what lure dudes into spending their dough ain't going to like Gene if he keeps on taking away their bait.

Speaking of predator killing Rangers reminds us of George Peterson, who got that lobo wolf last winter...

Fur Pieces: Our compadre on a trip through the White Mountains and the Tonto recently was the old River Rat, Bud Fox. Bud's all right, but those two dogs of his are more fun than a barrel of monkeys. Our bedrolls could have been a lot colder if there hadn't been a dog apiece snuggling in with us.

Georgie Daniels is still up around Clarkdale at last report.

Bud's portable office has been setting next to the P-R Building for a couple of weeks. He should be chomping the bit about now. In case you ever wonder why we don't mention anyone else in the Fur Department, the answer is that Bud and George are IT!

Wildlife Restoration: Went over to this office this morning and found nobody home except "Little" Vauding, the steno. Counting noses by the absentee ballot system, we find that Tom Wright is up on Anderson Mesa checking antelope; "Pop" Arrington is waltzing around the Grand Canyon Park, saying howdy to the lions and coyotes; Tom Kimball was up on Bard Ranch looking after his quail; Bud Knipe is back at Tucson looking over the desert mule deer situation south of the Gila, and, if our memory doesn't fail us, that takes care of everybody but Roy Gambrell, who was around somewhere, but we couldn't locate him...

Incidentally, Tommy Kimball has devised a gadget that hooks onto stock watering tanks that will allow quail to drink there from without falling in. Designed principally to salvage young quail that might get drowned, Tom would appreciate it if all you guys would look around and find some customers who would be willing to install the device. It hooks onto the tank, and consists, mainly, of an inclined ramp proposition. The Game Department will build the things and also pay the shipping charges. How about talking the gadget up in your vicinity and create a demand so that Tom can get going on this? They're free.

So far, the quail situation is ungood this year. Maybe the nesting is a little late, but all early data indicates that quail may not be on the open season this year unless conditions improve. How's it look to you?

June 29, 1946

Seasons: Nothing much new on this subject except that consideration of quail, turkey, elk and antelope seasons will soon get under way with an extensive survey to be made. Tommy Kimball will coordinate the quail survey, with the considerable assistance of the ever-reliable Ranger crew. Pop "buzz-bomb" Arrington will liaison for the other game surveys, and here again, the Ranger personnel will do the main job of getting the information necessary for the Commission to establish seasons.

Ranger Ramblings: Billy Hale, who has been holding forth in the Tonto since trout season opened, turned the whole thing over to George Peterson recently. Billy picked up two young javelina that had been in the hands of some well meaning, but misguided citizens, for transportation to the refuge at Tucson Mountain Park.

Speaking of people picking up young animals reminds us that Carl Jones has had his hands full of this up Prescott way. The folks up there are beginning to run across antelope kids, and the results aren't too good for the antelope. Seems to us that antelope have been having a tough enough time trying to survive without having the supply cut off at the source.

According to the version we got of it, Gordon Evans of the Flagstaff GPA should be the "Ranger of the Week" for having been on the spot when an over zealous hunter jumped the turkey season and bumped off a bird that Vance White had had his eyes on for some time. Results: Gordon saw to it that the turkey killer was promptly put into the hands of Vance and the local court. It was an expensive turkey.

Billy Baxter seems to be finding plenty of activity in his new territory over around Kingman. According to the JP reports from Mohave County, not all the people there are vegetarians...

Leo Gibbons, who has been supplementing the Ranger force in the Springerville district, recently got wind of a violation that was passed along to Blue Tharp down in Tucson. As it turned out, a conviction was simple, and Blue says that Leo can send him another "customer" like that any time.

Game Farm Hatchings: Yup, this is a new department, and darn well deserves a spot of its own. We have been keeping this one under wraps until the guy concerned got into production, and now he's done it.

Ramroddin' this spread is Louie L. "Buzz" Lawson, former PR technician, ex-GI and now the proud poppa and momma of a flock of new born pheasants and chukars. Buzz has put in a lot of hard work, and we mean hard, cleaning up the old Cluff Ranch, and getting it ready to harbor the latest experiment of the State Game Department.

Located at the foot of Graham Mountain, the Arizona Game Bird Farm should be a natural. It's a right pretty spot, and has the facilities to raise those several hundred little "peepers" that Buzz is riding herd on so anxiously right now.

And may we add that if hard work and a desire to make good is any insurance of success, Buzz has the stuff to make a go of this venture.

Fur Pieces: Bud Fox is still holding forth around Phoenix, and we can imagine that the big-little man is just about ready to blow a valve. We happen to know that Bud prefers a little fresh air to the hot sultriness of the Valley of the Sun. But who the heck don't?

We have been looking forward to another letter from George Daniels but it hasn't materialized, so we don't know what B. C.'s shadow is doing these days.

Which reminds us that Bud took a little air jaunt the other day, with Don Bell doing the chauffeuring. Bud insists that Don can fly him anyplace at anytime from here on out. Since Bud has done a little flying himself, we'd say that this speaks pretty well for the piloting ability of our Tempe Ranger.

Fish Division News: "Dud" Yoder pinch-hit for us as speaker at the Phoenix Rotary Club the other day, and the new Director of Fisheries did himself proud, as far as we are concerned, by putting the assembled luncheon straight on the current fish situation.

Incidentally, Dud and Herb Reid recently made a trip to the capitol city of New Mexico to confer with Fish and Wildlife Service officials on the subject of the Williams Creek Hatchery. Their results were highly gratifying and some definite progress was made towards further development and utilization of this much needed project. Arizona trout hatcheries and rearing ponds are in a bad way as far as further development is concerned, and the Williams Creek site is the only answer to Arizona meeting the increased demand for more trout...

Wildlife Restoration: Tommy Kimball is getting worked up to his annual quail survey, and if he doesn't lose a few pounds before he starts, we predict that he will afterwards. Did any of you ever see Kimball eat? WOW! Seriously, Tom is depending on the Ranger force for this important information. There was a lot of public criticism of the Department over last year's quail season. If the present indications prove out that a closed quail season is necessary this year, there is going to be a lot more wailing. The important thing is that when the season is set, or closed, that the information the Department used is correct...

More Stuff: Recently, the Commission stood up on its respective hind legs and made itself known as something to reckon with among some of the agencies who had, heretofore, looked down their noses at the Arizona Game people, if they looked at them at all. Frankly, the writer is a pretty small cog in this mechanism, but we can tell you this just as surely as Hector is our pet pup, it is a make or break proposition now. It is like getting a hold of a bear by the tail. We've got to hang on, or get chawed! Just as frankly, if the present personnel doesn't do the job, the sportsmen are going to see to it that they are removed and others put in their place. That's the way it is and you can take our word for it.

The way the surveys will work is this: Pop Arrington, whom most of you know, has been working night and day getting this thing lined out. He had originally intended to have Jay Klaus serve as liaison throughout the surveys, but since Jay's leave from the Department, Bud Knipe will probably pull out of his important work to help out.

Rangers who will principally assist are Bill Killion, Al Wilson, Orson Whipple, Gene Holder, Vance White and Bill Hale. There will probably be others, but this group is the nucleus because they operate in the principal game territories. It will, however, take the concentrated effort of all of us.

Commencing July 1, Arrington will make a statewide airplane survey of antelope... This animal is the best of all for airplane study, and the Department has two years coverage already by this method...

During the month of August, the survey will take place on elk... Each Ranger, in elk and turkey country will conduct the survey over the entire month of August. He has been furnished with a new type report card for these game species. He will be contacted regularly by a PR man...

Everyone in the Department wants to have an open season on turkey and elk. We hope that the survey will indicate that a season on turkey can be established more or less concurrent with the deer season November 1 to 17. We think the limit should be one turkey, if possible.

We know that because of the extreme drought, that more and more elk are forced into pastures to get food, and that they are damaging private property; that is, if the act of trying to survive should be considered as doing damage. Personally, we know of people who screamed "Dictatorship" when they were asked to give a pint of blood to save wounded servicemen during the war. We also know, that some of these same people didn't even murmur when they were paid for that blood. They just hated to part with anything without getting a profit out of it. We wonder, sometimes, just what kind of people will yell like a banshee when an elk or a deer gets on the wrong side of a fence to get a bite to eat. We heard a candidate for high public office yap his head off because deer got into the salt he put out for cattle. We heard the same bozo make the crack that he would like to see every deer, antelope and elk die. What kind of people are these, anyway?

Whatever they are, they are and will be, putting a lot of pressure on the Commission for an open season. Naturally, too, the sportsmen want to hunt, and they are entitled to hunt whenever there is a harvestable surplus of any game animal. Why not? They pay the bill. They are putting out good cold, hard cash to pay your and my salary, with the expectation of getting something for their money. The Commission's job, however, is to provide regulations that will ensure a substantial breeding crop of each game species, and to control the surplus by permitting a harvest to be made of our wildlife resources that is not incompatible with good conservation and management. How do they get the information they need to do this? That is your job, and mine.

Want to Buy Some Shoe Strings?

told by Cliff Sorrells

Cliff Sorrells and Carl Jones were both Game Rangers working out of Prescott in the 1940s. Carl started working for the Department in 1941 and retired in 1972. Carl became a Ranger Captain and later, when the Department re-organized to the Wildlife Manager system in 1960, he became a Ranger-at-Large. Cliff ended his carreer with the Department as Chief of Law Enforcement.

When these two Rangers were living in the Prescott area they often worked as a team, spending a lot of time together. Being compatible, they made an agreement that when buying meals they would just take turns paying the bill. That way they didn't have to figure out who owed what, or get separate tickets from the waitress. That was working well, but Cliff realized that he was buying dinner most of the time and Carl was buying breakfast. Dinner usually cost quite a bit more, but he didn't say anything or complain to Carl about it, figuring that it would all even out sometime in the future.

One morning the two were eating breakfast in a Prescott cafe. Carl was visiting with some of the locals near him talking about this and that and wasn't paying any attention to what was happening at his table. An old lady walked up to Cliff and asked, "Do you want to buy some shoe strings?" That seemed like a strange request so Cliff asked her why she was trying to sell shoe strings in this cafe. She said she was hungry and wanted to get enough money to buy breakfast. Cliff told her he would not buy any shoe strings but he would buy her breakfast, anything she wanted from the menu. Carl was still visiting with the locals and was not aware of this shoe string sales lady. She ordered a big breakfast and ate it in a hurry, thanking Cliff for his generosity and saying that her belly really felt good, being full of food. She got up and left. Cliff sipped his coffee.

When it was time to leave and get to work Cliff handed the bill to Carl as it was his turn to pay. Carl looked at the bill and with a startled look said, "Cliff, I didn't see you eat all this, are you sure this is the right bill ?"

Cliff responded, "Yep, and it's your turn to pay".

Was it an Ibex?

from the files

Some Department employees, especially those who have worked in Mohave County and the Region Three area in north-west Arizona have probably heard stories about the mythical ibex. (An ibex is a goat-like animal native to Asia and southern Europe) Some Game and Fish employees have probably even talked with local residents who are positive they have seen ibex wandering around the mountains of Mohave County. Here, from the Game Management files, is some correspondence that happened almost fifty years ago that may be the beginning of these ibex rumors.

207 So. Parkview St.
Los Angeles, 4, Calif.
May 1946

Arizona Game Commission
Phoenix, Ariz.

Dear Sir,

Some years ago, while fishing on the Colorado River, I met a man whose name, I believe, was Thompson.

He was a rather odd character and related to me a weird story of having been arrested once for shooting wild sheep or, maybe goats, in the desert. He claimed to have been accquited of the charge because of his defense that it was an ibex and not a sheep or goat. He further claimed that, because of his success with this defense, a law was passed against the shooting of ibex in the State of Arizona. This — notwithstanding the fact that no ibex are found in the United States.

This happened somewhere near Topock, Arizona.

I would appreciate any information that would throw any light on this case as I am interested in writing it up if there is any truth in it.

Thanking you, I am,

Yours truly,

Geo. H. Gibson

The Department's response to Mr. Gibson's letter is as follows;

May 11, 1946

George H. Gibson
207 So. Parkview Street
Los Angeles 4, California

Dear Mr. Gibson,

Your letter relative to the ibex case in Mohave County in Arizona has been referred to me for answer.

Such a case did occur. I cannot verify the name Thompson, but I am quite sure the first name of the defendant was Glenn. He had killed a mountain sheep down in the Chemehuevi Mountains. When brought to trial by Deputy Game Warden J. B. Edwards, who was able to procure as evidence only a small bit of hide and hair and a few bones, his attorney, Elmo Bollinger, based his defense on the statement that the animal killed had been an ibex and that the ibex was not protected by Arizona law.

The State, by bone structure, hair comparison and also by the absence of any evidence of the introduction of the ibex in the United States, proved their case well, but the jury ruled in favor of the defendant. The trial was held in Oatman, Arizona in either 1939 or 1940. While the defendant was not convicted, the publicity attending the case went a long ways toward settling the mythical ibex question in Mohave County, and resulted in building a strong settlement in favor of game law enforcement.

To the best of my knowledge, however, there has never been a law passed in Arizona protecting the ibex or acknowledging the possibility of its presence.

Yours truly,

Wm. L. Gambrell, Director
Federal Aid Division

WLG/VA

CC: Dan Gish

The Navajo Ordnance Depot Incident

from the files

At 10:30 am on September 23, 1948 the Arizona Game and Fish Department served a search warrant on the United States Army, resulting in a short term war of words and letters. Letters from Director Thomas Kimball went to Arizona's Congressional representitives in Washington D. C.. Among others there were letters in the file from the Capitol from Arizona Senators Carl Hayden and Earnest McFarland and General Omar Bradley, the Chief of Staff of the U. S. Army.

The incident began when Game Ranger Supervisor, Glenn S. Hunter of Flagstaff received what he believed was good solid information that deer and elk meat was being held unlawfully in the officers' locker in the Commissary at Navajo Ordnance Depot. His information also said there might be some illegal beef there also. He realized this case was too big for him to act alone.

He called the Director. The Director's advice was to contact the County Attorney to get a federal warrant. Hunter got in touch with U. S. Fish and Wildlife Service Agent Ray Lawhorn and conferred with the U. S. Commissioner and the U. S. Attorney in Phoenix. Based on the information and the advice of the U. S. Attorney, the Commissioner issued a federal search warrant to be served on the Commanding Officer of the Navajo Ordnance Depot. At 10:30 am on September 23, 1948 with a Deputy Sheriff from Coconino County, a Deputy U. S. Marshal, a State Deputy Cattle Inspector, Fish and Wildlife Agent Lawhorn, Game Ranger C. W. Womack and Game Ranger Supervisor Glenn Hunter left Flagstaff to serve the search warrant.

At 10:45 am they arrived at the gate of the Depot and the Military Police guard asked, "Where are you going?"

"To the Commissary", was the reply. The MP allowed them to pass. When they got to the Commissary the Cattle Inspector, the Fish and Wildlife Agent and Ranger Womack stayed to watch the doors while the Sheriff Deputy, the U. S. Marshal and Ranger Hunter went to the Commanding Officer's office to serve the warrant on the Colonel. They were met by the Colonel's secretary who advised them that the Commanding Officer was out. The Colonel had gone to Flagstaff, but he would take care of them.

After showing identification and stating the purpose of the visit, the warrant was shown. The warrant covered the Commissary and the lockers. After seeing the warrant the secretary advised that they would have to wait till the Colonel returned. The secretary made some phone calls and after a few minutes a Lt. Col. arrived, stating he was second in command. He was very pleasant and after examining the warrant said he wanted to cooperate 100%. He called the Captain in charge of the Commissary and advised him to let the wardens look.

The lockers in question were all locked with individual padlocks. It was clearly visible that they all contained wrapped packages of meat. The Lt. Col. agreed to have each locker opened by the officers as soon as they could be rounded up.

At this point, Ranger Hunter asked the Captain in charge, " Where is the deer that had been hanging in the cold room a few days ago?"

He replied that another Captain had ordered the deer cut up and given to the officers. Hunter asked if the Captain knew that this was a violation of the game laws. He replied, "No, he did not know."

At this point the secretary advised them that the Commanding Officer had returned and that he wanted to see them at his home, right now! The secretary, the Sheriff Deputy and Ranger Hunter went to the Colonel's home. They were met by his wife. The Colonel was still in bed! To open the conversation Hunter asked, "How are you?"

The Colonel replied, "Not good, and I am in a very bad mood."

The Deputy started to tell the Colonel what they were here for, but was quickly interrupted. The Colonel told them in no uncertain terms that they would not be allowed to search the lockers and then he asked, "Who in the hell reported us?"

Ignoring his question Hunter asked about the deer. The Colonel responded, "Yes, we have a deer. It ran into a fence and broke its neck. I ordered it cut up and given to the young officers that have never tasted venison. I also gave some to the hospital." He went on to say that everything inside the fence is just like another world and the State of Arizona has nothing to say about it. "It is entirely under my command. I could have you gentlemen shot for coming in here!" he shouted.

Ranger Hunter, in his report, described the Colonel as very officious and wanting to quarrel. He was one of the most disagreeable people he had ever met. The Colonel described the local peace officers as "yokels" and said that everything on the Depot was in his control.

Ranger Hunter tried to explain that the Department and Commission felt this was a violation of state law. The Colonel replied, "It isn't!" He went on to say that he could issue permits to hunt elk or anything else on the Depot and the State "doesn't have a damn thing to say about it."

Just then another Captain came in. He was part of the Depot legal staff. The Colonel told him, "... these gentlemen are here about the deer."

The Captain replied, "I did not see the deer killed but someone hit it with a car." He wanted to see the warrant. It was shown to him and he asked a lot of questions. How was it obtained? Who was the informant? And on and on. He said the warrant was illegal and malicious and wondered how the State officers were allowed onto the Depot grounds without him being called.

Hunter replied that he received information about what he believed to be an unlawful activity and it was his job to investigate. He then went on to say, "You gentlemen believe you own the game and the State thinks they do. Lets have a test case and see. I would like to have a portion of the deer for evidence." The Colonel declined but offered an affidavit instead. Knowing that the affidavit could not be introduced in Court, Hunter and the Deputy insisted on some of the meat. Finally the Colonel and the Captain agreed.

They found eleven packages of meat in the one locker they opened. Taking one package of meat with a leg bone, Hunter gave the Captain a receipt.

The search warrant was never served. Hunter, in his report, felt that if he had used the warrant, plenty of illegal game meat would have been found.

The meat was marked as evidence and placed in a cold storage locker at Babbitts in Flagstaff. It was all over at 2:30 pm. All over, except for the paper work, letter writing and meetings.

Ranger Hunter notified the Director about what happened and sent in a written report. The report describes in detail the attitude and some of the statements of the Commanding Officer. This disturbed the Director and he sent letters of concern to Senators Hayden and McFarland and a lengthy letter to General Omar Bradley. The letter to General Bradley got results. The Inspector General's office initiated an investigation not only about the behavior of the Colonel but also into the legality of state game and fish laws as they apply to military reservations.

A number of letters were mailed back and forth between the Department and the U. S. Army. One letter dated April 2, 1949 from the Chief of Staff's office to the Director said,

> "... It was determined by the investigation that the United States does not have exclusive jurisdiction over the entire tract of land comprising the Navajo Ordnance Depot; that in conformity with the provision of subparagraph 2b, AR 210-80, the Arizona game and fish laws are applicable on the premises of the depot; that the officials of the State of Arizona, particularly those engaged in fish and game conservation, and the present Commanding Officer, are not fully and correctly informed concerning the jurisdictional status of the area comprising the Navajo Ordnance Depot; and that the incident leading to the writing of the communication by Arizona State officials upon which the investigation was based, was the result of this lack of understanding.
>
> "The Commanding General, Sixth Army, is being directed to issue appropriate instructions concerning the jurisdiction of the Navajo Depot area to the Post Commander and to inform the proper officials of the State of Arizona regarding this jurisdiction. He is also being directed to cause a satisfactory agreement of cooperation to be made concerning this situation."

This was the beginning of a much more cooperative atmosphere between the two parties which finally resulted in a signed cooperative agreement dated December 14, 1949. In this agreement state and federal game and fish laws apply on the Depot. State Game and Fish field technicians shall be allowed to survey the area and determine the wildlife resources and that these surveys will be the basis of any future hunts. It permitted state law enforcement officers entry to the Depot after reporting to the Commanding Officer.

It goes to show that the actions of one Game Ranger, based only on some information given by a good informer, and the resulting investigation, can result in a tidal wave of activity that may go all the way to Washington D. C. Even though this case never went to trial, it had some positive results.

Why Don't Reporters Ever Get it Right?

from the files

Have you ever had a story about yourself published in a newspaper? If yes, then you know that the reporters hardly ever get it all right. Why can't they? Is it because of the short deadlines? Did they have time to check all the facts? Did they verify what they wrote? Did the editor change their story? Those may be excuses some reporters use, but I'm sure there are a few reporters that just like to stir things up to see what happens. This may be that kind of a story.

On December 22, 1949, Bert Fireman, a columnist for "The Phoenix Gazette," wrote a story about the Commission wanting to kill all the chaparral cocks or roadrunners in Arizona in order to help the quail population. In the same column he wrote about an Arizona Game and Fish Department Game Warden that was arrested for killing an antelope out of season. This column generated the following humorous response from Thomas L. Kimball, Director of the Department.

December 23, 1949

Bert Fireman
The Phoenix Gazette
Van Buren and Second St.
Phoenix, Arizona

Dear Mr. Fireman,

Relative to your column of Thursday, December 22nd, we cannot go along with the inference that "...wasn't a game warden of some sort recently arrested for killing an antelope out of season?" to quote from the above mentioned column.

We believe that you refer to a case occurring north of Prescott last fall when two members of a Prescott sportsman's club were arrested by Arizona Game Ranger Clifford Sorrells, also of Prescott, and subsequently convicted of illegally shooting an antelope from a vehicle. A "game warden" was involved only to the extent of being the arresting officer. The publicity incidental to this event has revolved to the point where the "game warden" has now become the culprit, an interesting play upon literary license.

In the matter of the chaparral cock and his legal status, we enclose herewith a copy of my letter to Mr. William Carr in reply to Bulletin #66 of the Arizona Wildlife Federation.

Please be assured that it is not the intent or desire of the Arizona Game and Fish Commission to exterminate the roadrunner; nor, if this is not an impertinent comment, do they advocate the extermination of all columnists.

Yours very truly,

Thomas L. Kimball, Director
Arizona Game and Fish Commission

cc: Commissioners

To Keep a Quail

from the files

Even though it's against the law, some people in Arizona want to keep wild animals as pets. They must feel they are doing something good and saving the life of a wild animal. Many times the capture and possession of wild animals results in the death of that animal because of improper diet and poor treatment by inexperienced handlers. Sometimes, in the case of larger animals, there can be property damage or injury to the "owner" from these captive wild animals. That is why there are laws in every state prohibiting the capture and possession of live wildlife.

There are, however, some exceptions in the law that permit individuals to keep wild animals, either as pets or as a method for promoting wildlife education. Even with all the education and information about it being unlawful to keep wildlife as pets, every year citations are issued for the unlawful possession of live wildlife. Sometimes, unfortunately, the press gets involved and the issue gets blown way out of proportion. The result is that the public feels sympathetic to the wildlife and to the person that gets arrested for keeping live wildlife. When that happens, the Game and Fish Department often becomes the bad guy.

It seems that when a Department Game Ranger or Wildlife

Manager issues a citation to someone for a quail in captivity, it brings out the worst press releases and the public's reaction is swift and almost always against the big bad arresting officer and the Agency. Quail do well in the sparsely developed areas. Many home owners feed quail and like them to be around. Seeing young quail without the hen makes some people feel the young are orphaned and therefore in need of help. The result is captive quail. Many past and present employees of the Game and Fish Department remember Hercules the Quail, and all the trouble that resulted from this one unlawful possession of wildlife. Many Commission meetings discussed the unfortunate incident of one little quail and the young boy who was trying to raise it. The bad press and many special meetings about this little Gambel quail seemed to go on for months. Hercules may have been one of the most troublesome captive wildlife cases involving a quail but it certainly was not the first. And almost surely it will not be the last.

In 1950, quail were confiscated from a resident of Tucson resulting in some national publicity for the Department. The arresting officer was Game Ranger W. P. "Blue" Tharp, somewhat of a legend in his own right, especially in the Tucson area. The following article appeared in newspapers across the country.

Kindness repaid by a $25 Fine

Tucson, Arizona, June 22 AP A Tucson resident who saved five quail chicks from drowning had his kindness repaid by a $25 fine.

Glen Malone was found guilty of illegal possession of game birds.

He told the court he and his wife rescued the baby quail when their nest fell in a stream two years ago. He made pets out of the birds and kept them in his backyard.

Last week they were confiscated by a game warden. Malone said he did not know he was violating the law.

The following two letters were sent to Arizona by readers of the news article. One was sent to the Governor who at the time was Dan Garvey, and the other to the Arizona Game and Fish Department.

From Asbury Park, New Jersey:

To the Governor of Arizona

Where as a man in Tucson was fined $25.00 for keeping quail in his yard, please consider they were saved by him from drowning and reared as pets, and he should be commended for conservation — not punished which latter serves in this case the letter, not the spirit. For the law killeth, but the spirit giveth life.

Converse Cleveland

And from Tyler, Texas

To State Game Department

Articles like this which was printed in our local Tyler, Texas paper are the ones that cause people to violate the game laws. I am a full time quail hunter in season and protect them out of season and it seems that a man should not have been fined for saving these lives.

A. E. Dennis

The Governor's response to Mr. Converse, dated June 29, 1950:

I have your card relative to the fine recently imposed on a resident of Tucson, Arizona, for keeping quail in his yard and I am taking the liberty of referring your communication to the Arizona Game and Fish Department for reply.

I can say to you, however, that while I know none of the facts of the case to which you refer, the party who raised the quail as pets could have received permission to do so had he made application to the Game and Fish Commission. If we were to let everyone who wishes to raise quail as pets to do so, there could never be any enforcement of the law against trapping.

With kindest regards, I am

Dan E. Garvey, Governor of the State of Arizona

The Department response to Mr. Dennis and Mr. Converse, dated June 30, 1950:

> Thank you for calling our attention to the clipping in your local paper concerning the arrest in Tucson for keeping quail without a permit.
>
> It is unfortunate that newspapers are not always able to get the complete story in the limited time which they have at their disposal before going to press.
>
> The arrest was made by one of our veteran game rangers after the defendant had absolutely refused to apply for a permit to keep the quail in the manner prescribed by law. I am informed that the defendant also became very abusive to the game ranger when he was requested to get a permit. I am further informed that the Tucson chapter of the Arizona Game Protective Association conducted an independent investigation in this matter and fully endorsed the action of our ranger.
>
> Under the circumstances I can only concur with the judgment of our local game ranger.
>
> R. W. Switzer, Chief Division Law Enforcement

My Beginning

by Wes Fleming

This story shows how it was in 1950 for a new Game Department employee. After spending two days in the Phoenix office getting supplies and instructions, I was detached to the annual elk surveys. These surveys started at Hannagan Meadow and continued for three or four weeks, ending near Flagstaff. When the antelope season started in September I was assigned to various checking stations.

Immediately following the antelope season I was sent to run the North Kaibab Jacob Lake deer checking station. The station checked through 10,000 hunters who had been issued permits. In addition, the Commission authorized 1,000 additional first-come-first-serve permits which I sold at the station. These permits lasted less than twenty-four hours, and my last ten or fifteen were sold to a group of Navajo Indians who came through at three in the morning. Finally, I was finished selling permits.

Then came the call from the Director telling me to issue eleven permits to a group of his friends who were on their way to hunt the Kaibab. I told him all the permits were sold and I couldn't sell anymore. He told me, "You better do it!" When the Director's friends arrived, I told them I could not sell them Kaibab deer hunting permits as they were all gone. There were eleven pissed off hunters who returned to Phoenix. I never heard much about this from the Director. At least he let me keep my job.

A day later four Hopi Indians came to the checking station to buy some of the extra hunting permits. I said the permits were all gone, but told them to go down Warm Springs Canyon off the mountain, hit the main gravel road, turn right and cross a cattle guard. This would put them outside the Kaibab hunt boundary and they could hunt there without the special permit. The next day they returned with four does telling me they had turned left into the Kaibab Forest Slide and Jumpup areas where everyone was killing does. Harold Pratt, Game Ranger from Fredonia, was in the checking station and I told him about the Hopi Indians and their four illegal does.

The first thing Pratt asked them was, "Who killed the does?" The youngest Indian proudly stepped forward and said, "I kill all deer, Uncles and Father too old, can't see good!"

Pratt stepped back and muttered something like, "Oh no! Oh man!" Then he told them the best thing they could do was cover up those deer and head back to Second Mesa as fast as their truck will go! He must have felt sorry for them and was trying to give them a break, which I found out later was not his usual behavior with game violators.

Somehow Game Ranger Captain Carl Jones, from Prescott, heard about Pratt and the four Indians. He transferred Harold to Yuma for six months. Being in the hot desert for that period was pretty tough on a native from Fredonia.

With the Kaibab deer hunt over, I was transferred to an elk checking station at Holbrook. I had more that $4,000 cash from selling the extra Kaibab deer hunting permits. I mailed the money to Phoenix for Harry Whitmer, the Department's Office Manager to take care of. He must have assumed the envelope with the money was just normal correspondence and put it in a pile of other papers. The permit money didn't show up when he expected it. It seemed to be lost. Frantically searching, they finally found the cash.

I was in Phoenix awhile and then it was back to the Kaibab's Slide and Jumpup area to help Curtis Earl in a deer trapping project. Earl had one helper called Dirty Jake. At the time we had two Jakes in the Department, the second, Clean Jake, was the chief mechanic. Dirty Jake was a roustabout and our camp cook. His food tasted like he scrounged around in the dumps for old rib cages, making lots of chili with beans.

Where did the Antlers Go?

by Phil Cosper

There are many important things to consider when deer hunting. Deer antlers are one. In 1950, I was in charge of the North Kaibab deer hunting check station. A few days after the season started an old guy and his wife came to the checking station. (they were about 55 or 60, and seemed old to me at the time) Both were upset and had tears in their eyes. They told me they had come all the way from New Jersey to hunt the famous Kaibab deer. There was a doe in the trunk of their car. The old fellow, with tears in his eyes, explained to me that when he shot this deer it had antlers, but when he and his wife got to the dead deer the antlers were gone. The doe was illegal and something had to be done.

Since I wasn't Commissioned yet (I received my badge the following year), I could not take care of the illegal deer. They would have to see one of the Department's Game Rangers. I told them Game Ranger Captain Carl Jones was staying at the Jacob Lake Lodge across the Highway and they should go see him. As they left for the Lodge, I felt sorry for them. Here was a nice couple that came from far away to hunt in Arizona and now they had to face the consequences of breaking a game law. And worse, they had to face the wrath of Carl Jones.

Over the years as a Game Ranger, Carl had established reputation as a hard nose enforcement officer and one that rarely, if ever, gave anyone a break. Those of us who knew Carl, knew he would gladly ticket his own Mother-in-law for such a little violation as fishing with two poles.

Half an hour later the old couple returned to the checking station. I asked what happened? They said Mr. Jones told them to turn the doe in at the checking station for me to take care of, and that they could go out hunting again the next morning, but this time to make sure the antlers stayed on.

Wow! So much for Carl's hard nose Game Ranger reputation.

The Alfalfa Eating Quail

from the files

It might be hard for us to believe, but in the 1940s and 1950s, some farmers in Arizona asked the Department for help to solve the problem of quail eating their crops. Quail in those days must have had a voracious appetite and consumed vast quantities of farm crops, especially alfalfa. The following correspondence from the old Game Management files tells a story about a farmer in the Safford area complaining about quail eating his alfalfa crop and the events involving some of the Department staff. The players are Charlie Luster, the local Game Ranger in the Safford area; A. W. "Dud" Yoder, the Department's Acting Director; O. N. "Pop" Arrington, the Chief of the Game Division; Jack Bennett, Game Ranger; Phil Cosper, Federal Aid Division; and Steve Gallizioli, Research Biologist. The farmer is Mr. Albert Morris. Max Layton was the Executive Officer for the Arizona Game Protective Association (AGPA) and a lawyer and lived in Safford. The AGPA became the Arizona Wildlife Federation.

The story begins with a letter from Mr. Morris dated Oct. 23, 1952 which follows:

Arizona Game and Fish Department
Capitol Annex.
Phoenix, Arizona

Dear Sirs,

Mr. Charlie Luster, the game warden here requested us to send to you for a special permit to take the quail with firearms, poison and traps. They are destroying the crops completely and feel we are justified to have protection.

Respectfully,

Albert Morris

P.S. We have seventy acres of young alfalfa which they are taking.

The Department responded with the following letter dated Oct. 28, 1952.

Albert Morris
Safford, Arizona
Dear Mr. Morris,

I have your letter of October 23 requesting permission to take quail with firearms, poison and traps.

I will take this up with the Commission at our next meeting which will be sometime in the early part of November, and will let you know their decision.

Thanking you for your inquiry, I am

Yours very truly,

A. W. Yoder, Acting Director

The next item in the file is a handwritten note to O. N. Arrington from Steve Gallizioli and is dated January, 1953. Steve was working on quail research at the time. It is as follows:

Pop

Today I had a highly unpleasant encounter with our old friend Morris of "Quail Depredation" fame. Last Saturday afternoon I was trying to finish up the overdue quail collections for this area. I was collecting on Morris' place since I thought he would appreciate someone shooting a few more of the little terrors that were ruining him as a farmer. When I went to drive off his place the gate which was unlocked when I entered had been secured with chain and padlock. There not being another exit I proceeded to the relatively simple task of breaking off the lock.

Luster came out this morning and told me he had had a call from the County Attorney to the effect that Morris wanted to press charges against me. The Attorney had stalled Morris off and suggested I go and see Morris, which I did. I consulted with Max Layton before doing so and was told I didn't have much to worry about. My subsequent visit with Morris left a pretty sour taste in my mouth. Both he and his son became so abusive I could cheerfully have committed murder.

After leaving this delightful pair I proceeded to the

County Attorney's office and told both he and the Sheriff (who had been called first by Morris) my side of it. While I was in the Attorney's office Morris and son showed up, so they were called in and we had a merry old time. It seems that the root of the trouble was that Morris still felt he had not received the consideration due him regarding his quail problems. He thought that by locking me in his place and forcing me to break the lock he could press charges which would result in some of the "Phoenix big shots" (his words) coming down to look into his problem. He retold all his troubles with quail, rabbits, crows, coyotes and Christ knows what else. One story was interesting because I had heard it from him twice before and in each case the details were slightly different. In telling of the damage done by the hordes of rabbits on his place he told of killing 50 cotton- tails a year or so ago in half an hour. The first time I heard the story it had been 35 rabbits in one hour; the second time 50 rabbits in one hour and in the interval since the second hearing the time had been reduced by 50%. Verily the truth is not in him!

To bring this narrative to a close, Morris was finally convinced he did not have much chance of making a charge against me stick. The County Attorney told him that while I was technically guilty of a misdemeanor there was little chance that under the circumstances the Judge would do anything but throw the case out of court. Since Morris was still insistent that one of you "Big Shots" come down and personally investigate his problems the Attorney asked me if I would get in touch with you and relay his request. I told him I would, as I have, but mentioned that it was unlikely that either you or Mr. Yoder could afford the time to personally answer complaints of this nature. But anyway I have done as requested. Frankly I would enjoy greatly being a by-stander to an encounter between him and a "Big Shot!"

When I saw Max today he reported that DeBord and Bull were about ready to open the season on the antelope on their place if something isn't done. They evidently think they can fence the animals out and want financial assistance from the Game Department in the project. I'll go out there tomorrow and talk to them again to learn what they have in mind. Max said if we could convince them only 30 to 35 animals are using their range (we found 32 on the aerial survey) that they would probably not be so upset. It may be a good idea to take one of their men so he could see for himself how many there were. I'll drop you a line after I've talked to their guys.

Sincerely,

Steve

P.S. I wish you would drop Morris a line and tell him you've learned of his desire to have you visit him and what you will do about it.

The following note from Arrington was attached to Steve's letter. It was directed to the Acting Director, Mr. Yoder and probably referred to both the problem Morris had with quail and the antelope problem Steve discussed at the end of his letter. The note has no date.

Dud,

Don't know how you want to handle this. If you don't know the story Jack Bennett does - - also Phil. I think it's about time we started twisting his tail if he can be caught killing game out of season - - and it's pretty pointless for anyone but Charlie and Steve to handle it. Do you want to write to County Attorney or Morris? cc to Steve ONA

Next is another letter from Mr. Morris dated January 26, 1953

A. W. Yoder, Acting Director,

I am still waiting for the reply to your letter of October 28th stating that you would take the matter of requesting permission to take the quail with firearms, poison or traps, up with the Commission and let me know their decision.

I am still feeding the quail, they are getting fatter each day while I wait for the answer.

Feeding quail an entire crop each year isn't putting any profit in my pocket.

Please look into this matter at once as I am very discouraged trying to get permission to do something.

Yours very truly,

Albert Morris
Safford, Arizona

Two Western Union telegrams dated February 3, 1953 reading as follows:

From Mr. Morris to Mr. Yoder

Action requested at once on quail destroying crops. Advise return wire. Albert Morris

From Mr. Yoder to Mr. Morris

Would like to help you on quail problem, but must have your cooperation. Will have Charlie Luster contact you and make recommendations. A. W. Yoder

And there the files leave us with no answer to the mystery of the crop destroying quail of the Safford Valley. Did Mr. Morris ever got his permit to take quail? What do you think?

The 1952 Elk Hunt Rescue

by Harold Van Sickle

The elk hunt of 1952 was a disaster. It started as a typical, warm, sunny fall day. Hunters left, prepared for a warm hunt. They worried how they could keep their elk meat cool and away from the meat bees. But a few days after the season started, the weather changed. It turned cold, snowed, and then snowed some more. Most hunters decided to stick it out, hoping it would stop snowing. Snow usually makes good conditions for hunting, but it got too deep. Many hunters were trapped. The snow closed the roads to all vehicles. Five hunters died from exposure.

The information for this story was provided by Harold Van Sickle. At the time he was a Deputy Sheriff for Coconino County, but he joined the Department soon after this search and rescue. Harold provided a news clipping from an unnamed paper as the source of this story. Bits and pieces came from others involved in the rescue.

The snow was piled high. The spruce trees squatted on the white mountainside like crippled grouse, and the far crack of a limb breaking beneath its powdery burden ran up the slope from the frozen valley below, and ricochetted among the nearby trees. The horses whickered and the animals breath laid a lazy steam against the dark trunks of the surrounding pines.

Heavy snows in the Flagstaff area have caused problems for wildlife and hunters. This is the 1968 snow that killed many antelope. It was a snow like this that trapped many elk hunters in 1952.

(Photo from the March / April 1968 issue of Wildlife Views)

One of the riders said, "What's the use, all this snow. Elk hunters are lost all over these hills. Snowed in. We'll never find half of them. And they will be dead. What's the use?"

Down the line of horses, Van Sickle saw Cliff Sorrells look at the man. Sorrells' voice was low and positive in the white silence, but it sounded loud. "We're going to find everyone of them!" The rescue party made no answer. Sorrells was their leader. They found them all, but here on the ridge they had no way of knowing that some of the hunters would be dead.

Sorrells nudged his horse's flanks twice before the animal budged. It was cold. Cliff was riding point, guiding the rescuers up one canyon and down the next. Doggedly, Van Sickle and the others followed, the horses breasting their way through drifts and stumbling on rocks hidden in the deep snow. The saddle leather was cold. A hot cup of coffee would be nice. But the great storm had trapped elk hunters, no one knew how many. Not for sure. Somewhere near here a group was snowed in, with their power wagons locked in this white prison, roads lost in the snow and wives in a panic back in Phoenix. The riders rode on, rested their horses, and rode on again. Van Sickle saw Sorrells pull up his horse, reach out and take something off a broken limb. It was a jacket.

In one pocket was an untouched candy bar. In another a box of shells. Sorrells met Van Sickle's gaze and prodded his horse sharply. A hundred yards further the muzzle of a rifle rose black and ominous from the snow. Sorrells kept on riding. Van Sickle leaned down for the weapon and followed Sorrells. It wasn't far.

A pyramid of pine cones had been scooped together in a small protected place in the trees. The tracks that went round and round the little pyramid were plain enough. A man had thought to warm himself. Lost from his camp, a man had stumbled through drifts, taken off his jacket and hung it on a limb. But the cones had never been lit. His boots stuck out of the snow. The man was dead. The hunt went on.

A bright flame showed from a small pocket canyon. Down there were two men. One lying down, the other sitting on his partner's chest. The man rose slowly. His voice was toneless, and he jerked his thumb at his partner prone by the fire. "He lost his head. Ran out in the snow and collapsed. I didn't have the strength to carry him so I rolled him back to the fire." Then the hunter put a hand out toward Van Sickle and fell flat on his face.

One of the rescuers came riding through the snow and Sorrells turned in his saddle and said to him, "This is the reason! This is why we keep riding." The rider said nothing and got off his horse and unrolled his chuck sack and fumbled with a coffee pot. These two hunters needed food and something hot. Van Sickle followed Sorrells. There were more lost hunters to find.

Sorrells and Van Sickle found the men with their power wagons. They had stuck close to camp. They were snug enough, but running out of food. Van Sickle told the hunters, "Beyond the hill, a plow has opened the road. I'll have a Weasel in here to take you out in a couple of hours." The hunters looked at each other. No smile touched their bearded faces and a small silence laid itself about the group.

Then one of the men said gruffly, "What about our power wagons?"

Van Sickle replied, "The Weasel comes in on top of the snow. Your equipment may have to stay right here 'til spring."

The hunter snorted, "If you got the road open as close as you say, it can come a little farther. We want this equipment out of here!"

"What about the other lost hunters?" Van Sickle asked. "No sir, we haven't got time to fool with your automobiles and your gear."

The man looked at his partner while his face darkened. He looked at the riders. "I'll guarantee you one thing," he said, "I'll take this to the governor!"

Sorrells laughed. "Then you better let us help you out of here to that road. You'd never make it out by yourself afoot."

Van Sickle has said that trip was the reason he switched from the sheriff's office to the Game Department. "You see," said Van Sickle, "Cliff Sorrells will help you do whatever you want, and what finer thing can any man do? Helping folks to live is about the most important thing I know of. Helping folks to stay alive, helping them to enjoy living."

* * * *

The Game Department was instrumental in finding all the hunters lost during that storm. Many people and agencies were involved. The Weasels were used until their tracks came off. Then bull dozers were used to open roads and get hunters out. Considering the amount of snow and how fast it came, it was remarkable that only five hunters lost their lives.

The Big Lake Squirrel

told by Robert J. "Kirk" Kirkpatrick

In 1952, I was called to investigate the activities of three boys camped on the east side of Big Lake. In those days all the camps were throw down camps and a person could camp just about anywhere he wanted. The Forest Service had not developed any real camping facilities like there are today. There was a small store and boats could be rented, but that was about it. These teenage boys were camped in a small tent next to the trees a few hundred yards from the lake's edge. There were a few other campers near them, including a bunch of Boy Scouts from Phoenix. The Scout Leader was the one that had called me to complain about these three boys.

It seemed to me that they were just being boys, raising a little hell, and doing the kind of things that boys do when they are off by themselves. I was told these kids were being noisy and loud especially when they went skinny dipping in the lake at night. They had, I was told, caught a raccoon in a snare they had built from a small aspen and had stuffed this critter in a canvas duffel bag, but it had escaped. What angered the Scout Leader the most was that these kids had chased a skunk toward the Scout's camp and had smacked it with a shovel right in front of the open door of their big wall tent. He was really upset about that and so were the Boy Scouts, because they had to move camp because of the bad odor. From what I had heard, I would not have been very concerned about these kids except the Scout Leader said he thought the boys had a gun. Now, that could be a problem. In those days, the Big Lake area was an established Game Refuge and no guns of any kind were allowed.

I got up early the next morning and watched the kids' camp, waiting until they left to go fishing. When they had been gone for about twenty minutes I went in to look around their camp. Sure enough, I found a gun under a bedroll. It was an old Benjamin pump air rifle. Not much of a gun, but it could easily kill some of the small animals found around this area. So I poked around some more. In the ice chest, along with a few trout, I found a dead spruce squirrel that had been shot. It was all wrapped up in paper. That was all I could find wrong, but it was enough.

Backing off from the camp I waited until the boys returned. After they had been in camp for about fifteen minutes I drove up and started to talk with them. They didn't act like they had done anything wrong. After we talked for a while, I asked if I could look around. "Sure, go ahead", they said. Well, the first thing I did was to look in the ice chest and unwrap the squirrel. I then asked for the gun. They fessed up and produced the air rifle. The boys were only seventeen. Since they were from Tucson, I asked them if any of their parents were with them in the area. One said his father was staying at Jess Burk's Beaverhead Lodge near Hannagan Meadows.

I went to talk with this man. He was a prominent physician from Tucson. He agreed to take the rap for the boys. As I remember, I think it cost him twenty five bucks and the air rifle. I never learned what the good doctor said to his son or the other two boys, but I bet he wasn't easy on them.

The point of this story is that years later, I did get to know one of those boys pretty well. He came to work for the Department in the early 1960s and worked with me in old Region VI out of Tucson. In fact, in January of this year he visited me to talk about old game ranger stories that I might know. He wanted to include some of my stories in a book about things that happened to Arizona Game and Fish employees. When I told him about the squirrel story he remembered it too! It's kind of like the TV show, "Now it can be told!"

The Summer Students & the Bear

by Daniel P. Schadle

In the early 1950s, before Arizona State University had a wildlife curriculum, the University of Arizona wildlife students were hired to perform many varied summer jobs for the Department. These jobs provided the students with funds to continue their education. Each summer these students came to the Department headquarters, and individuals were selected at random until all openings were filled.

The Game Management Division was constructing new cattle and elk proof fences in the Rim area. These fences protected stream bottom vegetation to improve turkey nesting habitat.

An exceptionally large crew of twelve students was hired and they, in turn, split into crews of four each. A permanent Department crew leader was assigned to each student crew. These jobs were called "camp-out" jobs as the crews camped around a small house trailer. The trailer was used as a cook shack and a refuge during rain, otherwise everyone slept on cots under the stars.

One rainy night the entire student crew, with sleeping gear, crowded into the trailer and were asleep when a large inquisitive black bear came into camp. Standing tall, the bear looked in several windows of the trailer. As the bear leaned on the back of the sloping trailer, his huge wet muddy feet slipped down the side, making a screeching sound.

A wet cotton mattress had been left out to dry and was draped over an oak stump. The bear focused it's attention on the mattress and proceeded to drag it from camp, leaving large balls of cotton stuffing along the way. I observed all this from the bed of my pickup where I was sleeping under a tarp. I was holding a steel reinforcing rod for protection.

At breakfast I mentioned the bear's nocturnal visit to the students. The sleeping men had heard nothing. To convince them, I took them outside for a tour of the camp and showed them the muddy claw marks on the trailer and the remains of the mattress. Seeing this, a student from New Jersey began packing his bag and begged me to take him back to Phoenix.

The Somersaulting Horse

by Steve Gallizioli

Unlike most Department field people, I was never particularly fond of horses. When I had to, I would use one, but I never had any desire to own a hay burner or to use one on a day to day basis. I always felt more comfortable on my own feet. So far as I was concerned, the idea that one could see more game from horseback than on foot was an old cowboy myth. Give me a sturdy pair of legs and a good pair of walking boots any day over a horse and a pair of pointy toed cowboy boots! But then, because of a decree from higher up, I found myself spending a lot more time on horseback than I had ever imagined I would. But I still wore hiking boots, even on horseback! It happened this way.

Back in the 1950s, the Department didn't have wildlife managers. We had a lot of game rangers and a few biologists. Game rangers for the most part were responsible for law enforcement, while biologists gathered the biological data needed to set hunting and fishing seasons. For years there was practically no overlap in the responsibilities of the two positions.

With my wife, Claire, and two toddling daughters I was living at Cluff Ranch south of Pima at the time. Word had come down from Mt. Olympus (okay, the Phoenix office!) that game rangers would henceforth assist biologists in making winter big game classification counts. As the southeastern Regional Biologist I had several game rangers in my area of responsibility, the nearest being a Department "old-timer," Charley Luster, Game Ranger for Graham County.

Charley was a long time resident of Graham County and particularly well acquainted with the massive Graham Mountains and the surrounding region. I knew he would be a lot of help in conducting my annual winter deer and javelina surveys.

I soon learned that while Charley was more than willing to help with the surveys, the only way they would be done was on horseback. Realizing that it wouldn't be practical for one of us to be on foot and the other on horseback, I resigned myself to spending a lot of time on a horse.

Since Charley had several horses, I didn't have to worry about getting one of my own. I did arrange to get a two horse trailer which we used to get our horses to the survey areas.

We spent a couple of weeks working the Mt. Graham area and had begun surveying east of Safford in the Whitlock-Peloncillo area when Charley came down sick and was out of action for several days. I tended to some report writing for two days and then decided to continue the surveys on my own. By now I had grown so accustomed to riding Whitey I decided to continue doing so, even without Charley.

On the day I was to "solo," I went to Charley's place to pick up Whitey. Charley suggested I use his one-horse trailer instead of my heavier Department trailer. He sent his son Pat out to help me hook up and load my horse, warning him to be sure the ball hitch was properly hooked up, since it was a bit tricky to get it just so. I was shortly on my way to the Peloncillo Mountains near the New Mexico border.

Daylight had broken by the time I approached my destination. I had to drive across Parks Lake, a dry lake bed. It was about a mile across the lake bed and I was barreling along at about forty miles an hour on the perfectly flat surface when it happened. Out of the corner of my eye I detected movement in the left rear view mirror. My first thought as I turned my head to look was: "What kind of triple plated damn fool is out here trying to race me across this flat?"

It wasn't any such thing! It was Whitey, my horse, trying to pass me in his trailer! The moment my eyes focused on the mirror, I realized what had happened. The trailer had come unhooked and was free-wheeling. Suddenly the trailer tongue dropped and dug into the soft dirt of the lake bed, bringing the trailer to an abrupt stop. What happened next made my eyes bug out and almost gave me a coronary! My poor horse came flying through the air over the front of the open trailer, did a perfect somersault and miraculously landed on his rump. Fortunately, I had left just enough slack in the cotton rope around his neck so he wasn't strangling though his neck was stretched.

Slamming on the brakes I jumped out of my pickup and clambered into the trailer whipping out my pocket knife as I did so. I had visions of at least one broken leg as I cut the rope and freed the horse. Whitey staggered to his feet and shook himself, looking more than a little dazed. He stood still while I checked him over. Amazingly there were no broken bones and the only sign of damage seemed to be some rope burns on top of his head. Boy, was I relieved!

I assumed I would have trouble getting him to load in the trailer and decided to ride him around the lake bed for a bit to calm him down before trying. After rubbing some ointment on his rope burns I rode him around for about ten minutes and then led him into the trailer. No problem! He walked into it as if nothing had happened. Amazing!

I continued on, after making damn sure this time the trailer hitch was indeed locked securely around the ball hitch, and once I reached the Peloncillos spent the next six hours completing my work in the area. Returning to my rig I dismounted and led Whitey to the trailer, confidently expecting he would walk in again without hesitation. I was in for a rude surprise! When he was about six feet from the entrance of the trailer old Whitey abruptly stopped and refused to budge! Evidently he had been thinking about his experience all day, and suddenly realized the trailer was the device that had unceremoniously sent him flying through the air earlier that day! He wasn't about to give that thing a chance to do it again.

With no experience whatever in handling recalcitrant horses unwilling to load, I had one devil of a time before I finally managed (two hours later and well after dark!) to coax him into that trailer!

While I never became a real horse lover, I always had a soft spot in my heart for old Whitey, the only horse I ever knew to do a somersault and live to think about it!

My First Three Days

by W. R. "Bob" Hernbrode

Memories of my first three days working as a Game Ranger are some of the best of my twenty six years with the Department.

On January 2, 1953, Cliff Sorrells, Chief of Law Enforcement swore me in as a Game Ranger and pinned badge number 55 on my new green shirt. I would answer to GF 55 on the radio. It was a serious moment and was treated as such by those observing or participating. Hands were shaken all around. I was now a Game Ranger, and a member of a group which I learned over the years was a close organization of good friends, like family. In addition to my badge, I was given a pocket size book of game laws, a citation book, some monthly report forms and a diary. I also got some black and yellow patches for my shirt that read "Arizona Ranger." This was the only uniform we had. A down jacket or windbreaker would cover up the uniform and we could work "undercover" anytime we wanted.

After some indoctrination at the Capitol Annex office I was ready. Game Ranger Captain Tom Barnes drove me to the Department's Papago Park facilities to get a vehicle. This was where the Phoenix Zoo is now, but in those days the Department had a warm water hatchery, shop facilities, and some offices there. At the shop I was issued a battered, black 1949 Chevy sedan with a long whip antenna on the rear bumper. It was equipped with a radio, the frequency belonging to the sheriff and Highway Patrol. The Game Department dispatcher only worked weekdays from eight to five. I also got a jack, a lug wrench, a shovel and an Army surplus five gallon gas can. That was it. I had to supply my own revolver, holster, ammunition and camping equipment. We never used motels.

My first assignment was to meet Jack Bennett, Assistant Chief of Law Enforcement at Quartzsite and be prepared to stay several days. We were to patrol in the Kofa Mountains during Arizona's first bighorn sheep hunt. My second day was spent traveling to Quartzsite where I met Jack. The trip there was uneventful. Listening to the police radio and using it for the first time was exciting. When I radioed my destination and asked for traffic, I knew I was a Ranger when the dispatcher answered, "10-4, GF 55." I met Jack at a coffee shop and we headed to our campsite.

We gathered a pile of mesquite firewood and put the coffee pot on. Setting up camp didn't take long. We laid out a tarp and put our bedrolls on it. As Jack started dinner I studied my new law book and asked questions. Jack was a happy-go-lucky guy and fun to be with, but he was serious about his work and was a good teacher. We talked a lot before calling it a night. Jack told me Cliff Sorrells would be pulling into camp later that night.

Sometime during the night Cliff arrived. I don't know what time it was, but it was late. Cliff set up a cot for his bedroll and went to bed. Really early the next morning Jack woke me up. It was still dark. Jack poked me in the ribs and told me to get up, but to be quiet because Cliff had come in real late and he wanted to let him sleep. At least that is what he said.

Jack was dressed and stirred coals from last night's fire, adding some wood. The coffee pot was the first thing on the fire. I was putting on my boots when I noticed Jack gathering handfuls of small twigs. I could not figure out what he was doing since the fire was burning. He quietly walked to the Chief's cot. Placing two handfuls of twigs under the cot, he arranged them as if he was going to start a new fire. I was fully awake now and watched Jack closely. Was he really going to build a fire under the Chief's bed?

That was just what he was doing. He looked over his shoulder at me, grinned and put his finger to his mouth telling me to be quiet. He struck a match starting the twigs on fire. He had gathered a bunch of green leaves from creosote and mesquite. When the flames were just right Jack added the green leaves. The smoke wrapped around Cliff's cot, lots of smoke for such a small fire.

Waiting for the right moment, Jack yelled, "Cliff, Cliff, get up, get up, your cot's on fire!"

Chief or not, I began to laugh. I did not know what to expect when Cliff realized what Jack had done to him.

Cliff sat straight up in bed and was engulfed in smoke. He threw himself off the cot, bedding and all. Rolling in the dirt he could see the small fire that Jack had set under his cot. Cliff looked at his assistant. Jack was bent over laughing at the good joke he had pulled on his boss.

"Damn you, Bennett" Cliff yelled. But he was laughing now. "Damn you, Jack, I'll get even with you."

I'm sure Cliff got even with Jack; he always did.

That was the beginning of my third day with the Department. There was a lot of hard work, long hours, low pay and exasperation during the years. And a lot of horseplay. I am sure it was more fun in those days than now.

Biscuits

by Daniel P. Schadle

In the summer of 1953, Ward Patterson, a wise, earthy, cowboy type, headed the University of Arizona summer student crew. Ward was the father of five fine sons and knew how to handle a crew of young men. In the order of things, the crew leader was assigned as breakfast cook. This was done to get the men up, fed and to work.

Ward's crew was always up early and well fed. The first morning in camp Ward made three dozen biscuits, and the crew ate them all. The second day Ward made four dozen, and not one was left. The third morning he made six dozen and one biscuit remained. Ward looked at the one remaining biscuit and said, "OK, if you don't like my biscuits, somebody else will do the cooking!" The lonely biscuit was quickly consumed!

A Tragedy at Apache Lake

by Wes Fleming

Every year Department biologists fly over the waters of Arizona conducting waterfowl surveys. Low level flying is fun, but it is not safe.

In 1954, Don Miller, a contract pilot for the Department, and I were flying the annual waterfowl surveys along the Salt River lakes. We were banking to the right as we flew through the narrow upper end of Apache Lake. I had just completed my notes about five American mergansers when "WHAM!" the super-cub hit something. The plane immediately dropped and slammed into the water. I was knocked unconscious either on the first impact or when we hit the water.

When I woke up, only half conscious, I crawled to the back of the airplane as it seemed that up was the best way to go. We were under water. Then, I realized that the only way out of the plane was through the passenger door. I pushed with no luck, it was jammed. I turned around and gave it a big heave with my legs. It opened. It was cold and dark as the plane was now twenty or thirty feet under water. I hoped Don was right behind me as I popped to the surface. The closest shore was to the north. I swam there and had difficulty climbing the rocky vertical shoreline, but finally was able to get out of the water. I never saw Don.

Since I was on the side of the lake with no roads or access I waited for three hours. A tourist stopping at the Apache Trail Lookout spotted me waving. They went back to the dam tender's house at Roosevelt to get help. He rescued me with his boat. As soon as I could, I called Johnny Hall, the Director. He came to find out what happened and take me back to Phoenix. I had black eyes, a sore back and skinned up legs and arms, but nothing broken. In two weeks Pop Arrington and I were back flying waterfowl surveys.

Don Miller lost his life in this accident. The cause of the crash was a three quarter inch cable strung across the lake. It provided a method to transport a few ounces of gold from Arrastra Creek.

Working as a biologist, wildlife manager or helper on these survey flights is a risky occupation, a hazard for which we are not compensated.

Down the Trail

by W. R. "Bob" Hernbrode

Rounding up buffalo from the rolling foothills of the Huachuca Mountains along the Mexican border requires no small ability as a cowboy, a degree of almost foolhardy nerve, and a great deal of damn fool luck.

One of the luckiest cowboys who ever "choused" a buffalo on this range was a wiry little redhead named Jack Bennett, who was Assistant Chief of Law Enforcement for the Department. Jack was practically born in the saddle, and among all the guys a man ever worked with, he would be remembered for his exuberant spirits under any conditions. He was known for his ability as a cowboy, and maybe most of all, for the scrapes he could come out of with hardly a scratch. This is the story of one of those scrapes.

January can be a nice time in the Huachucas, it's pretty cool 'long about sunup, but warms up real nice before the morning is very old. The skies are clear and the grass is rich and brown, reaching almost to the belly of a horse. This range was never grazed except for Post horses, and in more recent years only by the officers' polo ponies. The rolling, grassy ridges give way abruptly to the steeply rising slopes and canyons of the Huachuca Mountains. It is in one of these brushy canyons our story takes place.

Jack and Cliff Sorrells, his closest friend as well as Chief of Law Enforcement and Jack's boss, were hunting stray buffalo left after the main herd had been rounded up and shipped to the Department's Raymond Ranch. The military had cancelled the Department's Fort Huachuca Wildlife Area lease, and the buffalo that once roamed the area had to go.

With buffalo there are always a few renegade bulls that refuse to be corralled, herded, or handled in any way. They will fight any attempt to control them, so they are always the last to be brought in — if indeed they are. At the first sign of cowboys, the bulls scatter onto the high brushy ridges, and they are mighty hard to find and it's difficult to do anything with them. These animals are big, fast, cantankerous and as bad-tempered as any mother-in-law.

Jack headed up a narrow trail that rimmed the edge of the canyon. To his left the hillside dropped off steeply. The hillside was chaparral, almost impenetrable, with a few scattered junipers and pinon pines. Riding the trail allowed Jack to see into the canyon bottom and the opposite slopes. If he spotted a buffalo, the idea was to get above him and run him downhill into the open country below. Not as easy as it sounds.

After working to the head of two or three side canyons, Jack had lost track of Cliff. He hadn't found any buffalo, but was following a fresh set of tracks that seemed to be headed for the top of the Huachucas. In the meantime, Cliff had circled, also following fresh sign, and had gotten well above and to the right of Jack on the side of the mountain. The brush was so thick and the canyon so narrow and crooked that neither rider knew the other was near. There was no warning of what was about to happen.

Circling above Jack, Cliff cut ahead of the bull that Jack was following and turned him back. The bull evidently did not know that Jack was trailing him, so he spun and "sold out" back down the trail, with Cliff and his big black horse pounding along behind.

Jack had paused to let his horse "blow" and so he could roll a smoke. He was sitting "kinda slaunchwise" in his saddle, his right leg up over the saddle horn, completely relaxed. All of a sudden the side of the mountain exploded and what looked like the Santa Fe Chief came thundering down the trail right at him. Maybe that old bull wasn't a railroad engine coming down the tracks, but he was about the same size, coming fast and making a lot of noise. Before Jack could swallow the half lit cigarette hanging from his lips, the bull and his horse were practically nose to nose on the narrow trail.

Jack's horse didn't have to swallow a cigarette, so he moved fast, setting a new record for the sideways jump, right off the trail into the canyon below. The wild-eyed horse landed square in the middle of a big juniper tree, so straddled out that he stuck there. The lucky redheaded cowboy was still astride his horse right in the top of the tree. It took Jack and Cliff half an hour to get the horse down. But that was only after Cliff spent half an hour laughing, fit to bust.

The buffalo never looked back!

Fire in the Hole

by Wes Fleming

I think it was 1955. I know it was summer because it was hotter than hell. I put about eighteen boxes of ditching dynamite in my old Department banana wagon and headed for Mittry Lake on the Colorado River, just north of Yuma. In those days we had no refrigeration and we traveled with a wet towel wrapped around our head and neck and had a couple of desert water bags hanging on the car for cool water.

I met Johnny Russo in Yuma and headed for the upper end of Mittry Lake. Gabby Blaser had completed the dragline work as far as the water table would let him go. The balance of the ditch, about 500 feet was perfect for the ditching powder. We worked about half a day and had 200 feet of dynamite sticks laid, two sticks to a hole, three feet apart. We rigged up the electric detonator and yelled, "Fire in the hole!" Man, oh man! What an awesome explosion! The ground shook and mud flew a couple hundred feet into the air. Every stick propagated perfectly. We admired our work.

The Yuma Test Center, just east of the canal, went on "Code Red Alert." They sent a detail to determine the cause of the disaster. The sergeant in charge was chagrined to find two biologists standing near their beautiful new ditch, admiring their handy-work.

"Why weren't we notified of this activity, who in the hell do you think you are?" the angry sergeant yelled.

We told them, "This is Mittry Lake, not the Test Station, you have no jurisdiction over this project!"

They were upset, but we didn't care. There was more yelling by the sergeant, but in the end we went ahead and finished our ditch.

Russo had to go back into the desert on his bighorn sheep research project, and I needed some help to finish the ditch. I picked up a couple of winos at the labor hall to help lay a line of dynamite in the outlet ditch. We had worked about an hour when one of the winos complained about a terrible headache. He crawled under a bridge to get in the shade. Within minutes he came running out holding his stomach and screaming that something had bit him. He yelled, "It was a brown bug with big pinchers and a long tail with a hook on it!" He was convinced that death was imminent. He was so panicky I decided to take him to the Yuma Test Station Infirmary.

Boom! Explosions such as this one on Chevelon Creek Wildlife Area are often used to create wildlife habitat. It was a blast like this that woke up the military folks at the Yuma Test Station.
(Photo from the January/February 1968 issue of Wildlife Views. Photo by Robert Jantzen.)

The three of us, me and the two winos, were soaked with mud, slop and all kinds of stinky stuff. The medic didn't want us in his clean, white infirmary, but he finally let us in. I told the young doctor that the wino was stung on his belly by a scorpion . The doctor said, "Oh my God, you have to treat this the same way as a rattlesnake bite." He disappeared into his office and I could see him frantically searching his reference books. Soon, he came out and said, "No problem, just put some ice on the sting, and he will be OK." We didn't even fill out any forms. The medic wanted us out of his clean infirmary and he ushered us out the door — pronto!

On the way to town I bought a handful of popsicles. The last thing I saw was the wino holding two or three strawberry popsicles on his belly and walking down the highway.

The Horse Trade

told by Robert J. "Kirk" Kirkpatrick

When I worked out of the Clifton area in the 1950s I used to work in the Blue area a lot. It was good game country and I was there to look for poachers. While working there, I got to know DeWitt Cosper quite well. He was a rancher in the area and I liked to visit with him. He was a nice guy and always good for a hot cup of coffee. He was also the uncle of a Department employee, Phil Cosper. On one of my visits to his ranch, Game Ranger Pat Kelly was with me. Pat was kind of a rogue game warden. He was always trying to take advantage of any situation that provided him with an opportunity to deal. He never really cared about who came out on the short end of a deal as long as it wasn't him.

DeWitt had an old horse he was trying to sell. He said it was a good horse, even though it was kind of old. It grew up in the mountains and was a good mount to get around the hills and rocks. It was a steady horse, but he didn't need it or want it anymore and would sell it for $25.00. He asked me if I wanted it. I already had two horses and didn't need another. Pat Kelly told DeWitt that he could get fifty bucks for the horse if he would let him take it to Safford. DeWitt liked that idea so they loaded the horse into Pat's trailer.

Pat took the horse to Charlie Luster's house in Pima. Charlie was the Game Ranger for that area. Pat told Charlie that he bought this horse for him. He never told him what it cost and never asked him to pay for it. Charlie thought it was a gift. Pat never paid Cosper for the horse and probably never intended to.

Everytime I went to the Blue and saw DeWitt he asked me about his old horse and when he was going to get his money from Pat. This went on for months and I was tired of covering up for Pat. I kept asking Pat when he was going to pay for the horse but never got a satisfactory answer. I finally took the matter in my own hands.

The next time I saw DeWitt I wrote him a check for the fifty bucks Pat told him he would get for the horse. I also told him I wanted a bill of sale for this horse trade, which he gave me. I then went to see Charlie and told him I wanted my horse. Charlie was a little surprised that I wanted his horse, but when I asked him if he had a bill of sale, he could not produce one, of course. I then showed him my bill of sale from DeWitt. Charlie was a reasonable kind of a guy and a good man and he helped me load my new horse in my trailer. Right after that he called Pat to get an explanation.

Pat came over to Charlie's house while I was still there and we had a little confrontation about what transpired. I wanted my money! Pat, of course, wanted to keep his money and Charlie wanted his horse. We went around and around for a while but finally, with some arm twisting, Pat realized that I was serious and coughed up the fifty bucks. I gave the horse to Charlie and he was happy about the deal. I was happy. DeWitt was happy. Pat, of course, was not happy about buying a twenty-five dollar horse for fifty bucks. It's about the only time I know of that Pat Kelly got "chingered" on one of his own deals.

In the Silt and Sand

by Wes Fleming

In the early 1950s, the Department acquired the Robbins Butte Wildlife Area and started developing the site into a waterfowl refuge. The first Area Manager was a fellow named Sid Pearce, a political appointee of the Governor. He didn't last long. Charlie Copley became Manager, staying until he retired in 1984. Everyone thought Charlie did a good job.

Early in Charlie's career, a farmer from Buckeye didn't like the looks of the Wildlife Area. He thought there were far too many weeds in the farm fields planted with grain crops to feed wildlife. The farmer was a Game and Fish Commissioner and he asked the Director to check on Charlie.

This was a reasonable request, and would provide the Director a few hours in the field away from the office. So early one July morning, before daylight, a black sedan quietly drove toward the Robbins Butte headquarters. The sedan promptly got stuck in the silt and sand. At daylight Charlie heard a terrible grinding noise and the racing of an engine. He went to investigate. He found the Director shoveling and sweating, trying to free his sedan. Charlie must have known why the Director was there. No words were spoken. Charlie returned to the shop area, cranked up the tractor and pulled the black sedan from the sand trap. Again no words were spoken, except for a curt, "Thanks," from the Director. Both returned from whence they came. Charlie and I never heard another word about weeds in the milo fields.

Jack and the Roadrunner

by Levi Packard

In the mid-fifties I worked a lot with Jack Wheeler. I was one of the Game Rangers assigned to the Tucson area and Jack was the Game Ranger in Florence. Jack was a quiet man, very sincere, and a hell of a shot. He also liked big guns.

I had not been in Arizona very long having come from Wisconsin. I was a Game Warden there. Since I was new to Arizona, I was still learning about the game laws. I guess you could call me a gung ho ranger ready to catch anyone who violated the game laws. I spent a lot of time reading the Arizona and Federal regulations and I found out the Federal regs did not exactly agree with the Arizona code.

One time, Jack and I were patrolling in the Black Mountain area east of Florence. This is one of the best quail hunting areas in the state and we saw a lot of quail that day. We were driving slowly down a two track road. Jack was telling me that roadrunners would eat all the baby quail and how bad he thought they were. All of a sudden a roadrunner took off across the desert on Jack's side of the car. Out came Jack's .44 revolver and with one shot he killed the roadrunner.

I waited a moment, thinking about the laws I had read, and said, "Jack, roadrunners are members of the cuckoo family and they are protected by Federal Law."

Jack looked over at me and quietly said, "That one wasn't!"

My North Kaibab Buck

by Wes Fleming

In the 1950s, there were lots of deer on the North Kaibab. I mean lots of deer, way too many for the health of the herd. The management of the North Kaibab deer herd is the classic case that wildlife managers study in college.

In 1955, I was assigned to work the North Kaibab deer hunt. As was the normal standard operating procedure for the Department, I also had a permit to hunt. While hunting, I saw a big four point buck slowly work his way down the sagebrush slope of North Canyon. He headed directly toward me. He kept getting closer and closer and as he turned sideways my first shot dropped him. When I walked over to him I discovered that if he had been any closer the muzzle blast from my rifle could have killed him. He was that poor, nothing but skin and bones.

Arizona law provides that a very poor or sick deer can be condemned and a new tag issued to the hunter. I decided to take this wretched buck to Gabby Blazer, the Department's checking station operator and have him condemn the animal. After examining the buck, Gabby looked at me and said, "No way, Wes, if I condemn this buck I would have to condemn half of the deer being checked through the station this year." I had to take this poor deer home and make chili out of it.

This was how the deer were managed on the North Kaibab in the middle fifties. I hope today's managers do better.

The Lady and the Turkey

told by Harold Van Sickle

Turkeys are the poachers' choice. They are easy to shoot from the road, and since they are small, they are easy to pick up and hide. About 1955, I got a call from a Highway Patrolman who had seen a turkey poacher in action about five miles west of Flagstaff. I knew most of the highway patrolmen in the Flagstaff area since I used to be one of them. We had a really good working relationship. The Patrolman had given me a good vehicle description with the license number. This was going to be easy! Carl Jones, the Ranger Captain, was with me so we went together to respond to the call. On the way, we got another radio call from a Sheriff Deputy who had stopped the suspect's vehicle near Rogers Lake. He wanted to know how soon we would be there and what he should do. We told him we would be there in a few minutes and to hold the suspects.

When we got there everything seemed right. The vehicle and license number matched the description given by the Highway Patrol.

A man and a lady were in the car. We asked the man to get out of the vehicle and open the trunk. He did that and we found nothing. We looked under the car seats. Nothing. We opened the hood and looked. Nothing. We looked to see if the turkey was tied up under the car. Nothing. We radioed the Highway Patrolman that reported the poaching and asked him about what he saw. Yep, he was sure he had seen them kill a turkey.

Carl is a really good snooper and has a good nose for finding poached animals. In Carl's mind, there was only one place left that the turkey could be. He opened the passenger door next to the lady and asked her to lift up her dress! That's a pretty bold question to ask a lady. After a little gentle persuasion she did. Lo and behold, under the dress, there was the turkey stuffed between her legs! Case made!

Blow the Lines

told by Jack "The Printer" Thompson

In the 1950s, the Department's offices were in the Capitol complex on West Adams. The print shop was under the stairs in a small cubby hole. Since it was close to all the offices and we were a small outfit, I got to know everyone very well. It was hard to believe this story could happen to people I thought were pretty smart.

It wasn't too long after I went to work for the Department that I hired a young man by the name of Martin White. He was a part-time summer helper I needed to get out the new hunting regulations and license material. He was a funny guy and liked to play practical jokes. One day he asked me if it would be OK to play a joke on the Department secretaries. He didn't tell me what it was, but he said it would be harmless. I said OK. He was spending a lot of time on the phone, so I figured I better find out what he was up to. It didn't take me long to find out what the joke was. Moving in a little closer I overheard the following conversation. "Hello, I'm with the Telephone Company and we are having a little trouble with the phones. I need your help. We are trying to clean up the lines, it's called blowing them out. It helps a lot if the telephones are lower down, so we would like you to lay the phone on the floor for the rest of the afternoon. OK, that's great, thanks a lot for your help."

It sounded like fun to me, but I didn't think that many of the office girls would bite. A short time later I left the print shop and was wandering around the offices delivering some reports and to my surprise about half of the secretaries had their phones on the floor. I could hardly keep a straight face and just about busted a gut laughing.

The Turkey Lunch

told by Robert J. "Kirk" Kirkpatrick

I worked in the White Mountains in the 1950s for a number of years. I really liked to work with Jack Murray, Game Ranger from Winslow. He was an ex-railroad cop and was a good game warden. He knew his stuff and was a good man to work with. You could always depend on him to do the right thing at the right time.

One time we were working together and we heard about a bunch of big shots from Clifton that were camped in the Wildcat Point area. From what we heard they were taking more trout than the law allowed, so we decided to check their camp. The plan was that Jack would get on his horse and ride into their camp from the opposite direction of the road that I would drive in on. This would give Jack some time to check the area around camp while they were talking with me. Well, things didn't work out quite like we expected.

When I was about a mile from the camp I saw a man working on a fence. I thought it would be a good idea to talk to him. He might know something about what was happening at the suspects' camp. We talked for awhile. He knew nothing about the camp and seemed determined to continue with his fence work. Fence work isn't easy and it seemed to me anyone doing this kind of work would want a break. But not this guy. It was about noon when a lady in a car drove up. It was the fence builder's wife with his lunch. As a matter of habit I walked around to the back of the car and just looked around. On the bumper I noticed a small speck of blood about half the size of a dime.

"What's this blood from?" I asked the lady.

She replied that she didn't know what it was, but she was sure it wasn't blood. Being suspicious I asked her to open the trunk. She said she didn't have a key and couldn't open it. Well, I reached for my .38 and said that I had a key that would probably open the trunk. She responded quickly, having just found her key and then she unlocked the trunk. Inside were a bunch of turkey feathers, but no turkeys.

I had learned about the "persuasive master key" for car trunks from Jack. He told me about the time when he stopped a car that he knew had a bunch of poached squirrels in the trunk. The hunter would not open the trunk and would not produce the key. Jack then went to his patrol car and got a pair of handcuffs and a crow bar. The hunter asked, "What's that for?" Jack's response to the hunter was, "The handcuffs are for you and that small pine tree and the bar is for your trunk lid". Jack said it always works, and the keys show up quickly.

I then went over to the pickup belonging to the fence builder and looked inside the camper shell. There were a half dozen grocery bags and each one had a wild turkey stuffed inside. This guy had really got into the turkeys that morning.

About this time Jack Murray rode up on his horse, and was wondering what had kept me from meeting him at the camp. I explained what I had here and that I was glad to see him. The fence builder was related to one of the influential families in Springerville and was getting a little testy, but calmed down when he realized he was outnumbered. We got the turkeys out of his truck and into my sedan. We then issued tickets, gave receipts for the turkeys and took his gun for evidence.

I then asked the lady, "What's for lunch?"

"What do you expect, turkey!" she said. We had to take the lunch too and then went to her house to get the rest of the cooked turkey.

We had to file these citations in JP Court so we went to Eagar to see Judge Carl Hodges. We explained the case to him and told him about the evidence we had; the turkeys, the feathers, and the gun.

"Great", he said. "Hey, my daughter is getting married Sunday and I could sure use those turkeys for sandwiches at the reception. How about it?" Well, we explained to him that these turkeys were property of the State and it would be against the law for him to have them for that purpose. It took a lot of talking, but after a while he concurred.

We put the turkeys in cold storage for evidence, tagged the gun, put the feathers in a bag and headed back to camp. On the way we bought a jug of mayonnaise and a loaf of bread and had turkey sandwiches for dinner. Tasted good, but that turkey was sure dry.

Mac Dog

by Wes Fleming

Gabby Blaser was one of the best Department roustabouts. Since he could do almost anything, Pop Arrington sent him all over the state. Pop had sent Gabby to the Three Bar Wildlife Area to build holding pens for transplanted chukars. He had been there a couple of weeks and needed a few days off to restock his supplies. I was sent there to spell Gabby and to take care of the birds.

I took my dachshund, Mac Dog, with me. After a day's work, I ate dinner and crawled into my sleeping bag on a cot outside under the stars. Mac Dog promptly took his place inside the bottom of the bag, keeping my feet warm. In the middle of the night I felt something walking around on top of me. It was pitch black and I couldn't see a thing. I reached under the cot for my flashlight. Instead of a cold slick flashlight I felt something warm with long hair. I knew it wasn't Mac Dog, he was still inside my bedroll. I drew my hand back. Pretty soon I felt two critters walking on my bedroll. Mac Dog was still asleep. Reaching again for my flashlight I found it. I was moving in slow motion as I did not want to disturb the critters walking on top of me. I turned on the flashlight and there were two skunks pawing and poking around. The light made them nervous and they jumped off the cot and left. I didn't sleep much the rest of the night thinking about the skunks. Every time Mac Dog moved I thought it was the skunks, but they never came back. Mac Dog never knew of my trauma and it was probably a good thing. If he had discovered the skunks, it would have been weeks before Pop let me back in the office.

Rose Canyon Dam Construction

by Daniel P. Schadle

The construction of Rose Canyon Dam in the Santa Catalina Mountains was a nightmare. The Department had built several earthen dams with success, however this dam was constructed with rock rubble and it was a new experience. The rock and rubble used was quarried at the dam site. Getting the quarried rock to the rock masons was quite a challenge.

The constricted work area and topography around the dam site prevented the use of heavy equipment and only hand labor could be used to transport the rock. The Department signed an agreement with the Federal prison near Molino Basin for the use of prison inmates as a labor force. When the quarried rock was too large to handle, the inmates made them small enough to manage. The inmates had to carry the quarried rock to the dam site.

The work was going very slowly. The Department wanted to hurry things along and, consequently, the Director asked me to provide some supervision so the inmates would speed up production. I assigned Ward Patterson, a valued and long time employee to do the job.

Production did increase - - but not enough to satisfy the Director. Pop Arrington was then put in charge as project leader. To see why construction was going so slowly, Pop and I visited the Rose Canyon Dam job site. After watching the inmates work for a short time, Pop said, “Dan, those lazy inmates are only carrying one rock at a time. That has to stop!”

On returning to Phoenix, Pop told me he had a great idea which would really speed up production. The next morning Pop had the Department's welder at work making stretcher-type carriers with two-inch iron pipe as handles and a heavy metal mesh as floor between the handles. (They looked a lot like deer carriers without the bicycle tire in the center.) Pop's invention required two men, front and back, to carry it. Many of these stretchers were built and put on the job. Now the inmates could carry a bunch of rocks per trip.

On my next trip to Rose Canyon I noticed that all the stretchers were in use. Now, however, two men were operating the stretcher carriers as planned, but they only had one rock on each stretcher. This reduced the rock hauling production in half and took twice as long. The inmates must have really liked hauling rocks, because they could figure out all sorts of ways to work slower!

In spite of how hard they tried, Rose Canyon Dam was completed!

Raining Geese

by Wes Fleming

It all started in the living room of the Planet Ranch headquarters while I was taking a break from waterfowl surveys in the Bill Williams River area. I was telling Rusty Gibbons, the owner, about the fantastic concentrations of Pacific black brant in San Ignacio Bay on the west side of Baja California. Once, I had seen great numbers of birds during an aerial waterfowl survey. I told Rusty the area was one-hundred percent pristine, with no evidence of white man ever being there, only some old Indian camps and lots of turtle shells. There were packs of coyotes hunting the shore for food scraps. I knew a small plane could land on the hard packed sand below the high tide mark.

Rusty was getting excited and asked, "When do we leave?"

A date was set for our trip to Baja. However, as the plan evolved we had five airplanes and twelve guys willing to risk the adventure. One was Johnny Hall, the Director.

We checked through the Nogales International Airport and flew to Hermosillo, where we gassed up and tried to purchase hunting licenses. The local Mexican official said, "Oh no, señor, Baja is a separate state so we can not sell you their permits." We then flew to Santa Rosalia in Baja where the airport manager told us, "Oh no, señor, we don't have any permits, never heard of them."

Frustrated, we flew on over the mountains for San Ignacio Bay. The tide was out and the landing was perfect, as I had suspected. What a beautiful place. We spooked about 10,000 brant feeding on the exposed eel grass near our camp.

But it was no easy matter to bag a goose because the vast area had no cover and the birds were shy of any strange dark bumps in the flats. The first few days we killed enough brants for supper. For one night's dinner we caught a mess of sea trout. A fisherman in our bunch noticed a monster grouper feeding on the sea trout. Willard Skousen rigged up two beer can openers and attached them to a long throw line. He threw the "flashers" out into the channel as far as he could and began a slow retrieve. Directly, he had a giant tug on his line and the fight began for his monster fish. Willard stuttered a bit and as the battled progressed, the advantage slowly changed from man to fish. Willard fought hard and cried out in his stuttering voice, "I .. It's either go going t..to be hi..him or m..me, by g..god!" The fish fight took place on a long sand bank which finally gave away and Willard had to give up the battle.

Rusty and Johnny Hall came up with the idea of flying over to an island near the mouth of the bay. This would put them in a better position to shoot the brant as they flew on their way to the eel grass meadows. Flying to the island they neglected to land on the hard sand and flipped the plane over. Rusty got out quickly, but Johnny was stuck, hanging upside down in his seatbelt. Rusty yelled at him, "For Christ sake, Johnny, get out before this thing catches on fire." Johnny couldn't undo the latch of the seatbelt with all his weight on it. Rusty shouldered him up and when the belt unfastened Johnny fell, cutting his forehead. This wasn't the only blood Johnny shed on this trip.

We retrieved the radio from Rusty's plane and left the carcass laying upside down on the beach. Later, the Mexican Army found the plane which darn near caused an international incident. There was talk of spies, invasion, landing parties, dead bodies, and wholesale poaching by gringos.

The next day Johnny and I circled through a mangrove jungle to get in position in the shallows for a little pass shooting. As I worked my way through the water and soft sand I heard a scream from Johnny, and saw him jumping around on one leg. A sting-ray had nailed him right through his leather boot and into his instep. These poisonous critters really hurt, and the pain gets worse everyday. But he suffered through it.

We soon ran out of whiskey, so one of the guys flew to the village of San Ignacio. The mayor was a teetotaller and said, "We don't sell whiskey to gringos." Our pilot noticed a Mexican fellow motioning to him. So he followed him through town to his homemade still. He brought back a couple bottles of "date jack." This was beautiful stuff, probably 180 proof.

When we broke camp, we flew single file over the mountains, up the coast toward Tiburon Island for a leap frog across the Sea of Cortez. Johnny was flying with a pilot who was paranoid about flying over water. He was scared to death and started drinking the date jack. As we flew over the water the pilot's speech became more and more slurred and his flying became more erratic. We had decided to gas up at an airstrip north of Hermosillo. Our drinking pilot asked Johnny, "Can you land this thing? I can't do it!" Johnny was not a pilot and replied, "No way, I've never landed a plane in my life!" Between the two of them they got the plane on the ground with a fairly good landing. After we sobered up the pilot we took off for Nogales.

We had no hunting permits for the fifteen or so geese we had stashed in the planes and we knew we had to go through Customs. We also were not sure what kind of reception we would have because we had left with five airplanes but returned with only four. As we flew over Magdalena, Sonora, we tossed the geese overboard. The local Mexicans must have thought it was an Easter egg hunt and Christmas dinner all rolled up in one package.

As a note, Rusty lost his life in a airplane crash in Idaho not long after the infamous San Ignacio trip.

Was That for Real?

by Lawrence E. Powell

It was such a long time ago I might have forgotten some of the details, but it was an event that will stay in my memory forever. Most people who know me believe I am a reasonable person, a trained observer with a scientific education. I told only two people about what I saw that night. I only remember telling my wife, but Phil Cosper called and asked if I would tell this story for John's Game and Fish story book. I had forgotten I told Phil this story. He must have been a better friend than I remembered. Well, here it is.

In the late 1950s, when John Hall was Director, a rancher asked the Department to help build a road on his ranch. The rancher felt the road would serve his needs and provide hunter access to the Prescott National Forest. John asked me to look at the proposal.

The road into the area took off near where the Dewey Road meets Interstate-17. The rancher and I rode all day on horseback in the area south of I-17 and north and west of Squaw Peak. We finished our ride late in the day.

It was dark when I stopped to open a wire gate on the Highway right-of-way fence. I became aware of a humming sound. That noise was so different from anything I had ever heard it made me look up. There in the western sky I saw what appeared to be a distinct row of window cabin lights. There were ten to fifteen evenly spaced yellow lights. I was unable to judge my distance from the object I was looking at, as there were no references to help me determine its size or length. The object was oriented in a north south position and I watched it for several moments before returning to the truck. I looked again and moved my truck to align the lights in the sky with the gate post. The object was moving south slowly, and the humming sound continued.

After going through the gate and closing it, I turned southwest on I-17 toward Phoenix. After a few minutes I pulled off the highway, got out, and looked up. The object was still in sight and I could still hear the humming noise. Suddenly a very bright light appeared on the northern end of the row of lights and stayed on for several seconds. It then blinked on and off two or three times. Then the bright light came on the south end of the object, blinking on and off several times. Then the north end lights came on again as if in response to the south end lights. During this time the object continued moving in a southern direction toward Phoenix. When the lights were no longer in sight I continued south on I-17. Thinking I might see this strange object again I stopped several times to look. It was gone! No lights, no humming sound! Nothing. I thought to myself, "Was that for real?"

By the way, the Department did not participate in the rancher's road.

About Staff

by Wendell G. Swank

O. N. "Pop" Arrington was head of the Game Management Division when I came to work for the Department. He came to Arizona from one of the mid-western states; Indiana, I think. I don't know much about Pop's background or how he became interested in wildlife. He did hunt and loved to fish, but was always much too preoccupied with getting the job done to become really enthusiastic about either. I do know at one time he had something to do with the hotel business, because he always asked the price of a room before making a commitment. He said that in the hotel business there were always two prices, one for those who didn't ask the price, and one for those who did.

* * * *

Pittman-Robertson federal funds were just becoming available when World War II started curtailing almost all wildlife conservation activities. After the war, the Arizona Game Department had to grow in order to catch up, therefore most of us in the Game Management Branch were new to Arizona. We all did a lot of traveling around the State in those days, hence there was a lot of "eating out," and per diems were limited. Pop was rather fussy about food, and went out of his way to help the new arrivals eat in good places rather than bad. On the basis of his experience, Arrington prepared a list of "good eating places" by town. Under Holbrook he wrote, "Drive on to Winslow."

* * * *

In the early 1950s, the Department was transplanting antelope, catching them in fenced drift traps as they migrated off Anderson Mesa. When the weather turned foul we all gathered at Raymond Buffalo Ranch to lend a hand. Everyone brought their chuck box into the bunkhouse (it was a big bunkhouse in those days) and lined them up against the wall in the dining area. Pop was a late riser, and he detested pulling on Levi's over his bare skin on a cold morning. Who doesn't? So, when camping out he usually appeared for breakfast either in his pajamas or his clothes over his pajamas.

Pop was also a very civilized person, and believed in having a little bourbon and good conversation before dinner. Through experience he found that the bottle was frequently empty at critical times, because his friends had borrowed a little. Being cagy, he solved the problem by putting the bourbon in a Log Cabin syrup bottle, and tearing a corner off the label so he would be certain to get the right contents to suit the occasion. One morning Pop appeared as usual, late and in pajamas. Everyone was busy with breakfast when he entered the room and looking over the fare on the table he noticed that Brownie Holmes had the hallowed bottle in front of his plate, with pancakes swimming in a golden liquid.

Pop was aghast, and said, "Brownie, that isn't syrup!"

Without looking up, Brownie continued to chew away and retorted, "Don't you think I know it."

* * * *

Levi Packard was always ready with the right comment to fit the occasion, and one of those time was in the late fall of 1961. Levi, Arnold Kester and I were after ducks on small impoundments on Anderson Mesa. Other areas of the United States were down in duck numbers, but in the late 1950s and early 1960s, the Western Flyway had an abundance of birds, particularly pintails and widgeons (they were called baldpates then). The daily bag limit was ten, plus four bonus ducks, either baldpates or pintails, so there was an opportunity to do a lot of shooting. Levi and I hunted one impoundment and Arnold went to another close by, with the idea we would keep the birds flying between us. There were a lot of ducks in the area, and Levi and I limited out in about an hour. We field dressed our birds, listening to a lot of shooting coming from Arnold's area. Finally, Levi and I went over to where Arnold had set out his decoys. Arnold had a couple of ducks and there were empty shotgun shells all over the ground. When asked how he was doing Arnold said, "The ducks are flying high, and I guess my old 16 gauge can't reach up there to get them." Levi looked at the ground littered with empties and replied, "Arnold, if you crawled up on that pile of shells you would be a lot closer."

* * * *

Another fellow that always seemed to have an appropriate and humorous comeback was Bill Anderson who worked for the Kaibab National Forest in the 1950s. Forest Service and Game Department employees worked side by side in those days, checking hunters, making winter surveys and operating the Jacob Lake Deer Checking Station. One day Bill and I were driving toward the Grand Canyon National Park from Jacob Lake during the early hunt, and stopped to talk to a woman who was just returning to her car. We asked her how the hunt was going, and she replied that she had seen a lot of does but doubted that there were any bucks on the Kaibab. Bill, with a grin on his face said, "Well, I don't know about that, but there sure are a lot of fawns around." With that, he pulled away, not wishing to pursue that particular discussion.

* * * *

About a dozen Department and U. S. Forest Service people were trying to finish the 1952 North Kaibab winter deer surveys and had been snowed in for several days at the Big Springs Forest Camp. It was decided Bill Anderson would go to Jacob Lake to call Louis Jurwitz, the state meteorologist in Phoenix, to get a forecast, then we would decide to either stay and finish the survey, or postpone it and go home. Bill came back to camp and everyone gathered around to get the decision.

The first question was, "Did he say it was going to stop snowing?"

Bill replied, "Well, not exactly."

Our next question was, "Did he say it was going to continue?"

Bill answered, "Well, he didn't say that either."

We then asked, "Bill, did you tell him it has been snowing here for several days, and it looks like it isn't going to stop?"

Bill's comeback was, "No, you know how these weathermen are, I wasn't about to give him any hints."

* * * *

Before the Black Canyon Highway (Interstate 17) to Flagstaff and the Bee Line Highway to Payson were finished it was a long drive to get from Phoenix to the pine country or any place beyond the Rim. There were two paved highways, and to get from Phoenix to Flagstaff you had to go through Wickenburg, Congress Junction, Prescott, Jerome and Sedona; a four to five hour drive. The other route was through Globe, Salt River Canyon, Show Low and Springerville; again a four to five hour drive. A trip to the North Kaibab was a hard twelve hours on the road. As a consequence we tried to do as much on each trip as we could without returning to Phoenix. That put a lot of extra pressure on wives, and as we were mostly a young group, and that meant children as well.

Dennie Illege was a biologist responsible for the Payson area, and the road between Payson and Phoenix was not much more than an improved trail. Mary and Dennie had several young children, and Mary refused to live in Payson because there were no doctors available to attend the many ailments usually afflicting kids. This meant that Dennie was away from home most of the time. Because most Game Department wives had similar problems they used to get together at coffee clutches to commiserate with one another. The Illiges's Scottsdale house had a nice backyard, but you got there by going out the front door and around the house. Mary wanted to be able to put the kids out a side door with direct access to the yard so she could keep an eye on them.

In spite of numerous discussions and pleadings, Dennie kept putting off the new doorway because he couldn't work it into his busy schedule. One morning the wives gathered at Mary's house for the coffee clutch: Ski Smith, Bob's wife, Vivian Bumstead, Roger's wife, Waneta Swank, my wife, and of course Mary. In the discussion that ensued it was decided to solve Mary's problem. They drew an outline of a door on the wall where Mary wanted it, and proceeded to smash a hole with a sledge hammer. That made a rather rough opening, so they decided to make it neater. Later, when relating the event, Dennie said he didn't mind having to put in the door, but he sure was irritated because the women used his good wood chisels on the block wall to even up the edges.

* * * *

We were always short-handed and fall hunting activities kept Department personnel away from home over extended periods, sometimes several weeks. Waneta Swank was doing some early Christmas shopping with her two children, Bill, five, and Robin who was twelve. As they proceeded from shop to shop, Bill, probably noticing that most families had an adult male in tow, looked up at his mother and asked, "Is our Daddy dead?" So much for the good old days!

Get a Stick and Whack Him!

by W. R. "Bob" Hernbrode

About seventy miles east of Phoenix is a narrow, deep lake created by Horse Mesa Dam. Apache Lake is one of the chain of lakes built to provide irrigation water and hydro-electric power to the Salt River Valley. It is a popular fishing lake. North of the lake, rising abruptly from the Sonoran Desert habitat are the Mazatzal Mountains. The Four Peaks area there provides good habitat for white tail deer, mule deer, javelina, and black bear.

This story is about two Game Rangers, two fishermen, and a bear. It probably started in some back yard when they tried to raise a bear cub. When they found out that a big bear is not a good pet, it was released. The way the bear acted, it had only been in the wild a few days before these events took place.

After being on Apache Lake for awhile, one of the bass fishermen had to answer a call of nature. Putting the boat ashore in a small cove, one angler stayed in the boat while the other walked up a sandy wash. It was a quiet day and as this unsuspecting angler was about to complete his job he heard a loud "woof" off to the right. He looked into the brush and there to his surprise was a large black bear. He sold out for the boat and safety with his pants at half mast, yelling at his buddy to get the motor started, now! It must have been quite a sight to see this guy running down the sand wash, pants down around his knees, with a bear ambling along behind.

These fishermen had another problem. Beaching the boat they had raised the prop. When the fisherman in the boat saw the trouble his partner was in, he immediately tipped the motor, sticking the prop in the sand. With the boat stuck and the bear fast approaching, they both jumped into the lake and swam out of harms way. The bear stopped at the boat and looked around for something to eat as the two treaded water, twenty-five yards away. After searching the boat for food the bear left. The fishermen returned to the boat, leaving in a hurry.

Going down the lake away from the danger they flagged down two Game Rangers on patrol and told the bear story. Still soaking wet from their swim it was evident that they had a bad scare. It was a pretty wild story, but sounded possible. The Rangers went to investigate.

Buck Wallace, from Mesa, was a happy-go-lucky guy, always smiling, full of energy and the nervous type. He was six foot two, about 160 pounds. Bill Farrow, from Globe was a big, burly, slow moving, quiet spoken fellow, about six feet weighing 240 pounds. They worked really well together.

It didn't take long to find the cove the anglers described, as the Rangers knew every nook and cranny of the lake. The actions of the bear, looking for food and showing no fear of people, made them suspect someone had turned a tame bear loose. Landing and looking around they were not too concerned for their own safety. Following the bear tracks up the sandy wash about a hundred yards they were surprised when the bear popped out of the brush. The bear moved slowly toward the Rangers making grunting and whining noises, looking for a handout. Having nothing to offer Buck and Bill started to back slowly toward the boat, the bear following. The bear became agitated and took a swipe at Bill. Expecting something like this to happen, he was quick enough to get out of the way. Running to the boat was now a good idea, so he took off. The bear followed him and Buck followed the bear. Bill stayed a half step ahead of the bear on his race to the boat. The bear continued to take an occasional swipe at Bill's ample posterior missing only by the thickness of his Levis. Following the bear, Buck shouted at Bill, "Get a stick and whack him!" Buck must have forgotten that he was in the best position to do the whacking. By the time Bill got to the boat he must have torn up half an acre of catclaw and palo verde, going like a runaway Sherman tank. Reaching the boat he grabbed a paper sack with some candy bars and apples and threw it at the bear.

When the bear stopped to eat the apples, Buck launched the boat. Only then did they have a good laugh about what they had gone through. Buck praised Bill about his brush busting and sprinting in getting away from such a scrawny bear. Bill, of course, chastised Buck because he didn't, "Pick up a stick and whack him!"

After all the laughing and cheers, they talked about what should be done with the bear. Unfortunately, they decided it had to be destroyed before it hurt someone.

The Pie-wagon Pig

told by Don Vance

Picking up live animals from populated areas and taking them somewhere for release is routine. Most of the time this is a rather easy task and presents no problems for the wildlife manager. Sometimes a pick up goes bad.

This is about Henry Stotts, his Ford pie-wagon and a javelina. (At least I think it was Henry. If it wasn't Henry, it was someone just like him.) He started with the Department as a Game Ranger and after the 1960 re-organization, a Ranger-at-Large. He worked the Scottsdale and Buckeye areas during his career.

In the 1950s, the Department bought a few Ford pie-wagons. These cars were built on the same frame as a station wagon, except they had no windows behind the drivers seat. Henry had one of these pie-wagons as his patrol car. One day he was assigned to pick up a javelina that was in town. Capturing the javelina wasn't much of a problem. Putting it in a cage in the back of the patrol car was accomplished without much trouble. With that part of the task completed, Henry started to take the pig to its future destination. On the way, in the middle of Phoenix, the javelina got out of the cage. That was big trouble for Henry! A javelina loose in the back of a pickup is one thing, but loose inside of that pie-wagon was quite another. It had direct access to the driver, and it was not a happy pig. It could become a real western rodeo pretty fast.

Henry stopped, got out, and quickly studied the situation. He had a couple of options. He could just open the door and let the javelina out before it wrecked the inside of his patrol car. But, that would just cause future problems. Someone would have to catch that pig again, and it would probably be Henry. He didn't like the idea of trying to catch that pig again, especially in downtown Phoenix with everyone watching.

The second option was to try to put that pig back in the cage, while keeping it in his patrol car. That seemed like an impossible task to do by himself, and getting help would take time. By the time help arrived, his car would be a mess.

The third option came to Henry's mind quickly and seemed the best even though it might result in a big fuss. Henry acted quickly. He got out his service revolver and shot the javelina, while it was still in the back of his pie-wagon.

Problem solved!

I'll Accept

told by Phil Cosper

In the mid 1950s, Bob White was completing work on his whitetail deer feeding study in the Canelo Hills and was about to earn his Master's Degree from the University of Arizona. The Department was interested in hiring Bob as a biologist so they invited him to go to the North Kaibab with some of the staff, including Johnny Russo and Phil Cosper. Everyone stayed at Ryan Station, a remote Department bunkhouse on the west side of the Kaibab. They worked during the day and played poker at night. This went on for several days. After the work was completed Bob rode with Phil Cosper back to the Phoenix office. Driving down the highway they talked about the Department, the kind of work the agency did, pay scales, job prospects and on and on.

When they got to Grey Mountain, Phil put the direct question to Bob, "Would you accept a position with the Department?"

Bob thought about it awhile and finally answered, "Well, the Department sure doesn't pay very well, and that's not too good, but with what I can win from you in poker I think I can make it. I'll accept!"

Bob stayed with the Department for over twenty years and retired as the Region I Supervisor in Pinetop. During his years with the Department I'm sure Bob probably won a lot of poker hands from Phil and many other Department employees.

Trapping Geese

by Wes Fleming

In the 1950s, the Department trapped and banded Canada geese at Roosevelt Lake. The standard trapping technique was to bait an area with grain and use a cannon net. The cannon shoots a net trapping the birds feeding on the bait. Once and awhile the bait attracts other critters that may also be trapped.

For several days we had baited our trap location on the far side of the Tonto Creek arm of Roosevelt Lake. When the geese started to come into the bait we set up the cannon nets and waited. Don Taylor, one of the Department's best roustabouts, and I were in a blind waiting for the flock to take the bait.

Pretty soon a speed boat screamed down the middle of the lake making a ninety degree turn directly toward our trap set up. It was coming full speed at our blind. The boat twisted through some submerged mesquite trees and slammed against the rocks. Over the bow jumped this guy in a big white cowboy hat. It was Pat Kelly, the local Game Ranger. He was running toward our blind, confident he had just caught the most blatant poachers dead to rights. He knew we were "dead meat!"

When Kelly got within ten yards of our blind we stood up. He stopped short when he recognized us and hollered, "For Christ sake, what the hell are you damn biologists doing?" And he screamed, "Why wasn't I notified? Who authorized this project on MY LAKE!"

Communication within Department Divisions wasn't the forte in those days!

Duck, He's Shooting At Us!

by Steve Gallizioli

Today, wildlife managers, and other Department field personnel, are well equipped for practically any contingency. Everyone who drives off the pavement has a four-wheel drive rig equipped with a two-way radio that provides state-wide communication with base stations and other mobile vehicles. They are also well armed with semi-automatic pistols, riot shotguns, and even body armor.

While I seldom packed a sidearm in the course of my duties with the

Department, there was a time when I felt that something on the order of a surface-to-air missile might have been appropriate. It happened sometime back in the late 1950s.

Dr. Wendell Swank, who would shortly become Director of Game and Fish, and I, were paying an overnight visit to Sand Tank Well in the Sand Tank Mountains, a desert mountain range situated some twenty five miles southeast of Gila Bend. It was early July and temperatures had been running around 115 degrees for several days.

We were interested in learning whether whitewing doves were still concentrating at this famous waterhole. If they were, we intended to send a trapping crew to band a few hundred of this desert loving species to determine whether they contributed to the Arizona dove harvest or headed directly for Mexico after nesting.

Instead of today's standard four-wheel drive, air-conditioned pick-ups, equipped with two-way radios, we were in a two-wheel drive, un-airconditioned, Chevrolet suburban. This was long before the Department even had a two-way radio system. If we needed to communicate with the outside world we would have to do it the hard way — with smoke signals. Our most important "emergency" items were a five gallon water can, an axe and a jack.

To reach Sand Tank Well, we had to drive across the Gila Bend Gunnery Range, regularly used for target practice by aircraft from the local base. Standard Operation Procedure called for us to check in with the base and let them know we would be in the area, the type of vehicle we were driving, etc. The base in turn would notify us whether they planned any serious firing along our route of travel.

To expedite our trip Wendell and I had "forgotten" to contact the base about our intentions and destination. As we drove across the desert heading for the Sand Tanks we noticed that the military had hauled in a lot of old junked cars and scattered them around as targets for aircraft. Also we found a number of simulated bridges made of plywood over various sand washes, obviously being used for target practice.

Our trip in was uneventful and we spent the night near Sand Tank Well. The next morning, after recording information about white-winged dove abundance, we headed back towards Gila Bend just before noon. Our suburban had started acting up and caused us some concern because of its tendency to stall out when we gave it gas to get through sand washes. Still, we were making progress until we came to a particularly wide wash that military four wheel drive vehicles had pulverized in recent days. We had managed to get through it going in but our balky engine now got us stuck. And this is where our "adventure" really began.

We got out our massive bumper jack and proceeded to jack up the rear end. We used the axe to chop down brush and small trees to insert under the wheels. By now it was past noon and literally hotter than the hinges of hell. I don't know how many times we jacked up that vehicle, placed brush, logs and rocks under the rear tires and then "gassed 'er" to get through the soft sand. We were making progress, veeerry slowly.

The balky engine didn't help as it stalled on us every time we gained a couple more feet. Every three or four minutes we had to take a long drink from our five gallon can and rest from our exertions. The water by now was almost hot and had a most unpleasant odor, but drink it we did nonetheless.

While we had been working to extricate ourselves we could hear single engine military planes (they were propeller driven at the time) off in the distance, and frequently heard the planes fire single booming shots, obviously from some type of cannon. We didn't pay much attention until one appeared in the distance, heading our way. The same thought struck both of us at the same time: Would that fly-boy mistake our stalled vehicle for one of the junk car targets? Realizing that was a very real possibility, I got out in front of the vehicle and took off my T-shirt. When the plane turned in our direction I began to frantically wave the shirt over my head. On came the plane and I suddenly realized that we were about to experience something I had been lucky enough to avoid during World War II, the receiving end of aircraft fire. "Get under cover — fast" was my only thought. Frantically, I looked for a large boulder that might provide some cover. There weren't any! I looked back at the plane which was now pointed directly at us and saw a puff of white smoke. The pilot had fired!

Wendell was inside the vehicle at the moment and without giving any thought to what I was doing I yelled, "Duck, he's shooting at us!" and made a dive for the nearest palo verde tree. I heard what I thought was an explosion and a cloud of dust rose about twenty yards away. The plane pulled away as I jumped up and vented my frustration with the situation by using every invective learned during my three years in the Navy. The pilot must have heard me! Or perhaps he had suddenly realized we were something more than a wrecked car. Or maybe he was out of ammo! Whatever the reason, we were happy he did not come back for seconds, and watched with considerable relief as he disappeared in the distance.

Investigating, we discovered the projectile lobbed at us had ripped a furrow in the desert floor six to eight inches wide, four to five inches deep and about eight feet long. It had landed about halfway between our vehicle and one of the plywood bridges. Apparently it had not been armed with an explosive head. If the pilot had his sights on us we were thankful his aim was no better. It was close enough!

It took us another half hour to extricate ourselves from that wash. By the time we did we were both on the verge of collapse and badly dehydrated despite forcing ourselves to continue drinking the foul smelling hot water. The temperature was so high that the metal water can itself was almost too hot to handle.

We were too exhausted to talk about the experience as Wendell drove us into Gila Bend. We parked a short distance from an establishment that dispensed cold beverages and entered the dark and delightfully cool interior. Parking ourselves on a couple of bar stools we ordered two bottles of beer and two large glasses of water. For the next couple of hours we sat there alternating between beer and water, going over and over our recent experience as we slowly came back to life. We didn't head back to Phoenix until well after dark and the desert temperatures had dropped a few degrees.

That was the last time either of us visited Sand Tank Well!

A High Country Rescue

by Harold Van Sickle

We are all called from time to time to rescue people who get bogged down in the mud, snow, or with a disabled vehicle. As a Game Ranger in the Flagstaff area from 1953 through 1965, I was called out many times to help people in trouble in the high country. It seems to me I've rescued more people than anyone else in the Department. This includes hunters, fishermen, travelers, airplane crash survivors and so on. And yes, even Game and Fish people.

One rescue of three Department employees has stayed in my memory for a long time. It happened in late winter near Woods Canyon Lake. The Department had just completed the construction of Woods Canyon Dam and Bob Jantzen, Big Game Supervisor, wanted to check the water level. It had been raining and snowing and he thought the lake might be near spillway level. There was a lot of snow on the ground, and he did not want to go alone so Jack Murray, Game Ranger from Winslow went with him. Well, they didn't get there. They got stuck in the snow and radioed for help. Bill Farrow, Game Ranger from Claypool was in the area and he said he would go get them. He knew his vehicle would not get to where Jantzen and Murray were stuck. He went to the U. S. Forest Service Chevelon Ranger Station south of Winslow hoping to use one of their four wheel drive vehicles. No one was there so he "borrowed" a big Dodge Power Wagon and went to the rescue. Bill never made it to Woods Canyon Lake, getting stuck on the main road in the new snow. He had no radio communication and no one knew where he was. After two days had passed I got a call from Department Headquarters in Phoenix to advise me of the situation and to see if I could find out what was going on and if there was a way to help them.

The weather had turned really nasty and there was a lot of new snow. I needed something better than a four wheel drive vehicle. I contacted the State Highway Department and was able to obtain a Tucker Snow Cat. The Highway Department employee and I trucked the Snow Cat south of Winslow until the truck got stuck in the snow. Unloading the Snow Cat, we proceeded on to Woods Canyon Lake. We knew about where Jantzen and Murray were, but had no idea where Farrow was. On the way we noticed a large hump in the road. It was the Forest Service Dodge Power Wagon completely covered with snow. When I got out of the Snow Cat I went up to my hips in snow. I had not realized how deep the snow was as the Snow Cat traveled on top on the snow and made tracks only eight inches deep. We had to dig in the snow to open the door of the Power Wagon. At the time we did not know if Bill was inside. There was no sound coming from the vehicle. He was there, but he was not in very good shape. He had been without food for two days and was about to freeze to death. Because the truck heater did not work he had built small fires inside the cab from wood chips and gasoline to keep warm. I thought he was dead when I first saw him. He was all black with soot. He was unable to move by himself but we helped him into the Snow Cat and warmed him up with some hot coffee and a bite to eat. We needed to get Bill to a hospital, but we also had to find Jantzen and Murray.

We continued on and a short time later found our stranded pair. They were in good shape. They had food and were able to keep warm with the heater in their vehicle. We got Bill to the hospital in Winslow as soon as possible. The doctor told us that if we had not found Bill when we did, he would have been dead in two hours. He recovered without any problems.

I remember the rescue of a few other Department employees, but none quite as dramatic. I remember rescuing Game Rangers Carl Jones at General Springs and Jimmy Allen at Chavez Pass. I also got George Daniels out of a jam when he was in the East Pocket area above Oak Creek Canyon. I'm sure they remember the details of these events better that I do. At least they know how and why I had to come to their rescue.

Most of the time all we get for our rescue efforts is a thank you. And that's enough. But one time the Elks Lodge in Flagstaff gave me a beautiful Bulova watch for my efforts. I still have it and it reminds me of my days with the Department.

The Gila Monster

by Virginia Yates

Before the Department moved to the present offices on Greenway Road in northwest Phoenix, the administrative offices were located in the Capitol complex on the corner of 17th Avenue and Adams. The shop facilities and a warm water hatchery were at Papago Park where the Phoenix Zoo is now located. Because we were a wildlife agency, strange things sometimes happened.

One day someone brought a Gila monster to the office. The poisonous reptile had wandered into their backyard and they did not want it around and could not kill it. So naturally, they gave it to us to take care of. This giant lizard was put in a burlap bag for safekeeping, and placed under Phil Cosper's desk until someone could release it in the desert. That someone was Charlie Jordan, and he wasn't going to be in the office until the morning. No problem, the Gila monster would stay in the bag overnight.

The next morning the first thing Phil did was to check on his guest. Phil quickly stepped back when he discovered the bag was untied and empty. There was minor panic and everyone was going around carefully checking where they put their feet. We all knew that Gila monsters were slow, but we also knew they had a nasty bite and they did not like to let go. Everyone was looking under their desk and other places. I was trying to think like a lizard. Where would I be if I were a lizard and in a strange place?

I thought, if I were a lizard looking for a place to hide, I would try to find somewhere dark and cool. So I headed for the storage vault near Phil's desk, and there it was. As I recall, Paul Webb was one of our newest biologists, so we sent him in to "trap and transplant" the critter. As soon as that was done everyone relaxed and went back to work.

The Cibola Valley Information Center

by Wes Fleming

Pop Arrington was Chief of the Lands Division in 1958. He had a bright idea of developing a waterfowl area in the Cibola Valley along the Colorado River. He and I flew over the valley looking for Section 36, which was state land. After awhile we thought we located it, but needed to find the section corners to establish a legal description of the accreted lands between the river and Section 36. The southern half of Cibola Valley was a jungle of salt cedar and mesquite, with no roads, some wild cows, and a few squatters and woodcutters.

We had to find the section corners. Assistant Coordinator of the Wildlife Restoration Division Bob Smith, Pop and I drove into the area looking for a way into the jungle. Finding a two track road going into a mesquite thicket, we drove until we came to a log that had been placed there to block access. Bob and I moved the log and we continued on. We soon saw a campfire through the trees and a bearded character sitting on a log with a 30-30 rifle laying across his lap.

Pop looked at this character and then at Bob and said, "Bob, go check him out."

Bob looked at Pop and then at me and said, "Wes, go check him out."

Being low man on the totem pole I got out, mumbled something to myself, and walked toward the guy with the rifle. When I got about twenty feet from him he yelled, "Don't come any closer, my friend!" I may have taken one more step when a large animal came busting out from behind a log, running directly at me. Lunging, he stopped abruptly a foot from my neck when he reached the end of his chain. It was a large boar raccoon the old character had for a pet. Well, it scared the hell out of me. But, I introduced myself and we talked. In fact, we all talked for a long time about the Cibola Valley. He turned out to be a reasonable and knowledgeable man. He knew everything we needed to know.

This old guy had been born in the Valley and knew where every section corner was, who owned each parcel of land and when it was bought and sold. He was an encyclopedia of information. If he washed up, and dressed in a suit and tie, he would fit behind any professional's desk. We had found the source of information to locate the section corners for our waterfowl project.

A Ranger's Best Friend

by W. R. "Bob" Hernbrode

At the time of this story, Carl Jones was a Ranger Captain and working the dove hunt in the desert. He started working for the Department in 1942 as a Ranger in the Prescott area. His experience with hunters gave him a good nose for sniffing out violations. In fact, he was probably the best there was.

Dove hunters often hunt around stock tanks in the desert, shooting doves as they come to water in the morning or evening. Carl was checking stock tanks when he turned off the pavement onto a two track road leading to a popular dove hunting area. There were fresh tracks leading to the stock tank so he was sure he would find some hunters. This tank was surrounded by mesquite trees so he stopped short of the tank to listen and use his binoculars. He always liked to watch hunters before checking licenses and game bags. He looked and listened. He saw no one and heard no shots. As he was about to start his patrol car and move on, he heard the sound of a car coming from the direction of the stock tank. He waited. Coming toward him out of the trees was a sedan with a couple of hunters. When the car approached he waved at them to stop.

"Evening fellers, how's the shooting?" he asked. In the car with the two hunters was a black Labrador retriever. The dog had obviously been working hard, because his big red tongue was hanging out and he was panting heavily. Carl thought to himself that these hunters must have had a good dove shoot. One of the hunters answered, "Pretty good, in fact real good, lots of doves and a bunch of white-wings for a change."

"Great," Carl said. "I'd like to check your licenses and see your birds."

"Sure thing," the hunter replied. As they got out of the car the black Lab jumped out and raced back up the road. The hunter tried to call him back, but it wouldn't listen. It had something to do. As Carl checked licenses the Lab came back holding his head high and wagging his tail. In its mouth was a green wing teal. Whoops! Duck season was closed. Carl took the duck and got his citation book. The dog took off again and in short order retrieved another teal. And then, it did it again. Each time expecting a "Good dog!" and a pat on the head from his master. No such luck, at least not for these retrieves.

Carl never saw the ducks thrown out the window, but the Lab did and he had a good mark on where they landed. Carl thought it would have been fun to watch the Lab work, since he was such a good retriever. That dog would have made a good Ranger. Carl had good help sniffing out this violation, and it was from the hunter's Lab.

Three Springs in the Mountain

by Ted Knipe

Finding springs, following their performance and judging their value to wildlife as watering places, was part of my work as a wildlife manager. I recorded 191 springs in my field notes over the years and became somewhat of an amateur springologist. No two springs are exactly alike, but the following three had singular features not recognized in others.

In the Santa Catalina Mountains, at the foot of a cliff on the face of Pusch Ridge, a lone cottonwood tree grew. I could see it from the base of the mountain. There had to be water there because cottonwoods are water guzzlers. My concern was, did the wet spot provide water for wildlife in dry weather? So on a hot June day I set out afoot to find out. The three mile trip to the tree was over steep, rock strewn country, so my walking was slow, but not tedious. Along the way I came to a damp place at the base of a ledge. Several bees and one wasp were sucking wetness from the soil.

The essence of springology is knowing when to tinker with them and when to leave them be. I tinkered with this one because, as my cowboy friend would say, "I was thirsty as a mudhen on a tin roof." My tinkering produced a seep sufficient to fill a two ounce jigger in two or three minutes. I sipped the good water and tarried long enough for two refills.

When I got to the large cottonwood tree I found no surface water, it had exclusive use of an underground source. No water for me or the wildlife.

On my way back down the mountain I stopped at "Mudhen Springs" for another drink of the finest water I ever drank.

In Spanish, "ojos" are eyes on the face of living beings; they are also springs on the face of the earth, pouring out water from underground. Ojo Blanco is a spring on the eastern slope of Mount Fagan of the Santa Rita Mountains. Pelar el ojo means "keep your eyes peeled." That's what I should have done when I got down on my hands and knees and drank the mountain water. Raising my head I was eyeball to eyeball with a coiled rattlesnake on the opposite side of the spring, its poisonous fangs only a foot from my forehead. I reared back and tumbled a yard or two down the hillside. I got up, emotionally thanked the snake for sparing my life, then continued my journey, slightly bruised and deeply shaken.

Rural people in Mexico say there is a snake known to them as La Corûa. It lives in springs and protects them. Kill the snake and the spring dries up. They say it is harmless, which explains why the rattler didn't strike my forehead.

The third spring was an enchanting wildlife drinking fountain in a chaotic escarpment of towering rock cliffs, slot canyons and dusky coves. The spring water poured forth from a crevice in the face of a craggy bluff. The stream, the volume of a urinating fountain cherub, trickled down the moss covered rock, formed a small pool at the foot of the bluff, meandered through a tiny meadow, then sunk back into the earth's crust.

Springs of this nature are rare in semi-dry climates, but may be commonplace where precipitation is bountiful. For instance, in J. R. R.Tolkien's fantasy, *Lord of the Rings*, Frodo and eight other elfin hobbits were following a trail on their way to return a magic ring to Modoc. Rounding a hill "...they saw before them a low cliff, some 5 fathoms high, with a broken and jagged top. Over it trickling water dripped through a wide cleft that seemed to have been carved out by a fall." Tolkien, no doubt saw such a spring somewhere.

This spring and the landscape is the stuff that inspires poets. I'll leave it at that. It's best the wilderness solitude remains undisturbed and the wildlife unharassed by hordes of environmentalists, backpackers, bird watchers and so forth.

What's For Lunch?

told by Phil Cosper

In 1959, Don Berlinski was in training to become the new Assistant Waterfowl Biologist and Wildlife Area Manager. His boss was Wes Fleming, the state Waterfowl Biologist and the guy in charge of the Department's Wildlife Areas. Wes was a burly kind of guy, who prided himself on being rough around the edges and a little intimidating. One of the first assignments that Wes gave Don was some work at Raymond Buffalo Ranch east of Flagstaff. Wes told Don he would meet him at the Ranch the next morning. He also told Don to buy lunch and take it to the Ranch. They both arrived early the next day, meeting with the Ranch Manager, Jack Woolsey. They worked hard and it was time for lunch.

"What's for lunch?" Wes asked.

Don got the ice chest out of the back of the pickup and took it to Wes. Except for some ice, the only things inside the cooler were a case of beer, a big stick of hard salami and some crackers.

Wes looked inside the ice chest, then directly at Don. Then with the most serious expression he could generate, said, "Don, I wondered about you, but you just passed your trainee period with flying colors!"

Running Out of Gas

told by Al Essbach

There are a lot of stories we could tell about Howard "Bud" Bassett. He started in the 1950s with the Department as a Fisheries Biologist and retired years later as the Chief of Field Operations.

It seems that one day Bud was driving a sedan along a rocky, nasty road. At the top of the hill a rock jumped up and knocked off his gas tank. Being an old fisheries biologist, he wasn't too concerned with the loud noise associated with the rock hitting the underside of his car or the rumbling noise of the tank falling off. The engine kept running and the oil pressure gauge looked OK, so he continued driving down the hill.

Well, about a mile or so down the road the engine quit and Bud had to figure out why. After a while, he came to the conclusion that gas wasn't getting to the carbureter. So he started to check out the lines. When he finally traced the gas line back to the gas tank, he knew what had caused the loud noise. It took time and some effort walking up the hill to find the gas tank, carrying it back to the car, putting it on and hooking up the broken lines. But eventually, Bud got to where he was going!

Kill and Run

by Harold Van Sickle

The following story was published in the June 1990 issue of the Department's Wildlife Views. The story takes place in the 1950s. It has been abbreviated for inclusion in this book.

I listened intently in the dark forest. The hum of an engine echoed again, but was fading! It seemed to be vanishing toward my partner. We were staked out trying to catch the most vicious, illegal, big game killer in Arizona.

Pressing on the button of my microphone I called my partner. "Subject passing in your direction. Do you see him?"

"No I don't," came the prompt reply. "I thought he was on your side."

"What!" I gasped as I stared into the dark forest. No sound echoed now. I had suffered this failure before trying to bring this game law violator to justice. He foxiness was uncanny.

We will call this man "Willie Manson." Willie had been convicted of illegal game killing many times. His record stretched back for years. For every fine he paid, Willie got away with a hundred kills. His game killings made a warden's blood boil. He was a professional poacher. The peculiar thrill of it was in his blood. He was the slickest poacher I had seen.

Bright starlight makes it a cinch to accomplish night kills. We had known for weeks Willie was invading the forests on a new spurt of wildlife destruction. On this stakeout, we closed in on him with our radio equipped cars. Tracing him to this stand of timber, we hid beside the only two roads out of the area. A rifle banged once in the night. We waited expectantly, believing he would fall into our trap.

Instead, Willie disappeared! After so much tedious stalking, I promised myself I would devote all possible time to apprehending him. He was responsible for destroying more wildlife around Flagstaff than all other poachers combined.

People like Willie obey one iron clad rule: kill and run! But that's not all. They also shoot at game rangers! We had to be careful.

Professional game killers, such as Willie Mason, are dead shots with a rifle and have no scruples. Trying to pierce the silent darkness, I wondered if he was now scouting his escape route, with rifle held at ready. Unconsciously, my right hand shifted to my revolver.

The radio broke the silence. "Van. He's out! He's going over the hill! I can see his lights." Tricky Willie had somehow driven through the timber without lights. Once on the road he was forced to use lights. Willie had made monkeys of us so often it seemed we would never nab him. He fled right out of our grasp. We raced after him, down the dirt roads, then along the main highway to town, but when we reached his home, we found him all washed up and wearing clean clothes. He stood snickering while we searched his house. "I told you," he said, "I done quit shootin' game after that last fine."

He was referring to a $500 fine he paid for killing an elk out of season. At the time, he had remarked with a sly grin, "I can afford this as long as I stay in business!" During that same period, he also forked over $1,350 in fines for bootlegging liquor. Willie also made money from big game killing, but I never knew how.

The radiator of his pickup still steamed. There was fresh blood and deer hair in the bed of his pick up, but this evidence was no good without a carcass. We left him. That infuriated me, whetting my decision to keep after him.

Doing detective work on Willie and watching him while trying to cover my territory proved tough. My area was huge. I knew it would not be long until Willie went out again. Once more I returned to stalking Willie. Waiting for him to make his move, I mapped the sites of his known kills. They formed a definite pattern, and the dates proved illuminating. It appeared he never went near the site of a previous kill. I gave closer study to Willie's habits than any other criminal.

He employed tricks that took time to crack. He had a secret cache for freshly killed game meat. He also changed cars and tires. He used extra tires to leave a confusion of tread marks. Frequently he borrowed a friend's car, using it only once. One evening I saw him leave town.

Studying my map I decided he would enter a refuge where he had not been before, or at least I had no record of his kill and run jobs there.

Traveling east on Highway 66, I turned south at Toonerville onto a road I felt sure he would use. A mile out, I parked in the juniper country. If Willie came up the road he would not recognize the Department car until he was too close. Traffic on the road was light. Time drifted. A few cars passed, but not Willie. Then headlights broke around the curve. That could be my man. When the car came near, I turned on a light shining it on the identifiable Game and Fish car.

The car did not slow down, increased speed, forcing me to leap to safety. It was a coupe with a medium sized man. He was not Willie, but because he didn't stop I tore after him. When the driver slowed for the junction I caught him.

To my surprise, the driver of the car was a long time resident of Flagstaff. I searched his coupe and found a small deer, but that's another story. Once again I lost Willie.

Nothing was going to distract me now until I apprehended Willie. I returned to work, trying to ferret out his cache. If I couldn't get him at the site of his kill, catching him in possession of game meat would be just as good. I prowled after dark examining three dozen buildings near his home. Failure. Willie seemed too slick for me. Then one night while inspecting his neighborhood, Willie drove away in a pickup. Running to my car, I followed him. Heavy traffic slowed him and I saw him at a stoplight. He went to the Fort Valley Highway, a route taking him to game country. Forced to maintain distance to avoid discovery, I lost him. Speeding up, I reached the edge of Fort Valley, five miles from Flagstaff. The road was empty. Willie had turned off on a side road.

Pulling onto Snowbowl Road, I parked. I moved on foot to a timbered area. I had passed three side roads, one to the north and two to the south. Willie could have taken any one of them. My hope was to spot his lights returning to the main road. I heard no rifle shots, but the glare of headlights soon flashed in the treetops. It could be Willie. He worked that fast.

Into the car, I followed. Soon I was doing 90 miles per hour, but no tail lights were in view. I kept going. Still no lights. I rolled on and began to meet traffic at the city limits, I reasoned Willie would take the shortest route to his secret cache. A red traffic light prevented me from crossing Santa Fe Avenue. Across Santa Fe, and parallel to it, ran the railroad and I saw Willie crossing ahead of an oncoming train. A dirty canvas covered something in the bed.

With the train blocking my path, I went to the underpass and rolled east to where Willie disappeared. I headed south and braked as I turned into Bottle Alley, so called because it was literally paved with broken wine bottles. Some hundred feet beyond was the only building I had not searched. Was this Willie's hiding place? It was half a block from his house.

I left the car and scooted against a wooden wall. There was no sound but then Willie's heavy voice echoed clearly! "All right," he said to someone, "you get the meat out of sight and go to work on it. I'll get rid of the car."

Reaching for my gun, I sprang forward, only to fall flat on my face in a tangle of wire and tin cans. The racket was enough to rouse the neighborhood dogs. Willie's pickup roared off. I raced to the front of the building, the other man had also fled. I found the building unlocked and entered. A board table had been used to cut up meat. The floor was swept clean. I had discovered Willie's secret place.

I didn't think I had a chance to find Willie with the evidence, but I went to his house anyway. Willie appeared hulking toward Bottle Alley but came back in a few minutes. I turned the corner where I met two liquor control agents. They asked what I was doing, and on hearing, exclaimed, "Come on! We saw him sell a jug of wine with a marked bill."

They were anxious to catch him with the marked money. We entered the house and Willie regarded the agents with apprehension. He gave me a look that reaffirmed my belief that it wasn't my turn. He stalled when emptying his pockets. He carried a large wad, but no marked bills. While the agents searched him, I stepped into the kitchen and looked toward the service porch. The door was closed, yet I heard someone moving. I looked back at Willie and saw a crumpled dollar bill on the floor near the couch.

I picked it up and handed it to the agents, saying, "This is probably what you are looking for." Then I hurried to the service porch and yanked open the door. I surprised a man busily cutting up a deer carcass. This was the first time Willie was careless. I learned later, the men had run from the cache when they heard my clatter, then decided to cut up the deer and dispose of it at Willie's house.

"I didn't shoot it! I didn't shoot it!" Willie's friend babbled when he regained the use of his tongue. "I was just cutting it up for him!"

Willie looked sad. The liquor agents laughed. They had him for bootlegging, and I for two game violations. In court the next morning the judge fined him $500 for the deer and gave him 90 days for bootlegging. "The next time I see you," the judge warned, "it will be the limit, $300 and six months in jail on every count."

At last I had caught Willie, but I knew it would be impossible to reform him. He wouldn't go back to his old pursuits right away, because he was facing six months or a year in jail if he got caught. But he would get restless. I figured it wouldn't be long until he'd kill and run again.

E = MC² - 10

by Paul Webb

The tall, thin biostatistician teaching the class twirled the long lock of hair near his receding hairline and frowned. Calculations were not working out. Three times he had tried to fit the math to known results but nothing was coming out as expected. The place was a hotel conference room near Nogales. The participants were Department biologists and game rangers, the instructor, and "one dirty dog."

In 1958, the Department hired a new biologist with knowledge and expertise in statistical analysis. Ron Smith was hired to perform the statistical analysis required of many research projects and to conduct the hunter questionnaire program. Ron was instructing the group with an example of how the Lincoln Index works.

As a model he had chosen a large glass jar filled with white and black marbles. He confidently explained to the class that the white marbles represented an unknown population of deer or other wildlife while the black marbles represented a known or marked population. The same principle applied to tagging or marking wild animals and recapturing some of them along with others in the population. By knowing how many marked animals there were, the estimated population could be calculated. Ron's demonstration would take a sample of marbles from the jar. By calculating the ratio of black to white marbles he could accurately estimate the total number of marbles in the jar.

In fact, Ron explained that he had counted the number of white and black marbles and knew the exact number.

With these explanations out of the way, he asked someone from the class to take a sample of marbles so he could show the group how the formula was used. Someone did the sampling and counted the white and black marbles. The counts were entered into the formula and calculated on the blackboard for the class to see. Whoops! The answer did not come anywhere close to the expected results. Oh well, it must be due to chance.

Twice more samples were taken and twice more calculations were conducted in front of the class. Again they were way off. This was embarrassing to the math expert the Department had just hired and a good reason for the biostatistician to twirl his hair.

He did not know that from this group of biologists and game rangers there was "a dirty dog" that snuck in his classroom and removed a fair number of black marbles from the jar. His math was correct, but he never knew his original count of black marbles had been changed!

Pop and the Lynx Creek Irregular

by Bud Bassett

Orville Nathaniel "Pop" Arrington was Chief of the Planning and Development Division in the 1950s and 1960s. He was a dignified, smooth-talking salesman whose passion was finding dam sites and building recreation lakes. Most of the lakes built by the Department are a monument to his passion.

In 1959, the Department was seriously considering creating a fishing lake on Lynx Creek east of Prescott. Negotiations were pursued with the Forest Service concerning a dam site, and with rancher Norman Fain over water rights. Determining if there was enough runoff to maintain a lake at the selected site was of primary interest. To further such determination, Pop installed a Cipoletti weir in Lynx Creek slightly upstream from where Lynx Creek Dam now is.

The installation of the weir created a need for someone to take twice daily water flow measurements and to keep a log of the results. The most promising candidate for the position was a retired miner whom we shall identify only as Jim. Jim was a squatter, who luckily for us, was doing his squatting within 100 feet of the weir. He was 78 years old at the time, a leathery old fellow who was the proud owner of a single front tooth which he freely exhibited whenever he opened his mouth. He had scabbed up a two room dwelling for himself next to Lynx Creek. The walls were constructed of chicken wire covered with mortar and the roof was formed of old scraps of galvanized sheet iron. Jim owned a tired looking 1930 sedan which he used to go to town whenever his small pension check arrived. He maintained a bountiful vegetable garden on the bank of the creek and used a small gasoline powered pump to draw creek water to irrigate his garden. On pay day he might be found on Prescott's Whiskey Row trolling a bottle of busthead wine seeking feminine companionship to give him solace back at his digs on the creek.

Pop decided Jim was our man. After some negotiations it was decided that Jim would receive the remarkable salary of five dollars a month to work the weir. Jim quickly figured that this money translated to ten bottles of good busthead wine a month. The horizons this opened were nearly overwhelming. Setting to work, he became an "irregular" Game and Fish employee.

From time to time Pop would drop by Lynx Creek to check on things and to pick up the weir logs. He normally would have a cup of coffee or two with Jim. This routine continued for some time right up until that day. Pop and a crony dropped by to visit Jim and were having the normal cup of coffee among the bits and pieces of discarded furniture that made up Jim's kitchen set. If things were running true to form, Pop was doing a good amount of the talking. At some point the old blanket that was hung to divide Jim's entertaining area from his bedroom was drawn aside. One of the fruits of Jim's Whiskey Row trolling stepped out and stood demurely behind him. She was attired in nothing but a smile. Pop, gentleman that he was, was not one to totally ignore a well turned ankle. He was not prepared, however, for her completely unadorned 75 year old system.

Jim couldn't help but notice that Pop's jaw had frozen in mid swing and that his eyes were riveted on something(s) just behind his shoulder. Jim turned around to see what Pop was staring at. With savoir faire given only to few, he playfully reached around and gave the lady a directional pat and said, "Better go get some clothes on Honey, you're a big girl now." He then calmly turned back to the table and waited for the conversation to continue, which took a little time to get restarted. Pop told this story better, but then he had a lot more practice; I'm only telling it once.

At the time I was a fisheries manager in Clarkdale, so I was showing up on Lynx Creek fairly regularly and thus was keeping abreast of this rural soap opera. Our "irregular" continued his weir duties in spite of this small embarrassment with his Department "boss." The lady in question gathered her belongings and moved in with Jim and his new reservoir of wine. I don't recall that Pop ever dropped by to see Jim again, although he might have.

One day catastrophe began to loom on the far horizon. Jim said that his "woman" had gone south for six weeks to visit friends. A couple of weeks after that announcement I found Jim's digs unattended and the door wide open. However, his gasoline water pump was still in place. Two weeks later Jim was back, but visibly distraught. A touching tale was forthcoming. Jim, it seems, had lived the bachelor life for about a week after his "woman" went south. He then evidently caved in to loneliness and lust (old miners were a healthy lot) and headed for town to troll a fresh bottle of busthead wine up and down "the row." His efforts were soon rewarded and he headed back to Lynx Creek with another vintage damsel who had a taste for the grape. On the way, one of Yavapai Counties finest made the outlandish allegation that Jim was the inebriated victim of his own bait. The Deputy took Jim to the slammer where he subsequently spent a few days on a drunk driving charge. The lady took Jim's car on to Lynx Creek. When he finally made his way back to Lynx Creek he found that lady number two had made off with his car and other sundry articles, but worse yet, she had absconded with all of lady number one's possessions, including her clothes.

Jim was emphatic on a couple of points: "I wasn't drunk, dammit. It was the worn out kingpins on my car that made it weave all over the road. I only had one or two beers, dammit, and that dumb cop thought I was drunk because my car wouldn't drive straight."

Then with more urgency: "That _____ (a miner's term doesn't lend itself to the printed word) took all of ______'s stuff." (Her name is left out, protecting her presumed innocence) "She's coming back next week and when she finds out she's gonna kill me!" I could tell by his excited state that he wasn't using "kill" as a figure of speech. He was using "kill" as in "dead as a doornail!"

Next time I hit Lynx Creek the house was empty, the pump was gone, and the weir was unattended. Our Lynx Creek "irregular" had forfeited his five dollars a month and fled for his life. He wasn't seen again. Pop decided we had enough stream measurements, although we were still a partial season short.

Today, a 55 acre lake sits right on top of where old Jim used to grow his vegetables and entertain the ladies. It's probably just as well because today wine has quadrupled in price, and about all you can troll for on Whiskey Row are tourists.

Welcome Aboard

by W. R. "Bob" Hernbrode

It's not that I can't remember the names of the individuals in this story, I can. How could I forget? I have reminded them many times about this incident. This time, I'll just let it ride, there may be a few Game and Fish people that remember. If you ask around, you might find out who they were.

The boat left a lazy, curling wake as it skimmed the glossy surface of Lake Mohave. It was summer, one of those one hundred and twenty degree days, and the two Game Rangers sagged on the old boat seats. Only their eyes, hard squinted against the sun, were active, probing the shadowed coves for the occasional bass fisherman.

Ahead, and towards the shore, a slight disturbance on the mirrored surface of the lake caught one of the Ranger's eyes. "Hey! Over there, a snake swimming across the lake!" he said.

The boat slowed and curved to intercept the moving reptile. As momentum was lost, the boat settled deeper into the water, finally wallowing to a stop across the swimmer's route. The two men eyed the snake, identifying it as a rattlesnake, and admired its effortless, rhythmic movement. Unthinking, they watched the snake as it slowly approached the boat. Suddenly, spying the apparent solidity of the boat, the snake increased its speed and in a moment was alongside. Sensing trouble, the pilot twisted the throttle of the tired, old Johnson outboard. The engine stalled.

At almost the same instant, the snake's flat, triangular head appeared over the side of the boat, instantly followed by four feet of looping, coiling body caboosed by a rattle-tipped tail. For a moment the boat's three occupants eyed each other - and then, with a scrambling urgency, each headed for a different part of the boat.

The pilot achieved a precarious perch atop the hot cover of the outboard motor, feet widely braced against the transom. His cohort, equally agile, found himself posing as a backward figurehead on the bow. The snake, meanwhile buzzed his war song and rapidly twisted his glistening coils into fighting position.

The first Ranger, terrified of snakes, had drawn his .38 revolver during his climb to a seat on the motor, and almost before the rattler had coiled, he fired.

An excellent shot, he sent six well aimed bullets slamming through the snake's head and body — and on through the fragile, plywood bottom of the old boat.

Tales from the Arizona Strip

by E. Harold Pratt

Harold Pratt spent his career with the Department working the Arizona Strip. Last January he was interviewed by reporter Barbara Pyles of "Southern Utah News" Her story about Harold was published January 26, 1994. Harold sent me a copy from which I chose a few stories to share.

My Most Satisfactory Case

One night I received an anonymous call about poaching in Grand Canyon National Park. I was given a good description of the poacher's car. I decided to go the Park's entrance and wait for the car to leave. I waited all night, but I never saw the car leave. I saw some nice deer which made me even more determined to catch the poachers. The next morning I drove into the Park to look for the poacher's car. I found it parked at the Park Ranger headquarters. I felt I should contact the Park's law enforcement ranger, but he sent me on a wild goose chase. The next day I went into the Park by way of a back road. Looking around without their knowledge, I found several quarters of deer buried in a manure pile at the mule sheds.

I had enough evidence to convict two of the head donkeys. I mean the Park Rangers.

A Scared Game Ranger

After giving several tickets to some men for fishing without a license at Lake Mead, I started back to my truck. One of the fishermen walked in front of me keeping me separated from my truck. He kept this threatening manner up as the others watched and snickered. I knew they were going to try and make this Game Warden go swimming in Lake Mead. I was determined not to go swimming, even though I knew they were about to force me into the water. I put my hand on my pistol and kept walking. "Is the Warden scared?" bellowed the man.

"You bet I am," I said. "And there is nothing more dangerous than a scared officer!" The man backed off. He knew this Warden had made up his mind not to go swimming.

The Las Vegas Crowd

During my early career, I spent a lot of my time policing hunting camps, and writing tickets for infractions of the law. I recall many owners of the casinos in Las Vegas hunting quail and deer. I got acquainted with them, and over the years we became pretty good pals.

Old Charlie of the Riviera and I were good friends. He often invited me to visit him in Las Vegas, and I did. Once, my supervisor and I came to his hunting camp and he insisted we camp with them. The men had sleeping bags and all the modern conveniences of home. Levi Packard and I had hardly anything. Once when we were washing up for supper we started to use paper towels, but Old Charlie broke open a whole bundle of Riviera bath towels and threw one at us. The next morning we reached for our same hotel towels and Charlie yelled, "Oh no," and threw us another new clean towel. They even had their own cook. They hunted in style.

When Levi and I came back from patrol, the Las Vegas men were gone but they left us their supplies. At noon, we decided to eat. They also left a bottle or two. Levi said, "Boy, this is the stuff you read about." It went down so smooth. We were still enjoying what they left us at dark.

Later, I got a call from Old Charlie and he wanted me to go hunting with him and a friend. I was prepared to go with them to show them the best places to hunt deer on The Strip. I got a call a week later and he told me the trip was off. I asked who his friend was and he said, "Jimmy Hoffa." What he was looking for was another gun around camp.

I was glad I didn't meet Hoffa. Those people live in a different world. Around the camp fire they are having fun with you and you with them. It gets down to their telling stories among themselves and then you're left out. They ask what happened to so and so. An answer might be, he got his throat cut. It was a world that I didn't want anything to do with.

It Was a Rough Road!

by John N. Carr

New Department trainees sometimes remember events that the "old timers" have long forgotten. I was one of the class of 1961, seven new college trained wildlife managers still wet behind the ears and ignorant about Game and Fish business. The first group of new "wildlife managers" was hired in 1960. Before the re-organization in 1960, there were game rangers and biologists, and they had their differences. When the changes came, there was a lot of heartache. Some of the game rangers sure as hell did not want to be a biologist-wildlife manager. And there were just as many strong feelings from some of the old district biologists who sure as hell did not want to be a game ranger-wildlife manager.

We were the second class of new wildlife managers to be introduced to the internal strife of biologist verses game rangers. The Department's "trainers" had a year of experience and knew how to use these seven new guys. The six month wildlife manager trainee program was a lot different in those days than it is now. We did all sorts of wild and interesting things; we fed fish at the hatcheries, cut fire wood for Regional Supervisors, built corrals, worked lots and lots of hunt checking stations, cleaned out storage bins, drove the gut wagon and skinned carcasses at the buffalo hunt, sorted and delivered mail, counted deer pellets, measured browse twigs and helped with hunt drawings. On a few occasions we were allowed to help with wildlife surveys, and sometimes we even got to ride along with an experienced wildlife cop during a hunt. That was the Departments training program. What I remember most was that we had about 5 or 6 days off during the entire six months. I really think the whole purpose of this training program was to find out who was willing to work and who was not! But, I bet we had a lot more fun than today's new trainees.

During the antelope season in Unit 21, north of Phoenix, I got to patrol a big game hunt with a long time game ranger. The season lasted three days, but we were out for five. We camped in the Bloody Basin area. The camp included Bob Jantzen, a game biologist and the Big Game Supervisor. He later became the Director for three terms. Bill Farrow, Regional Supervisor, and one of the old game rangers and Tom Barnes, the District Wildlife Manager, previously a Game Ranger Captain. There were some wives also: Bill's wife, Arlene; Bob's wife, Bo; and my wife, Sally. Tom and I each brought our small camp trailer, and I believe the others were in tents or camper shells. It seemed to me that everyone tried to out cook and out do the others. We ate really well. Sally and I didn't contribute much because I had no idea what to expect or to bring. I just brought what we needed.

Bob brought his giant 24 inch frying pan and cooked bacon, eggs and fried potatoes. One of those big frying pans holds more eggs than a guy really wants to eat! Tom cooked his famous buckwheat pancakes, and Bill, who was in the butcher business before joining the Department, brought plenty of meat. There were dutch ovens and the works. Well, here was this new green wildlife manager and his new bride in the middle of these "old timers" who really knew how to set up camp and cook. They put on a great feast every meal. (I had camped and hunted before joining the Department but I was used to warming up a can of beans or Dinty Moore stew.) I didn't know at the time but this was just the normal way they fixed meals and camped. I was really impressed.We also had horses in camp. A lot of the wildlife managers (pre-1960 game rangers and district biologists) had horses and used them for surveys and law enforcement. One story I heard was about Game Ranger Ralph "Mutt" Morrow using his horse during the weekdays of big game hunting seasons. When he found a hunter he would saddle up and follow him until he committed a violation. Ralph said he came up dry only about 20% of the time. Ralph Morrow, a Game Ranger-Wildlife Manager in the Chiricahua Mountains from the 1930s to 1963, became a Commissioner after he retired.

Bill brought horses to use on this hunt. Bob and Bill practiced roping the rancher's calves in the early morning, and they probably messed around with the horses, leather, hooves, tail hair, curry combs and feed most of the time. From my observations, it always seems that's what most horsemen do. I never had much use for horses unless I had horse work to do. I never liked to play with them. And I even grew up on a ranch! I know that Bob and Bill went on patrol with the horses and in their vehicles, but I am not to sure just how they spent their days since I spent my time on this hunt with Tom.

As I said, Tom was a Game Ranger Captain prior to the wildlife manager system. He later became a Regional Supervisor and Chief of Law Enforcement. Tom drove a Ford sedan, because, like most game rangers, he hated pickup trucks. It was not his style and besides, Tom believed he could take a sedan anywhere a pickup could go. In those days all Department pickups were two wheel drive, but they did have a few four-wheel drive bob-tail jeeps. After driving around with Tom for a few days, I believed him. On one of those days my wife and I rode with Tom while looking for antelope hunters. We went for miles on some really nasty roads.

We started on the Bloody Basin road and came out the Dugas road. It was slow; we never got stuck, but once we hit a large rock and nearly knocked the gas tank off. We spent an hour or so fixing the damage with bailing wire. We were lucky we didn't punch a hole in the tank. We made a big loop on that nasty rocky road and finally came out on a graded dirt road. There we met two antelope hunters heading in the direction that we just came from. They were driving an old Army 3/4 ton four wheel drive weapons carrier. It had big wheels and lots of clearance. It could probably go anywhere. It must have been a rough riding SOB. After checking them for licenses and tags, I couldn't believe what I heard next.

Tom warned them in a very serious tone, "Be careful, fellas, we just came from there and it was a rough road."

I'm sure Tom, Bob and Bill don't remember that antelope hunt as anything special. It was just another routine hunt patrol for them. But as a new wildlife manager trainee, I remember it as one of my more pleasurable learning experiences. I learned you can cook anything in camp that you can cook at home, and you can take a sedan anywhere a pickup will go. And in spite of what I had been told, these old game rangers really were pretty good guys!

Don and the Windmill

by Daniel P. Schadle

At one time the Department had about twenty windmills scattered throughout the southwestern desert. These windmills provided water for wildlife all year. The water in some of these shallow wells was salty and brackish which caused problems with the operation of the windmills. They had to be maintained often.

This maintenance required the removal of the pistons and replacing the leathers. To be safe, the fan and the tail had to be feathered so the mill would not turn or the head revolve.

Don Taylor, a newly assigned crew leader, was performing maintenance on a twenty-foot windmill tower. I noticed that he had tied down the fan but had not feathered the tail section. I mentioned this hazard to Don, but he told me he knew what he was doing. He didn't want an interfering biologist telling him how to do his job.

Just then, a large gust of wind spun the tail section around knocking Don from the twenty-foot tower to the soft desert floor.

Don landed on his head, so he was unhurt.

Charlie, a Crack Shot

by Wes Fleming

Charlie Copley and I spent a lot of time together. For many years Charlie was the Manager at Robbins Butte Wildlife Area west of Buckeye. He worked for me. Charlie would often help me with waterfowl surveys or work in the mountains. Once, while working in the White Mountains we decided to hunt turkeys. As we talked about hunting, Charlie said he always killed his game with a shot through the heart. It didn't matter if it was a deer, squirrel, rabbit or even a turkey, right through the heart!

Taking advantage of his bragging I said, "Charlie, I'll bet you a bottle of Jack Daniels you won't shoot your turkey right through the heart!"

"You're on!" Charlie replied.

We camped near Mexican Hay Lake and were out before daylight looking for turkeys. Just at sunrise we saw some turkeys, and Charlie shot the last straggler going over the hill. Needless to say all Charlie had to shoot at was the rear end of the bird. The posterior end of the turkey was decimated. I had won my bottle of Jack Daniels! But Charlie insisted on a postmortem. We fumbled through the mess of guts and blood and sure enough, one, and only one pellet from his shotgun shell had perforated the heart. Charlie was correct, it was right through the heart. I lost, but we both enjoyed the campfire that night with our mutual friend, "Jack."

The Mistletoe Kid

told by Jack "The Printer" Thompson

In 1993, Hollywood released a movie starring Jack Lemmon and Walter Matthau called "Grumpy Old Men." I think the Department had the original mold for grumpy old men. His name was Ed Barrett. He was the Purchasing Agent for the Department and ran the shop facilities at the Department's Papago Park administrative and hatchery site. Later he lived in the residence on the south side of Greenway Road at the Department's new facility. Most of the time Ed was not a pleasant man, and it was not fun to be around him. Many of the people who knew Ed thought he was just born grumpy. Although his non-humorous attitude might have grown from many wildlife biologist and game rangers trying to acquire equipment and supplies and not signing for them. At any rate, Ed thought everything on these Department properties belonged to him, and it was not easy to get needed equipment. It was almost always an unpleasant conversation when Ed was involved.

One morning, about Christmas time in the early 1960s, a courageous Department employee somehow managed to tie a piece of mistletoe to the belt loop of Ed's pants, just over the name on his belt. Ed carried that mistletoe around most of the day and he got more and more irritated as the day passed. The people around him seemed pleasant especially when they saw Ed leaving. Ed could not figure out why everyone kept laughing when he left the room and it was upsetting him.

Just before lunch, he discovered the nasty trick that someone had played on him. Then he was beyond being just grumpy. Ed had to be separated from the next person that laughed, assuming he must have been the one that tied the mistletoe over the place that some employees called him!

It Happened at the Gate One Day

by John N. Carr

There are a few people in the Department who like to play practical jokes, especially on new wildlife manager trainees. Most jokes played on the new kids are for fun, but some are tried to see how these new greenhorns will handle it. This is about a joke that was played on me.

As a new wildlife manager trainee I was assigned to work the early elk hunt in the Mogollon Rim area with Bob Hernbrode, the Wildlife Manager in Payson. On this particular day we were with Bill Farrow, the Regional Supervisor, and Buck Wallace, a Wildlife Manager from Mesa. All three had been with the Department for a long time and I was the new kid.

We were on horseback looking for elk hunters. Bill also had a elk permit and was hunting. Around mid afternoon we were heading back to a cabin where Buck and Bill were staying. Bob and Bill decided to ride down a canyon to hunt for a bull elk while Buck and I continued on to the cabin.

Buck was riding his old horse Pard and I was riding a young filly that belonged to Bill. He warned me that this young mare really liked to run, so I had better keep on my toes. Buck was aware this filly liked to run.

When we got to the gate, about 300 yards from the cabin, he asked me to get down and open it. Being the new kid on the block, I did as he asked. After going through the gate and closing it, I had just put my foot in the stirrup when Buck gave a yell, slapped the filly on the rump, spurred Pard and took off on a gallop to the cabin. He thought the young filly would leave me in a cloud of dust laying on the ground. The filly took off as expected, but it didn't quite work as he planned.

Buck didn't know I grew up on a ranch and rode horses every day in my early years. I knew what to do! I had just enough weight in the stirrup and with my hand on the saddle horn I was able to pull myself up into the saddle while the horse was taking off. Being on a young fast horse, I passed Buck and Pard just before we got to the cabin. Both horses crow-hopped to an abrupt stop at the corral. Buck came out of his saddle, but didn't quite leave his horse. Being new I didn't say anything. I just unsaddled, went into the cabin and poured a cup of hot coffee. I didn't offer any to Buck and he didn't say anything to me.

A few years ago, I told this story to my son, who writes cowboy poetry. He was inspired to write this poem.

It Happened at the Gate One Day

by John M. Carr D.V.M.

We were workin' up near Payson,
a friend o' mine an' me,
ridin' along the fences,
to see if there any mendin' be.

My friend, 'is name was Denny,
an' he didn't have much sense,
but he was a pretty fair hand,
at workin', an' ridin' fence.

We were about as far as we could be
from the bunkhouse an' the grub.
I was sweaty, dirty, an' smelled
like horse,
an' could've used a tub.

We were about to pack it in,
an' to call it a day,
but before we headed back
we had to cross one more gate.

This gate it was a tricky one
'cause it was strung mighty tight,
an' I had to get down off my horse
to be sure I'd closed it right.

As I was down there on the ground
an' strugglin' with the wire,
Denny smacked my horse in the butt,
an' took off like a fire.

I guess it was his idea of a joke,
but I didn't think it funny,
I was holdin' reins in my hand,
an' my mare she started runnin'.

I grabbed for the horn with my
left hand
an' barely got a grip,
I tried to swing up to the saddle,
but landed on 'er hip.

I crawled up to the saddle
by slitherin' on my belly,
I don't know how I found the stirrups,
my legs had turned to jelly.

The prospect of bein' stranded
had got me quite upset,
an' Denny was almost out of sight
almost, but not quite yet.

The mare that I was ridin'
was very fleet of foot,
I wanted her to catch ol' Denny,
cause I wanted to whip 'is butt.

When I finally caught 'im,
the ranch house was quite near,
but the boss was standin' right outside
an' there was no fightin' here.

I was pretty darn upset,
an' my horse was in a lather,
but the only sound that I could hear
was the sound of Denny's laughter.

What I wanted to tell ya'll
is that if you're gonna cause trouble,
you'd best just be prepared,
to take it back, an' double.

Three Bar Deer Pellet Transects

by Norm Woolsey

During my twenty-nine years as a Research Assistant for the Department, the Three Bar Wildlife Area deer pellet transects figured prominently.

It seemed everyone from supervisors to trainees, helped read transects and pick pellets. Being assigned to read pellet transects on the Three Bar was a lot like drawing KP duty in the Army. It was long, hard work and everyone was glad when it was over.

The Three Bar was a special place. Bob White, a Research Biologist and later Region I Supervisor, once said, "Everything on the Three Bar either sticks, stings or bites." The lay of the land is either up or down, with very little else in between. Groves of jumping cholla cactus are common, as are rattlesnakes, scorpions and Apache red ants.

When I hired on in October 1957, Dr. Wendell Swank was Project Leader and John Hall was Director. I was the first Project Assistant hired for the project. Wendell had a deer study on the Three Bar's Peters Mountain, which included belt pellet transects that were read two or three times a year. These belt transects were soon replaced with circular pellet plots at four chain intervals and were established randomly. The idea was to grid as much of the Three Bar as possible. Before the study got underway, Wendell took leave from the Department to study wildlife on Africa's dark continent.

Steve Gallizioli became the acting leader, and Biologist Ed Webb was assigned to establish the Three Bar deer pellet transects. I was to assist him. We bought a horse and a mule to pack the heavy iron rebar pellet stakes and other gear to the transects sites on Granite Springs Trail and other hard-to-get places. The stakes were made of half inch rebar and were 28 inches long. Some transects had over 40 plots at four chain intervals, making some over two miles long. These transects were laid out on a north south bearing, which as many know, made the transects cut all the steep hills and deep canyons at right angles.

Ed Webb and I started with the grand idea using a heavy transit, tripod, and plane table so we could shoot perfectly straight lines for the transects from Mills Ridge to Apache Lake. The mule, however, had other ideas. He balked at the heavy load and wrecked the tripod. So we reverted to the hand held Silva compass to establish transect lines. During the early work, Ed Webb often was busy with work in the

Phoenix Office, and I worked alone establishing the pellet transects. Some of these early transects were the longest and roughest. One I created with a "dog leg" through a saddle instead of over the nasty and rocky Hackberry Peak. "What a blessing to future pellet pickers," I reasoned. That was the only transect with a "dog leg" although I was tempted many times to deviate from the compass bearing to make it easier.

Ed Webb moved on to the Bureau of Land Management in the early 1960's, and Dr. Clay McCulloch arrived from Oklahoma State where he just received his Ph.D. He came to the Three Bar to see what was going on. Harley Shaw came a few months later to replace Webb and stayed long enough to add a few more pellet group transects. To find space for these new transects Harley went to the top of Vineyard Mountain. "There is a road to the top," he argued, "and we have four ways to get there, horseback, foot, jeep or tote-goat."

We found out the only dependable way to get there was by foot. Mishaps with the tote-goat on the steep trails were common, and driving up and down with the jeep was very hazardous. We had to reverse up some of the switchbacks, and no one wanted to drive, and no one ever wanted to be a passenger. But, you could get a great view of Roosevelt Lake in the rear view mirror. Horses were better, but they were not always available and some of us didn't like them.

Clay was now ready to start a study to monitor the U. S. Forest Service's Experimental Watershed programs on the Three Bar. The Forest Service was giving different treatments to the various watersheds of Rock Creek to determine which treatment would produce the most water. Clay needed to know how these treatments affected the whitetail deer population in the chaparral belt, so of course, more pellet group transects were needed. Clay wanted plots at one chain intervals and we used smaller stakes. This made it a little easier.

With all the pellet group transects now on the Three Bar, manpower to run them was a problem. Greg Massoro, a former Forest Service employee, was hired as a second Research Assistant. About this time Harley left the Three Bar to study turkeys on the Moqui, and Al LeCount came to replace him. With a new biologist I feared new transects would be required, but Al felt the existing transects were enough. He was instrumental in changing the sequence of reading plots, from two or three time a year, to once, in the Fall. And we were grateful for that.

Al moved on to his bear studies on the Three Bar and the nearby Four Peaks. Jeff McMichael came to take his place. Also, Clay had branched out to a study on the Hualapai Indian Reservation where he had combination pellet group and vegetative transects. His goal was to study the effect of pinion pine and juniper control on the deer and elk herd.

During Jeff's stay on the Three Bar, the nine foot chain link enclosure was built on the upper Loop Road to keep predators out. The enclosure encompassed one square mile of mule deer and javelina habitat. Once again pellet group transects were needed, inside and outside the enclosure to compare effects of predation.

Jerry Day, a long time Biologist for the Department, was busy capturing and marking deer and javelina on the Three Bar. He was always available when it came time to read Three Bar pellet group transects. At different times he had three assistants, Frank Machamer, Joe Stanley, and Tice Supplee who helped read transects.

Jim Wegge, who was assigned to help Al LeCount with his bear study was a regular participant on pellet counts. For the first few years Steve Gallizioli, Project Leader and Chief of Research was also a regular crew member as was Research Statistician Ron Smith. Wildlife Manager Don Vance also helped, although I don't remember him picking pellets. He often picked us up on Apache Lake in his boat and ferried us across the lake to our vehicles.

In the late 1960s, Clay moved lock stock and barrel to Fredonia to become the Senior Biologist on the North Kiabab. Later, Jeff McMichael left the Department to go into private business. Ron Horejsi was then selected to succeed Jeff.

In 1974, I left Mesa and moved to Prescott to assist Harley Shaw on the Spider Ranch Lion Study. Later I assisted Dr. Don Neff when he started the antelope, coyote study on Anderson Mesa. During my time on the Spider Ranch I seldom missed the Three Bar pellet counts, probably because I was one of the few people who knew where all the transects were. The only time I remember missing the Three Bar pellet counts was when I was attending coyote traps on Anderson Mesa.

Ron Horejsi was not to be outdone by previous Three Bar biologists. His new deer study required more pellet group transects. His study on the Three Bar and adjacent Tonto National Forest was to determine effects of grazing. More transects were placed with the help of his Research Assistants Bill Powers, Jim Wegge, Cathy McCoy, Patty

Glinski and others. Others in the Department had the dubious pleasure of counting and picking pellets on the Three Bar and they included, Richard Ockenfels, Ron Day, Gerry Perry, Denny Haywood, Bill Foldish, Chip Lewis, Norris Dodd, Becky Benda and Bill Carrel.

Three Bar pellet pickers in the earlier years included; Charlie Wallmo, Don Neff, Bob Jantzen, Dave Roe, David West, Dave Brown, Richard Brown, Wes Martin, Mike Yeager, Jack O'Neal, Kenneth Clay, Art Queenan, Juan Romero, Wayne Anderson, Tom Barnes, and yes, even John Carr. All, at one time or another, had the pleasure of counting and picking up the deer droppings of the Three Bar deer. Others who I remember helping included Tony Crilly, Jim deVos, Miles Rodda, Keith Zanther, Don Randall, Jim Scalero, Kim Murphey, Don Rinker, John Theobald and Lee Fitzhugh.

Some of the remarks made by helpers were interesting. A few I remember include the following.

Steve Gallizioli asked if it was it by design or accident that he was assigned to read the Hackberry transect with the "dog leg" in it. He knew it was one of the roughest on the Three Bar. I can't remember Steve's exact words, but I do remember they were not fit to print.

Tom Barnes made a remark that still sticks in my mind. After running a particular steep pellet transect he referred to all the zeros on his data sheet by saying, "No deer can get there to drop anything!"

Another Three Bar pellet picker who I can't remember, once found a *Homo sapiens* dropping on a deer pellet plot. He felt it might be an indication of that person's complete disgust of our method of obtaining deer population information.

As of this writing, I understand the Three Bar pellet transects are a thing of the past. In those days, however, they were an important tool in obtaining deer population trends.

In 1981 when I was nearing retirement age, the Research Branch presented me with the "Three Bar Golden Pellet Award" at a get together on the North Kaibab. It was bigger than life, a 24 inch length of over-sized re-bar mounted on a nice wood plaque. The stake was painted "gold" and all my friends names were inscribed on it. One thing I can say about this award is that I know there was never another one like it and never will be. Thanks again to all my Three Bar pellet picking friends!

Gino Learns About Deer Surveys

by Steve Gallizioli

Wildlife biologists have been using fecal pellet group counts to estimate deer populations for many years. While the technique is one of the better ones for getting a handle on deer numbers it has one distinct disadvantage. It's difficult to talk about without cracking up your audience. A good example was the barber I used to go to many years ago .

An inquisitive soul, Gino had plied me with questions on my first visit several weeks before. He was particularly interested in how a kindred soul, a paisan' really, both of us having come from the old country, had ended up working for the Arizona Game and Fish Department. By my second visit, he already knew that I was a wildlife biologist and that I had attained that exalted position after receiving a college degree from Oregon State College (now University). A hunter and a fisherman himself, Gino was much interested in the affairs of the agency that collected his license money. Before I entered his shop, he hadn't realized there was any job other than "game warden" connected with hunting and fishing.

Gino was somewhat less than fluent in English. On my second visit, his first question after the usual preliminaries was, "Wot my biologo fren doin' dees day?"

I wasn't eager to talk about my current project, deer pellet group counts, for obvious reasons. It was a difficult subject to discuss even among Department people without ending up on the receiving end of sarcastic jibes about the "science" of pellet picking. Perhaps, I thought, I can get around the problem by not being too specific and by resorting to euphemisms instead of more easily understood four letter words.

I proceeded to tell Gino about the deer surveys, via pellet group counts, we were doing on the Three Bar Wildlife Area near Roosevelt Lake northeast of Phoenix. But I did so without mentioning pellet groups. I talked about transects, circular plots, sample sizes and about converting the data we got into an estimate of deer per square mile. Not a word about pellet groups. Gino got part of it at least.

"You say you count da deer, huh?" Gino sounded genuinely interested. "I no unnerstan how you do dat. Mus be hard to do. Tell me, how you count dos deer."

I hesitated a moment trying to think of words to use which might satisfy him without really telling him about pellet counts. No way, I thought. I'll just have to explain it all.

"We count pellet groups on small circular plots placed along transects extending across the area." I said. "It's really an excellent technique," I assured him, "the most reliable we've ever come up with for estimating deer numbers."

Gino frowned as he finished with the electric clippers and began snipping away with scissors and comb. Obviously he was trying to digest what I said. Finally he stepped back, scissors upraised, like a conductor about to begin the overture to Rigoletto, and gave me a puzzled look.

"Pell' group? You don' say." Obviously my explanation had left something out. "Wot dees pell' group, anyway? I nevair hear tell about pell' group before. Wot happen to da deer?"

Still wanting to avoid the short Anglo-Saxon word that would clear up the mystery but leave me open to ridicule, I said: "These are fecal pellets, Gino. Wildlife researchers have found that deer defecate about thirteen times a day. By knowing the size of the circular plots, number of plots, and the number of days since the plots were last cleared of pellet groups, we can calculate the number of deer per square mile."

Gino snipped away quietly for a few more seconds while he mulled that over. I could tell from the look on his face that I still hadn't dispelled much of the fog, if any. He stopped again and gave me a blank look. I might as well have tried to explain why $E = MC^2$.

It was clear that my attempted snow job was working too well. I was also certain that Gino wasn't about to give up on me, and that I would have to clear things up with less gobbledegook. "I guess I gotta tell him or I'll never get out of this chair," I thought. Reluctantly, and perhaps desperately, I looked around to be sure no one else had entered the shop, lowered my voice to a whisper and said, "We make deer estimates by counting piles of deer shit!"

Now I know Gino had to be as familiar with that expression as with the Italian equivalent, but he reacted as if I had hit him across the face with a five day old carp. He studied me from a distance of three or four feet, his brow wrinkled in distaste, as he tried to sort out my totally unexpected remark. I could almost see the wheels going around as one emotion on his expressive countenance was replaced by others; Did I think he was a fool? Why was I pulling his leg with such a ridiculous explanation? What a lousy thing to do to a fellow paisan'!

Evidently my red-faced, embarrassed look slowly convinced him I must be serious. Slowly the frown disappeared and his face began to light up. He grinned, smiled, and broke into loud laughter. Waving his lethal looking scissors under my nose he managed, between guffaws, to squeak out, "You count da deer shit! DEER SHIT!"

I gave him my best Mediterranean shrug, wondering how I could get out of here before the situation got any more embarrassing.

"And you go college four year to learn count deer shit? Mamma mia, now I'm hear everting!"

Since Gino hadn't shaved my neck yet and I was still a prisoner in his barber chair, I continued explaining the procedure, hoping to convince him I wasn't a complete nut. I tried to stress the scientific validity of the technique by bringing out the fact that the number and location of the pellet plots was determined by a statistician who had even more book learning than me. Gino, however, apparently couldn't dispel the mental image of a college graduate on his knees counting deer do-do. He was still chuckling as he punched the cash register and accepted payment for the haircut.

Before I could escape, another customer entered the shop and Gino couldn't pass up the opportunity.

"Hey, Joe, you neva gas wot my young fran here do for livin," he paused for one pregnant moment as Joe looked at me inquiringly. "HE COUNT DA DEER SHIT!" Gino broke up again as I slunk out the door vowing to find another barber or let my hair grow — and to never again mention deer pellet groups to anyone!

Knock and He'll Tell You

by John N. Carr

When I was a Wildlife Manager trainee in 1961, one of my assignments was runing the bighorn sheep checking station in Kingman. In those days, the sheep checking stations were open 24 hours a day, from two days prior to opening day until two days after the end of the season. This December hunt was to last about three weekends and I would be at the station by myself. I was given permission to bring my wife and my own small 15-foot camp trailer which we parked at the checking station site, the downtown parking lot of the Kingman Chamber of Commerce. I also had my dog Rosco, a large German

Shepherd, who was very friendly but also very protective. After setting up the checking station signs and plugging a 50 foot extension cord into the Chamber's electrical outlet we were ready to check in the first sheep hunter. Don Wingfield, Regional Supervisor for Region III, Kingman area, came by to see if I needed anything. At that time the Regional Office was in a rented motel room a few miles from the checking station. Since I had no radio and only limited access to a telephone, Don said that he would stop by occasionally to see how I was doing and to give me a break so we could resupply our groceries.

I did not feel really sure of myself since I had never even seen a bighorn sheep, and I didn't have any idea what to expect from these hunters and their experienced guides. There were about 12 permits for this year's bighorn hunt in the Kingman area, and they all had checked in before the opening day. I only remember two of them and their guide. The hunters were from Pennsylvania, one was a very large man, 6 feet 4 inches, weighing about 240 pounds. The other was 5 foot 8 and weighed 145 pounds. Kind of like Mutt and Jeff. Their guide, well known in the Arizona hunting circles, was Bob Householder.

After the season started not one single person came by the checking station for five days. I mean no one! Being couped up in a little 15-foot trailer, just waiting for a hunter to check in or out can get boring. We couldn't even spend time outside because it had snowed and the famous Kingman winds made it too cold!

Finally, we had the first sheep check in. How exciting! What a welcome break after a bunch of dull days. I sure didn't let on to that hunter that this was the first sheep I had ever seen in my life. Another few days went by without any visitors. Finally, Don Wingfield stopped by to spell me for a few hours and we were able to stock up on some badly needed groceries.

Then, Householder brought one of his hunters back to check in his sheep. It was the little guy and he had a fairly decent sheep. The sheep was all there, they had carried it out in one piece. After doing all there was to do to check out the hunter, we talked and visited and became pretty well acquainted. Even Rosco and Householder became "friends". Then more days with nothing.

One afternoon I was resting, I might have even been asleep. I had read all the *Reader's Digest* we had and the best way to pass the time was to ignore it. All of a sudden Rosco woke me up with his loud growling and barking. But he was not inside the trailer. Well, I jumped up, looked out the door and there was Rosco standing and growling over a prone and very scared Bob Householder. The large hunter stood there and watched.

I called off the dog and Bob stuttered, "John, why didn't you tell me that dog was in the trailer."

My response was, "Bob, if you had knocked instead of just opening the door, the dog would have told you!" Bob was a good sport about being taken to the snowy ground by my dog, and fortunately he was not hurt, but it was an incident I am sure he remembered for a long, long time.

I began to check out the big fellow's sheep. It wasn't very big and they had brought only part of the sheep; the head, hide and the backstrap. Being a new trainee, I didn't know how, or if I could, check out only part of a sheep. Fortunately for me, Don showed up. Don and Householder went round and round about why only part of the sheep was brought to the checking station. The hunter claimed the rest was all shot up and not fit to eat. From examining the hide it didn't look that way to us. The hunter did get to keep the sheep and no tickets were written. However, I think this particular incident was the primary reason for the rule that now requires that the entire sheep carcass be checked out.

The Navajo Code Talker

told by Paul Webb

A long time ago, the Department and some of the Indian tribes in Arizona had a very good working relationship. We worked with them and they worked with us. This was especially true for the San Carlos Apache, White Mountain Apache Reservations and the Navajo Nation. We helped them with game surveys, issued their big game hunting permits, and often rode along with their game wardens. Their wardens often attended the Department's in-service training schools. No so today, but that is a different story.

In the early l950s or 1960s, I don't remember exactly when, I was working with a game warden from the Navajo Nation. His name was Homer Bluehouse. We were patrolling during deer season in the area south of the Grand Canyon National Park on the Kaibab National Forest. Homer was working with me looking for Navajo Indians who sometimes liked to hunt off the Reservation without the proper licenses. If we found a Navajo Indian hunting in the area, Homer did all the talking and determined if he was legal or not. I took care of all the other hunters we came across. We worked well together and got along well.

We spent several days together, talked a lot about this and that. I learned quite a bit about the Navajo Indians from Homer, although he did not talk much. I learned that his name came from his grandfather, who got a good deal on blue tar paper to roof the new hogan he was building. His house was in a remote area and it was often used as a landmark when directing people to places on the Reservation. They were told to "just go down the road till you get to the blue house and go ten more miles," or some other directions related to his grandfather's hogan with the blue roof.

Homer did catch one Navajo Indian hunting without a license. I don't know what Homer told him, he spoke in Navajo, but a lot of the words spoken by both Indians must have been one of the best strings of cuss words ever delivered. It was a pretty heated exchange, especially from Homer, as he really chewed out that Navajo for being in the wrong place. Homer was a pretty good warden and he was in control.

After that event I tried to get Homer to teach me some Navajo. It's a difficult language and I was a poor student, but I did learn a few words. Once when I was talking on the radio with another Game and Fish officer I signed off with the common radio code, "10-4."

After I signed off Homer asked me if I wanted to learn the Navajo phrase for "10-4." Of course I said, "Sure."

Homer looked at me with a grin and said, "Oh Keh." Then he laughed because he knew that he had pulled a good one on me.

You'll Come When?

by John N. Carr

I can't remember who told me this story, I guess it's because I heard it so long ago. I think that either Bob White, Region I Supervisor, or Rex Hansen, Wildlife Manager from Eagar told me about this event. Or, it could have been Harvey Palmer, Wildlife Manager from Taylor. I believe one of these fellows told me the story when I was part of the Department's crew conducting dead deer fawn surveys in the White Mountains in the summer of 1970. It's a good story and about one of the guys who started to work for Game and Fish the same day I did.

In January 1962, Wes Martin was a brand new Wildlife Manager in Region I, assigned to the Nutrioso district in the White Mountains. The new bunch of Wildlife Manager trainees completed training in December and moved into their Districts in January. Not the best time of year to move into a high mountain district. Wes was new to Arizona, coming from California. He had seen a lot of Arizona during his six month training period, but now was the time to learn his district. And that's what he set out to do, driving the open roads and getting familiar with the lay of the land.

One afternoon the Pinetop Regional Office received a radio call from Wes. "Officer needs help, my vehicle is stuck and I can't get it out. Can you send someone to help me?" He then proceeded to tell where he was and what roads to take to get there the fastest.

Bob White was listening to the conversation on the radio and determined it would be more than an hour before anyone could reach Wes to help him. Bob took over the radio controls and talked to Wes. "Listen Wes, it will take more than an hour to get to you and by that time it will be dark. I'll tell you what! Why don't you just plan on staying there for the night and we will come and get you in the morning. Anyway, it will be easier to get you out in the morning freeze. Look for us a little after daylight. 10-4?"

There was a long pause from Wes. "OK," he said. "I'll wait for you."

About thirty minutes later, just before the office was to close, the radio cracked again in the Regional Office. It was Wes. "Tell Bob I got out. I guess I wasn't stuck as bad as I thought I was. I'm on my way in."

Bob was glad he didn't have to send anyone to help Wes. Laughing to himself he thought, "The new guys have to learn to get themselves unstuck and if you put the pressure on they can figure it out."

In the Soup for Two

by Ron Smith

Here is a story that I can't help but recall with a certain warped relish.

The occasion of this incident was a research work trip to the Three Bar Wildlife Area sometime in the early 1960s. The principles involved were Bob Jantzen, Bob White, Ed Webb and myself. The biologists had returned on this winter day to the old wooden cabin for lunch. Jantzen was quite proud of his skills as a camp cook. On this chilly day he had agreed to add oven biscuits to our lunch of soup and sandwiches. His biscuits, however, were a sorry lot. The only edible part of the biscuit was its crusty exterior. I finished my soup, and not wanting to hurt his chef's pride, I ate the outside of one biscuit. I also absent mindedly rolled the biscuit's center into a soggy one-inch ball. Finished with lunch, I headed out the cabin door, ready to return to work. As I went through the door I did a rather uncharacteristically impulsive act. I turned, and with a high-arching shot that would have made any high school basketball coach proud, sent that soggy missile in the direction of Jantzen, who had just started his soup. To my horror, that mushy biscuit center came home, landing in Bob's soup bowl, thoroughly soaking him with his own soup.

Bob White convulsed in laughter and I exploded out the door, fully expecting that bowl of hot soup to follow. It's hard to apologize for an act that is quite intentional and gives such intense pleasure. Jantzen and I simply kept our distance for the rest of the day.

The Javelina Map

from the March 1967, Quail Calls

In the 1960s, Regional Supervisor Ted Knipe and his gang in Tucson arranged to have a regular spot on the local TV station to talk about the Region's wildlife issues. Every Thursday the Wildlife Managers took turns on this two minute show.

Ron Anderson, Wildlife Manager from Nogales, spent the entire morning of February 22nd preparing a large map about the upcoming javelina season to use on the Channel 4 show that evening. He labored over it continuously for hours, even cutting out a picture of a javelina and pasting it on the map so the viewers would have an idea of what they would be hunting.

All who saw his map agreed it was a work of art. The map was an enlargement of the javelina hunt areas, showing which of these areas would be closed the first two days and which would be open during the season. The open and closed areas seemed to be confusing to the hunters but became very clear on the map Ron had made.

Then the moment came. Ron walked into the studio only minutes before air time. His basic presentation for that TV show was around the map, his talk and areas of reference were all geared to the viewer being able to see his beautiful map. But as Ron walked into the station just minutes before going on camera, he realized he had left his fantastic production back at the office. Punt!

The map wound up being on display at the Regional Office for hunters that walked in. It sure would have been a nice map for television viewers, but that's the way it goes sometimes!!

The Road Kill Deer

by John N. Carr

Joe Hill, the Deputy Sheriff in Patagonia, called me real early on the opening day of the 1963 deer season because two deer hunters had stolen a road killed deer. Joe said he wanted me to meet him at the crash site just across from Patagonia High School. Joe got a good description of the hunter's vehicle from the person who hit the deer and he believed they were still in the vicinity. A few minutes later when I arrived, Joe was trying to calm down the driver while arranging for a tow truck to take the car to town. The damaged car had a caved in front end and a busted radiator as a result of the collision with the deer.

The driver of the car was from Hermosillo, Mexico and did not speak English. He just kept repeating the same statement over and over again in Spanish: "They said they would take the deer to the hospital and then they got a gun and SHOT IT!" He was really agitated, waving his arms and going through the motions of shooting a gun. He must have thought that a doctor would treat this poor injured deer. Except for the excited driver, Joe had things under control, so I started to look for the hunters that had taken the deer. Joe and I both thought that they took the deer so they could tag it and keep it for themselves.

I described the vehicle to several people I talked with in Patagonia. One person had talked with the two men and saw the deer in the truck. He told me they had gone up the Temporal Canyon Road. On my way, I stopped at the U. S. Forest Service District Ranger Office. To my surprise there was a very large 4 x 4 whitetail buck laying dead on the front steps of the office. It didn't take long to figure out that this was the deer that had been hit by the car. Those two "honest" hunters left the deer at the Forest Service office so it could be given to the "hospital." These hunters must have known that the Department donates the meat of salvageable road kills and confiscated wildlife to charitable organizations.

I never found out who those hunters were and I am still amazed that they didn't tag it for themselves. The whitetail buck probably would have scored about 110 Boone and Crockett points. When I skinned it out to prepare it for the "hospital," the meat was hardly damaged, except for the bullet wound in the neck. I gave the meat to the County Welfare Agent in Patagonia, who in turn probably gave the meat to some of the better deer poachers in Santa Cruz County!

Checking Station Games

told by Robert J. "Kirk" Kirkpatrick

What do you do when there is nothing to do? There are often slow times at wildlife checking stations. You wait and wait for a hunter to drive down the road. Once and awhile the hunters will turn around to avoid the checking station and then it may get exciting when you go after them. But most of the time it's feast or famine. When the hunters come by there is plenty to do. You have to check the game, sometimes you weigh it, sometimes you age the animal by toothwear, sometimes you have to check for parasites or other things the biologists are looking for. Licenses always have to be checked, and sometimes citations have to be issued or game confiscated. But most of the time it is boring. You wait and wait for things to happen. When it's really boring you can make fun things happen by playing checking station games.

One of my favorite checking station games is to race pop cans. No, we called them "beer can races". How in the world do you race beer cans? Since you can't drink them on duty, it's not a chug-a-lug race, although that might be more fun. You race empty beer cans. If you have ever been to the Three Points - Sasabe Highway west of Tucson you probably know that the wind blows most of the time. The wind is the beer can engine, it's what makes them go. There must be at least two players. The race begins when the two players set their beer cans next to each other on the center line of the highway. On the count of three you each let go. The winner is the beer can that gets off the pavement first. The loser pays up. The standard bet was ten cents a race. With a good beer can I could win a couple of bucks a day at the Three Points checking station.

If we were in a remote area we had another game we played. It was "drive the nail". We would take a nail, any nail we could find, and start it in a fence post. We would then take turns trying to drive the nail into the post with .38 wad cutters. It was not only hard to hit the nail on the head, but it was almost impossible to drive it all the way in. Most of the time the nail bent. This was especially true when all you had to deal with were old hard mesquite fence posts. But it was good practice and it lead to another event that involved accurate shooting.

Once on the Sasabe Highway checking station during javelina season, I was working with Dave Brown, the Wildlife Manager for Unit 37B. We had already played our beer can races and drive the nail, when we got to talking about how hard it would be to hit the antenna on the top of the patrol car. That sounded like a challenge to me, so I bet Dave I could do it with one shot. He didn't think I could, so the bet was on. I can't remember how far away I was, but that one shot took the antenna clean off the car. It just disappeared. A piece of barbed wire fixed Dave's radio antenna and it worked well for several months until it was replaced at the shop. Next year, same place, same parties, same bet! Same result, except this time the antenna was just bent into a big V shape, and it stayed on the car.

Bopping Heads

told by Warner Poppleton

In the early 1960s, I was a Wildlife Manager in Saint Johns when the Department held the first legal blue grouse hunt. Bob White, the Regional Supervisor, didn't know how many hunters to expect or how many birds might be killed, so he planned to patrol the area with a lot of men. A bunch of us camped out at the Department's old Big Lake cabin because of its central location.

Al LeCount, the Wildlife Manager in Alpine, and I were assigned to work on Escudilla Mountain. Near the top in Terry Flat and Toolbox Draw, we were in good grouse country. To our surprise we were the only ones on the mountain. While we were patrolling we saw a big bunch of blue grouse. Al and I got our shotguns and went after them. We got into the covey and each got one on the rise. The rest flew away and landed in a big spruce tree. The limit was three a day so we each had two to go. We walked to the big tree and the grouse never flew. So we walked around and around the tree, shooting a grouse whenever we had a clear shot. We each got our limit and the rest of the birds never did leave that tree. It was really easy.

At the end of the day Al returned to his home in Alpine and I returned to the Big Lake cabin. I decided to cook up two of the grouse for dinner and offered some to the other guys. For some strange reason, I had no takers until Steve Gallizioli showed up. He was eager to taste one of Arizona's blue grouse. He had a bottle of white wine so we simmered the grouse in wine for about 45 minutes. Boy were they good! We ate it all!

The next morning was another patrol day. Al arrived at the cabin before daylight. Bob White had decided to split us up to get more coverage. I was to go alone to the Hannagan Meadow area. Since Al was really familiar with the area I asked him where I might see and hunt for some more blue grouse. He told me about a little meadow along Highway 666, between Beaverhead Lodge and the Hannagan Meadow store, where he almost always saw grouse. "Great," I said. I left thinking I would take home a limit of grouse.

As soon as I got near the meadow I started looking and sure enough there was a big bunch of grouse near the highway. I pulled off the road and got my shotgun. Walking into the meadow I expected the birds to flush at any moment. I couldn't find them. I walked back and forth, back and forth and could not find any birds. Giving up, I was returning to the truck when a hen took off and I got her with one shot. After retrieving it I returned to see if I could get up one more bird. Since I had a grouse left from yesterday I only needed one more to fill my limit.

Well, I got into the birds but they would not fly. They were running around on the ground at my feet. I yelled at them, stomped my feet at them, but they just would not fly. They just danced around. One bird stood at my feet looking up at me, and in frustration I swung my shotgun like a nine iron. "Bop!" Off came his head! I had my limit. I cleaned the birds, continued to patrol for the rest of the day and returned to Big Lake at dark.

That evening at dinner time I told my story. I had to brag about how good my shotgun golf swing was and that I got two grouse with only one shot. Everyone there thought it was a good story and had a good laugh. Everyone except my boss, Bob White.

Bob come over to me and said, "Come outside, Warner, I want to talk with you."

"What did I do now?", I thought to myself. We went outside.

Bob became serious and said, "Listen, Warner, I don't ever want to hear you talking about golfing the head off of a grouse again. You know it is not legal and I really should give you a ticket and take away your birds."

He was serious as hell, and he meant it. He didn't think what I had done was funny at all. Especially when I told everyone about it. He must have thought my actions had put him in a bad position. My response to Bob took him by complete surprise.

"Look Boss," I said. "the law is clear, it says that you can take blue grouse with either a bow and arrow or a shotgun. It doesn't say you have to shoot them. I killed all of the grouse with my shotgun, even the one I got with the golf swing."

Bob's jaw dropped and his eyes opened. "Damn! I guess you're right, that's what it says. I guess we don't have a problem." It was about the only time I ever saw Bob speechless.

I took those three grouse home and had some really good eating. I have enjoyed telling about that hunt for years.

The Come-Along

by Wayne Anderson

One of the Department's legendary figures was Levi Packard, Region II Supervisor in Flagstaff. I feel fortunate to have worked under Levi's direction for a little more than 18 years as a Wildlife Manager in Unit 5. Working with him was anything but dull. I transferred to Flagstaff in December 1963. It actually took me about 10 years to kind of figure him out. A sense of humor he did have.

Once in the spring of some year in the mid-60s, Levi and I were near Willow Valley Dam in Unit 5. We had stopped to look at a dirty camp left by hunters. When we finished scrounging around, we got into his carryall to leave only to discover we were stuck in the mud. The bed of pine needles had disguised the mud. Rocking the vehicle back and forth was of no avail. We got out the come-along and a long piece of cable. Under Levi's direction the cable was hooked to the vehicle and then to the come-along which was chained around a tall stump.

Levi told me to work the come-along while he was in his carryall with the engine running. He would be ready to put it in gear after I pulled him out of the mud hole. Diligently I cranked on the come-along and the cable got tighter and tighter. SNAP! The cable broke near the vehicle and came whistling just past my left ear.

I knelt there in a mild state of shock, realizing what would have happened if the cable had been two inches or more to the right. I continued to kneel, staring straight ahead at the vehicle and Levi sat there in the drivers seat, not moving. After what seemed a small eternity he got out of the vehicle, looked at me, and said, "I was waiting for your head to fall off!"

You Got Us!

by John N. Carr

I clearly remember one early morning deer patrol in the Huachuca Mountains with Jack Davis, a Wildlife Manager from the Payson area assigned to work the white-tail deer season and Dave, a friend of mine. We took some time to do a little deer hunting in Brushy Canyon. We went there because I always saw some nice white-tail bucks during my winter surveys. By mid morning we started back to the truck because was time to check deer hunters. We had seen a few deer, but no big bucks. I had heard some barking dogs, but didn't think much of it as I thought they belonged to one of the local ranchers. On the way back to my truck, we walked past a parked Ford pickup. Out of habit I looked inside. There on the dash was an open box of 22 Hornet shells. In 1964 the 22 Hornet was not legal for deer hunting so there was a good chance we had a ticket here. We decided to continue the short distance to the Department truck instead of waiting, since there was no way they could drive out of Brushy Canyon without going past us. After coffee and a sandwich we drove back to the Ford pickup. It was gone!

Since the truck had not gone past us, I knew it had gone the other way. At the end of the road there was a one room line shack and an opening in the canyon bottom just large enough to turn a truck around. Sure enough, when we got there we saw the Ford pickup. There was also a nice white-tail buck hanging in a tree. And dog tracks everywhere! But no hunters. Jack and I decided to hide our truck down the road and then we went inside the cabin and waited. Good idea! We waited for what seemed a long time. In about a half an hour a large Doberman pincer dog appeared. The first thing it did was to jump up to the hanging deer trying to tear off a hunk of meat. Suddenly it lifted its head, sniffed the air, and headed directly for the cabin, growling all the time. That dog knew we were inside and didn't like it. He patrolled around the cabin, sniffing the air and growling at the windows and door.

Soon more dogs showed up, two mutts; one looked like a hound, the other was a large dirty, scruffy lap dog. They were more interested in chewing on the deer than joining the Doberman on his cabin patrol. The Doberman still growled and circled the cabin.

In ten minutes or so three hunters showed up. All were carrying rifles. It looked to us as if one of them was continuing to hunt after killing his deer. Here was at least one more ticket. They were whispering and we could not hear what they were saying, even though they were less that 25 feet away. The Doberman still patrolled! The hunters paid no attention to the Doberman and started loading the deer in the truck. The Doberman was now looking in the broken windows and still growling. We were trying to keep out of sight and quiet, still trying to hear what the hunters were whispering about. After loading the deer, they called the dogs and put them in the truck. Two of the hunters got in the bed of the pickup with their rifles placed over the cab. The driver started the truck and as he drove past the cabin (within five feet of the door), Jack and I stepped out.

The startled driver slammed on the brakes, almost throwing his partners over the cab, threw up his arms and yelled, "Oh my God, you got us!"

Up to that moment Jack and I had not decided what we had "got them" for. Since they admitted they were guilty of something, without hesitating we said the charge would be hunting deer with the aid of dogs.

"OK", the driver said, "How much is it going to cost?"

I gave him the standard answer, "The fine is up to the judge".

After signing his citation, one of the hunters, out of the clear blue sky, pleaded, "Please don't tell Jerry Day about this, he goes to my church."

I don't know why he told me that. How was I to know that he was an acquaintance of Jerry? (Jerry was a Research Biologist with the Department.) I never did tell him. When Jerry reads this story, he will hear it for the first time.

Dangerous Encounters

by Jerry Day

After 35 years of bushwhacking and rock hopping, one encounters all kinds of mishaps and dangerous situations that could have been life threatening. I am not thinking about the potential dangers of driving vehicles or as a passenger on low level helicopter flights. No, I would like to relate some of the more insidious things that befell me over the years.

My first painful episode occurred on July 25, 1953, after only two months on the job. Paul Webb, Ed Webb and I were camped at Burnt Corral along Apache Lake. We were looking for transplanted chukar partridge. The main release site was on the Three Bar Wildlife Area, so we used a boat to check the nearby lakeshore for birds. As I sat on a cushioned boat seat, a scorpion nailed my exposed calf. The venomous critter slipped back under the seat unharmed, but it left its poison and a lasting impression on me. The initial pain was excruciating. It felt as if sharp needles were going up my leg to my groin. We did not have enough ice to relieve the pain, so we drove to Roosevelt Dam to get help from the dam caretaker. In those days there was a man living in one of the towers who was always friendly and helpful. He provided plenty of ice, first aid instructions, and comforting words, assuring me I would survive. By this time I had a headache, dry mouth and a tongue that felt swollen. During the night, while applying ice packs, a childhood ditty came to mind. "I went to the dam man to get some water, but the dam man would not give me any dam water, so I told the dam man to keep his dam water." Thank you, dam man, for giving me frozen water.

* * * *

On March 1, 1954, a foxy story happened when I was making a deer survey in Hog Canyon of the Santa Rita Mountains. Around midday, I was standing on a rock in a wash and spotted a gray fox bounding along. I thought the fox would pass by, but it came right up to me. I was able to kick it away and had time to pick up a rock. On its next charge, I hit it squarely between the eyes with the rock, stunning it. Then I jumped on its rib cage, killing it.

End of the story? Hardly, just the beginning. For some reason, I decided I needed the fox skull for my mammal collection. So I cut the head off and skinned the hide from the skull. Back in Tucson, I hung the skull on the clothes line to dry. Three days later, I mentioned the fox encounter to Professor Roger Hungerford at the University of Arizona. He thought I used poor judgment by handling the fox skull, because it could have been rabid. Since the skull was still available, he recommended that I get it tested for rabies. I promptly took it to the state health lab for testing.

The next day I was talking to a rancher in Gardner Canyon about the Kaibab deer that had been released there. He provided deer information, but also reported a large number of dead foxes in the area which he thought was probably due to a hydrophobia epidemic. This was not encouraging information for someone who may have made a fatal mistake.

Five days later my landlady reported that the authorities were hunting for me, because the fox indeed tested positive for rabies. I went to see Dr. Howard at the state health office. I related the story and told him I was not bitten by the fox. He checked my hands and saw the usual nicks and abrasions that were not protected during the skinning and handling of the skull. He seemed to think my chance of contracting rabies was slim, since I had not received any puncture wounds. Also it was probably too late to take the shot treatment. However, he recommended that I check with my regular doctor for his advice. Not having a doctor, I went home and back into the field. Believe me, I had some anxious days waiting for the incubation period to elapse!

* * * *

During my years of field work, I had numerous close calls with rattlesnakes. One that could have been serious occurred sometime in July, 1963, along the shores of Lake Mohave. I was staying at the Willow Beach Hatchery with two summer students. We were trying to capture desert bighorn sheep. When bighorn watered at the lake shore, they could sometimes be approached within range of capture guns. On one occasion, about six sheep were at the water's edge. As we approached in our boat, they spooked a short distance, so we backed off and waited. I got the bright idea to stalk them on foot by going along a narrow ledge that would be out of view and lead me right to them. My equipment included a loaded powder charge gun and a Ambu resuscitator in a canvas bag that hung on my left side. I was able to negotiate the ledge with the bag scraping the side of the cliff. I came to a gap in the ledge that I would have to leap over. Stopping, I looked at the boat idling twenty feet below me and decided it was too risky to safely move the bag to my right side. As I made the short leap, out of the corner of my eye I saw a movement close to my neck and then heard a buzzing sound. For a few minutes, I was unable to move because I was shaking so badly from this close call with a rattlesnake. Those in the boat wondered why I was not moving toward the sheep. Eventually I moved on, but the ledge petered out too far from the sheep. I was forced to turn around, back to the gap in the ledge. The rattlesnake was still there, so I had to kill it before I could safely pass. To this day, I believe that if the canvas bag had been on my right side, I would have been close enough to the snake for a fatal strike in my neck or head.

My Truck

by Don Neff

The old time cowboy, and even the new ones, they say, would tackle just about anything if he could do it on horseback. If it couldn't be done on horseback it wasn't worth doing. And besides that, any cowboy would not want to leave his horse.

So too, the wildlife biologist, wildlife manager. But it's his truck. There seems to be a psychological bond between the wildlifer and his truck. Most trucks are well equipped and organized with everything vital to the work and survival in the field. They become part of your life. Everything you need to do your job, to travel in tough country, to make repairs, to live anywhere you want to or have to is in your truck. To disrupt that secure and orderly existence and have to travel in an alien vehicle is a terrible wrench. It was awfully hard for supervisors to get biologists to car pool to far away jobs, like the North Kaibab. To go in someone else's vehicle was awful. You knew that you would leave behind something terribly important, and that usually was the case.

In early 1965, I was living in Prescott. I drove my trusty old green Chevy carryall to Flagstaff and parked it next to Levi Packard's Region II warehouse. I was to car pool to a Western Conference in Gallup, New Mexico. I rode with Doug Morrison, a biologist with the Coconino National Forest. Most of you know that Forest Service vehicles are never equipped as well as your Game and Fish truck. I just felt that something would go wrong and what we needed would be left behind in my old Chevy. But we made it to Gallup OK and after several days of meetings we were on our way home. As we drove into the Region II office area in the cold and gloom of evening I saw my carryall. I remember being very glad to see it, and I said so. Doug looked at my well-worn green carryall and said, "Well, things have come to a pretty pass when that old truck looks like home and mother."

Me and the Bear

told by Howard McDonald

Sometimes bears wander into picnic grounds looking for food. Bears usually do this when it is dry and their normal food sources are low. It often results in problems for the bear. I remember clearly being involved with a campground bear in Oak Creek Canyon one summer in the early 1960s. In this case no one was hurt, nor was the bear. Oak Creek Canyon is a very popular summer recreation area for trout fishermen and people looking at the scenic red rocks.

John Russo, Big Game Supervisor and I were working in Oak Creek Canyon near the June Pine Resort when we got a frantic call about a bear terrorizing a family in one of the campgrounds. No one had seen a bear in Oak Creek for a long time so we thought we had better have a look. When we got there we were told that a small bear had come into camp, surprising a family having a picnic lunch. It was obviously looking for something to eat. When the bear approached the picnic table, everyone scattered. Everyone except a four-year-old girl who was confined to a wheelchair. She was too small to move the wheelchair by herself and had been left alone when everyone ran off. The bear picked the table clean and then started sniffing and licking the little girl's face and neck. Seeing this, the mother ran back to rescue the girl and hit the bear on the head with a frying pan, chasing it off. By the time we got there the bear was gone, but the family was upset and concerned about the wild bear in the area.

Russo and I started to look for the bear. We found him a short time later with his head stuffed in a grocery bag in the back of a small car. The car owner had thrown a lantern and other things at the bear trying to scare it away. Yelling, I ran at the bear, and it ran off and treed. Thinking we could capture it and move it to another location, I went after a rope. The bear wasn't very large, a yearling, maybe eighty pounds, and we thought we could handle it. When we got back to the tree with the rope the bear was gone. But we found it again, this time with its head inside a garbage can. I gave it a swift kick in the rear and it ran off. This time we saw it go up and out of the canyon. I thought we had seen the last of it. There were no more reports about bears in Oak Creek Canyon, so my trusty boot must have done the trick.

A few days later we heard about a small bear hanging around the base of a Forest Service lookout tower. This fire lookout was about three miles from where the bear licked the small girl in the wheelchair, so we felt it was the same bear looking for some easy food. There was a lady manning the lookout tower and we heard that she did not come down from her station for three days after seeing the bear.

About Commissioners

by Wendell G. Swank

Why anyone would want to be a Commissioner has always puzzled me. They get no pay, only expenses for official duties, they spend a lot of time attending meetings on week ends when they could be having fun, and an enormous amount of time reviewing information sent to them by the Department prior to official Commission meetings. They get little praise or recognition for their efforts and a lot of guff from the general public. Yet, my association with Commissioners has convinced me that there were few who would not like to have been reappointed to additional terms. They may have griped at the duties while serving, but most remember their terms as enjoyable experiences.

To paraphrase an old quote, I agreed with some of the Commissioners some of the time, most of the Commissioners most of the time, but none of the Commissioners all of the time. Like everyone in the Department, I had my favorite Commissioners, but I can't say that my favorites were always the best Commissioners. However, I don't want to go into that here. What I want to do is relate certain facts that may shed some light on the association between Commissioners and personnel in the Department, and some background known to few in the Department.

When I first came to the Department in 1952, there were only three Commissioners; Fred Faver, a farmer from Buckeye, Dr. Richards, a veterinarian from Kingman, and Jack Mantle, a Pepsi-Cola Bottling Company owner from Tucson. Fred may have been a native of Arizona, but I don't know about that. I do know that he punched cows under the Rim in the Payson area for a long time before moving to Buckeye to grow grain and cotton. He was a great supporter of the Department, and believed in managing wildlife on the basis of facts. One of his favorite comments was, "if you told a wildlife biologist a red car was parked there, the biologist would say it's red on this side, but let's walk around to look at the other side before we draw any conclusions."

* * * *

When seat belts became more recognized as a safety device, the Department urged the Commission to adopt a policy to install belts on all Department cars and require personnel to use them. At that time vehicles were not delivered with seat belts, and it cost about fifteen dollars for two lap belts in front, plus they had to be installed, which probably cost another ten dollars. Twenty-five dollars was a lot of money in those days; about the amount paid to a game warden or a biologist for half a week's work, and the Commission deliberated for about two years before approving the expenditure to carry out the proposed policy. Not long after the policy was adopted I picked Fred Faver up at the Adams Hotel, where all the Commissioners stayed when on business in Phoenix, to go to the House Chamber where the big game season setting session was in those days.

Fred got in, and I said to him, "Fred, you will have to fasten your seat belt before we go." He looked at me and said, "If I'm going to need it, I'm not going."

* * * *

Jack Mantle came to Arizona sometime in the late 1930s, and quickly became involved in the Tucson Rod and Gun Club, an affiliate of the Arizona Game Protective Association. He was an enthusiastic quail hunter, but probably the most conservative member of the Commission when we were trying to get increases in length of season and bag limits on quail following the droughts of the late 1940s. To get more information on quail, the Department began studies at Oracle Junction in 1951 and at Pinnacle Peak in 1956. Those studies demonstrated that hunting was not a factor in influencing quail populations. One of the reasons for selecting Oracle Junction was its close proximity to Tucson where quail hunting had first priority for Jack. In their deliberations Commissioners always gave more weight to the leanings of the Commissioner who would be most affected by that decision. Jack's hunting partners, Jack O'Connor, Manny Drachman and Tom Ellingwood, were wheelers and dealers in the community and they weren't bashful about expressing their opinions at Commission meetings, in the local paper, and to the community at large. So, to get a quail season with a reasonable bag limit we first had to convince Jack, and that wasn't easy. We encountered the same response when we tried to get a hunting season for Mearns' quail, but when convinced by research results, Jack supported the program, as he did other Department activities. Jack's influence on the Department was extensive because he was on the Commission a long time.

* * * *

Marcel Forman came on the Commission in 1960. He told me he came West from Missouri as a young man and settled in Goldfield, Nevada, I would guess about 1915. Sometime shortly thereafter he came to Yuma to work for his uncle in a shoe store "downtown." While Marcel was on the Commission we made quite a few trips together in the field. On one trip the fisheries people were taking samples on the lower Colorado River when Marcel and I discussed the similarity of this habitat to the good holes for flathead catfish he remembered in Texas. We then decided that we would try to interest our fisheries people in introducing flatheads in the lower Colorado. After getting approval from the other state members of the Colorado River Management Committee, flathead catfish were released in the lower Colorado River. So, if you like fishing for flatheads, give us at least some of the credit, and if not, I'll take half the blame.

Marcel's stint on the Game Commission wasn't his first experience as a Commissioner. He formerly served on the Highway Commission,

Director Wendell Swank addresses the Commission. From left to right are: Director Wendell Swank and Commissioners Ralph Morrow, Martin Johnson, Lee Hover, Maury Sizer and Milton Evans. (Photo from the May/June 1964 issue of Wildlife Views.)

but felt that political pressure on the Game Commissioners was less. According to Marcel, Governor Hunt, the first Governor of Arizona with a reputation as an old time political dictator, called Marcel into his office before appointing him to the Highway Commission and had him sign a undated letter of resignation. Governor Hunt commented as he put the letter in a drawer, "Just remember, I have this in case I ever need it."

For several years I accompanied Marcel, Game Rangers Joe Wiltbanks and Don Moon, and biologist Warren Kelly on spring trips looking at the bighorn sheep habitat between Quartzsite and Yuma. That was desolate desert, with nothing but nothing for miles and miles. On the first few trips we went into the back country and set up camp, sleeping under the stars in the open, and sometimes erecting a canvas fly for shade to eat under. We always took two one hundred pound blocks of ice which we wrapped up in a tarp and buried in a deep hole in a sandy wash to keep things cold, because even in mid March noontime temperatures were conducive to the consumption of a lot of cool drinks and cooled fruit. Later, Marcel wanted a little more comfort, so he took his truck and camper and we went as far into the outback as we could, without abusing the equipment and the country.

There was a lot of country to wander around in, but Marcel usually didn't ramble far from camp and prepared the evening meal, frequently consisting of biscuits and something else.

I came in one evening, and opening the door to the camper I said, "Marcel, I smell gas; don't you know that this thing may blow up?"

Marcel, bending over the stove peering into the oven, looked up over his bifocals and retorted, "In case she does, where shall we meet?"

Cut Off My Finger or I'm Gonna Die!

by Art Queenan

Years ago when I was a Wildlife Manager in Region I, one of our responsibilities was to help with browse transects. We did this by measuring the new growth of twigs on selected browse plants, marking them and then later measuring the same twigs to see how much utilization there was on these plants. Presumably, we were measuring the use of these plants by deer. We did these browse surveys on the winter range, since this was the critical habitat for deer in the Region. The staff of Region I conducted several of these browse transects on the Blue Primitive Range every spring and fall.

In the Spring of 1965, I was part of a browse survey crew consisting of Region I Supervisor Bob White, Wildlife Managers Harvey Palmer, Rex Hansen, Al LeCount and Paul Webb, a biologist from the Game Management Division in Phoenix. We were staying at Joy's Blue River Lodge, riding horseback to the various browse transect locations. One day we rode to the Red Hill transect and I was paired with Paul Webb. This Red Hill transect was located on a very steep hill and we had tied up the horses at the bottom of the hill and walked to the transect sites.

At one particular browse plant, I reached up to pull a branch down so Paul could measure the twigs and mark them. At that moment I felt a sharp sting on my index finger. I jerked my hand back. I knew what had happened even though I did not see the bee. He had, however, left the stinger in my finger. I whipped out my knife to flick the stinger out and in my excitement I mashed the little bulb on the stinger pushing more poison into my finger. I knew I was in trouble.

While I was in college I took a bee keeping course as a filler for some of my science requirements. Once, while working with bees in that class I was stung nine times. I went into anophylactic shock and almost died. I had no pulse and no blood pressure and was given a shot of epinephrine directly into the heart along with cortisone. I recovered, but the Doctors told me at the time that very little was known about this allergic reaction to bee stings but it is known that future bee stings could result in a quick death, especially if medical care was not readily available.

Here I was, miles away from a medical facility and I knew I was going to die. I decided to cut off my finger to keep the poison from spreading, but I just couldn't do it. I handed the knife to Paul and pleaded with him, saying, "Cut off my finger or I'm gonna die!" Well, thank goodness Paul couldn't do it either, but he did gouge a sizable chunk out of my finger.

Harvey Palmer was nearby and heard the commotion and came over to see what was going on. My impression of Harvey at the time was that he was a tough, old, grizzled, mean Game Warden. I knew he thought all these new college trained boys were wimps and not worth much. I guess I must have been whining about dying from a bee sting because Harvey told me, "If you're gonna die you better walk down to the horses because you're too damn big to carry!" Even though I'm about six feet four, Harvey always seemed bigger and I knew he was an ex-pro boxer, so I just did what he told me to do. Except I ran.

When I got to the horses I passed out, I think from the shock. I came to in a few minutes and felt woozy for awhile but recovered nicely. I'm really glad now that I gave the knife to Paul and not Harvey, who I'm sure would have cut off my finger!

Pop! There Goes Donna's Weasel

by Wayne Anderson

Levi Packard is an avid hunter and oversaw Region II's wildlife management programs during the many years he was Supervisor. His wife, Donna, is anti-hunting as much as Levi is pro-hunting. Even in spite of these diametrically opposed views, it has been a very good marriage. I state this as an outside observer who spent many hours in their home eating, drinking, and watching TV. They made me feel like a member of the family. Donna, in her own right, is as much of an individual as her husband. Donna always had food on the table for any stray that Levi might bring home, including me.

One weekday, Levi was off duty at his Department home behind the office on Lake Mary Road. For some reason, I stopped by, probably hoping for lunch. When I arrived, Levi and Donna were in the back yard, and I could sense a crisis existed. To digress a moment, Donna was not only anti-hunting, but liked animals. She fed a good number of golden mantle ground squirrels that lived in the wood pile and among the rocks in the back yard. These were some large fat squirrels. The number of Donna's golden mantle squirrels had decreased over a period of time and she could not figure out the reason for this diminishing population. By the time I got there the reason had been seen. It turned out to be a small least weasel enjoying life at the expense of Donna's golden mantle squirrels. A crisis!

Levi had tried several things, as I remember, but with no success. The weasel would end up under one of the large flat limestone rocks that no one could lift. As we studied the problem Levi said if we could get the little $#@&* to run out from under the rock he might be able to shoot it with his .410 pistol. We tried banging on the rock with a sledge hammer, but that didn't work. We could think of nothing until a sudden inspiration hit me. Off to my truck I went and pulled out one of the greatest inventions of all time: the Handyman Jack, a very large heavy duty bumper jack.

I thought of the Handyman Jack because of a construction problem my parents had when I lived with them in Phoenix. At the time I was the Wildlife Manager in Unit 21. My folks decided to add a large living room to their home for extra space when my brother and his family visited. The grandchildren needed more room, as any grandparent knows. Anyway, there was a concrete slab out front that had to be removed and the contractors crew was banging away with their sledges trying to break it up. Tired of the noise I went out and got my Handyman Jack, borrowed one of their shovels, dug a hole, set the jack down with the hook under the concrete slab and started jacking it up. A piece about three feet in diameter broke off. Their job became easier, and this idea was imbedded in my psyche.

Well, that started it. I got under the rock with the jack and Levi was poised and ready with the pistol. I started levering the jack. In a short time, out came the weasel and POP! Levi would take a shot. Missed! Under another rock went the weasel. Another hole dug. Levi in position, jack levered, POP! Another miss. After several series of holes, rocks, POPs and misses, Levi finally figured out that he was too close and basically his charge pattern from the pistol was not spreading enough. Finally, with Levi standing further away, the weasel's next charge was his last.

Mounted, and residing on the fireplace mantle, the least weasel is a permanent reminder that although Donna is an anti-hunter, she is not against vigilante justice when it came to messing with her critters. How do I know this? I ate well that night, because Donna fed me and I heard the discussion at the dinner table.

The Rockets Red Glare

by Wes Fleming

Duck are always hard to find along the Gila River west of Phoenix. Especially, it seems when you are hunting. In an airplane they are easy to see, and large flights of pintails are often seen flying over and around Gillespie Farms. From my surveys I knew ducks often piled up in a few small ponds below Painted Rock Dam. Sometime during the 1965 waterfowl season, five fellows from the office wanted to try their luck duck hunting at these ponds. It was still dark when I dropped off the first hunters. Making their way to the ponds they had to struggle through thick salt cedar, crawl down cliffs and wade across wet areas to the pond where they set out decoys and built blinds. Then they waited for the flights of pintails.

Wendell Swank, the Director, and I were the last in line to set out decoys on our pond. About noon we gave it up. Picking up our decoys, we returned to the truck. Stopping to pick up Paul Webb, Small Game Supervisor and Bob Jantzen, Chief of Game Management, we could see their decoys setting in a small pond. Using binoculars from our advantage on the hill I could see a single teal swimming with the plastic decoys. Webb and Jantzen were obviously fast asleep in their blind.

I happened to have a few depredation rockets in my truck. The Department uses these rockets to scare birds off farm fields when they are causing crop damage. These rockets are pretty big and mean. I positioned a rocket toward the pond with the decoys and the lone teal. I lit the bugger and off it swished, sounding like a big flight of pintails cupping their wings for a landing. The rocket twisted and turned and then headed for the hunters' blind. Jantzen was the first one out of the blind, he must have thought the Korean war was starting again. Webb knew he was back in Germany. The teal didn't think at all, it just got the hell out of there.

Swank didn't think it was very funny, but I was almost hysterical watching the two confused characters race up and down, blasting away with defensive firepower. The rocket also scared all the ducks out of the area. Steve Gallizioli, Chief of Research, didn't think it was funny either. He was at another pond and had a flight circling his decoys when the war started.

Let Her Burn

by Phil Cosper

I think it was about 1965, when Wendell Swank, the Director, and I went to Sky Harbor Airport to pick up a visiting dignitary. We were driving east on Jefferson following a Volkswagen bug when we noticed black smoke coming from it's engine compartment. When the driver noticed the smoke he pulled over to the curb. We pulled in behind and parked at a safe distance. The Department had just installed certified fire extinguishers in all vehicles, so we grabbed ours and ran over to the VW, thinking we were about to become heroes.

Just as we were about to pull the trigger on the extinguisher the driver of the VW boiled out of the car and yelled, "Don't you bastards dare put that out! Let the son of a bitch burn!" Well, we backed off. And before the fire department could get there, it did indeed burn to a crisp! So much for our attempt at a good deed that day.

Let's Eat it All . . . We Might Die in Our Sleep Tonight

by Art Queenan

As Wildlife Manager in Page from 1966 to 1974, I had all of Lake Powell and the North Kaibab. It was a huge district to cover and I had a lot to learn. I talked to many of the locals when I first got there to find out what I could. One of my best sources for good reliable information was Harold Pratt, Wildlife Manager in Fredonia. Harold was born and raised in Fredonia and started working for the Department in the 1940s as a game ranger. He knew the country and the people. He told me that there used to be bighorn sheep in Kanab Creek all the way to the Colorado River. When I asked him if they were still there he said he wasn't sure. The last time he was down in the depth of Kanab Creek was before he went to the Pacific as a Marine during World War II. He didn't care to go back. He reminded me that Kanab Creek was all in the Grand Canyon National Park anyway.

Bighorn sheep in Kanab Creek perked my curiosity so I studied the topo maps of the area and discovered that the Park boundary was defined as following the upper rim on the west side of the canyon. This meant all of the interior of Kanab Creek canyon was within the boundaries of the North Kaibab National Forest. The topo map shows Kanab Creek as a squiggly line making it hard to measure the distance to the Colorado River. If bighorn sheep were still in Kanab Creek there might be a possibility of a hunt. I wanted to find out.

I had just bought a second horse for my son and had a packsaddle which I had never used. I needed a buddy to go along with me so I called Jim Higgs, Wildlife Manager in Prescott. Jim was a horseman, a cowboy and an experienced roper, but not a packer. He agreed to come up and do this bighorn sheep survey in Kanab Creek with me. I remember telling him it depended on how far we could trailer the horses down Snake Gulch but I thought it was about twenty miles each way. Snake Gulch is a feeder canyon to Kanab Creek and provides the only vehicle access to our starting point. Anyone should be able to ride twenty miles in a day, right? Wrong! At least not in Kanab Creek as we were about to find out.

We got permission for this excursion from Levi Packard, Region II Supervisor. He also wanted to know if bighorn sheep were still in Kanab Creek. He suggested we take Chic Wayne, a new employee the Department had hired to do creel census work at Lake Powell. Chick was a young cowboy type who knew horses and would be a good addition for this trip. Chic had never packed before either, but all of us had plenty of experience working in the country and we felt confident. Well, we packed up a bunch of food in our ice boxes and trailered to the Kaibab and down Snake Gulch to Kanab Creek and camped at the trucks for the night. This is big country and to this day I don't know of anyone trailering horses as far as our jumping off point. We had studied the pack books and the maps and were ready. The next morning we packed all our gear on the packhorse, saddled up and were on our way. We figured on one night out and back to the trucks the second night. Just in case, I packed a canned ham for a second night if that was necessary.

Our first day down the canyon was slower than we anticipated. We knew we were still a long way from the Colorado River so the second morning we decided to continue riding down the canyon till noon before starting back. We would eat half the canned ham that night and still have half for the third night if we needed it. At noon all of us felt we just had to see what was around the next bend, then the next and the next. We just couldn't stop now, we were so close. After such a long tough ride none of us wanted to quit till we saw the Colorado River.

We finally got to a rock slide that blocked the canyon and it was impossible to continue. We were disappointed but we had seen one band of bighorn sheep and plenty of sign so we felt the trip was a success and worthwhile. On that second night I wanted to split the ham and save half for the third night which we all knew we would spend in the canyon. Jim Higgs was convinced that we could make it out and back to the truck in one long day if we'd just ride hard. His final comment was, "So let's eat the whole damn thing, we might die in our sleep and never get to eat the second half."

Since both Chic and I were pretty hungry too, we ate the whole ham and rode like hell the next day and the next day after that. That third day all we had to keep us going was one Pepsi apiece and the knowledge that we had food and beer at the truck. I know that Jim and Chic felt the same as I did when we finally saw the truck. What a ride! What an experience! That night we had the best steaks and all the trimmings I think I ever ate. And beer!

I learned a valuable lesson on that trip. Always, I mean always, bring along extra rice, beans, oatmeal or something for that next bend in the canyon or that extra day that was not planned for.

As a result of this survey the Department did authorize a bighorn sheep hunt for Kanab Creek. Three permits. Jim Higgs and I drew permits with Fred Peters. It was without a doubt the toughest hunt of our lives. Fred Peters was the only lucky hunter, getting a nice ram. His story is written in the *"Arizona Wildlife Trophies,"* 5th edition, 1990.

The California Poet

from the November 1966 Quail Calls

Most of the time when a hunter, fisherman or boater gets a citation, he goes to court, pays his fine and that's the last of it. He is never heard from again. But, once in a while the Department gets a letter. Usually it's because the violator is mad and feels he was treated unfairly by the arresting officer and or the judge, but most often it's just because he's mad. He may not realize it, but he is mad at himself for being stupid, or not reading the regulations and then being caught by the game ranger.

It's pretty unusual when a poem is mailed to the Department after a citation is issued. At least it shows that one hunter has a touch of wit, although the ending of this poem leaves some doubt about this poet's sense of humor. The following poem was sent by a California dove hunter after Jim Higgs, Wildlife Manager in Prescott issued a citation.

While hunting in Arizona, one fair day,
We ran into old "Higgs" just earning his day's pay.

He chatted, he chortled, discussed previous weathers,
Then gave us a ticket for birds WITH NO FEATHERS!

We were angry, chagrined, but gave forth with no chants,
But Jim was close to getting a good kick in the pants!

After twenty-five dollars and sixteen nice birds,
We were left standing there .... just biting our words.

The thing that's upsetting and causes such distress,
Is now .... darned Judge Hagley now wears my new dress!

We're not hard losers and sportsmanship will prevail,
We'll be there next month to shoot at your quail!

As for you .... our dear warden, do don your warm clothes,
Cause come deer season .... you OWE US TWO DOES!!!

A word to the wise .... could be or could not ....
Just don't turn your back .... I'm one heckuva SHOT!!

I Wonder What Those Tracks Are!

by Wayne Anderson

The Thiokol Spryte sno-cat is a two-tracked enclosed vehicle that carries three people. Our plan that January day in the mid-60s was to haul the sno-cat to the Kinnikinick Lake junction on the Happy Jack-Long Valley Road or down to Sawmill Springs junction. In those days, the road at Mormon Lake dropped down to near the lake level (if it ever filled), not its present location along the edge of Anderson Mesa. As it turned out, we ended up at the Sawmill Springs turnoff.

Something had occurred along Mormon Lake that should have tipped us off that things were not in order with our communications equipment. We could hear Paul Miller, the Wildlife Manager for Unit 9, trying to call Levi from the Grand Canyon, but we were not able to contact him on channel one, the frequency that is relayed through the repeater towers. When we came out of Mormon Lake and gained a little elevation, we were able to talk to the Flagstaff Region II Office on channel two. This frequency is used in a car-to-car situation in a direct line of sight for short distances. Expecting to continue our radio communication, we put the "pancake" from the carryall into the radio of the sno-cat. We should have realized something was wrong with the radio, but we didn't.

Unloading the sno-cat from the trailer, we headed east on the Sawmill Springs Road looking for elk or elk sign on our way to Lower Long Lake to take water samples, the main purpose of the trip. Traveling over a good depth of fresh snow, resulting from a very cold low pressure system, made conditions perfect for the sno-cat and finding fresh game sign easy. Around noon we were on the east slope of Jay Cox Mountain, eating a lunch that Levi's wife, Donna, had made for us. We ate in the sno-cat and watched a herd of twenty to thirty elk.

We then headed for Long Lake. As we approached the lake shore from the north, I hesitated at the controls. Should I turn right or left before going to the center of the lake? Levi's voice from behind me said, "Take it down the middle." A direct command from my supervisor. So I did.

No problems. We got to the center of the lake and cut a hole in the ice. There was eight to ten inches of good solid ice. Actually the sno-cat puts less pounds per square inch of pressure on the ice than a man does. We finished collecting water samples and returned to the sno-cat to head back to the trailer. I was still at the controls.

Again the voice from behind me said, "I wonder what those tracks are?" A single set of tracks led to the east bank of the lake and then away from it. Once again I thought this was a direct command. Levi still claims that all he did was just ask a question and that he had no desire for me to drive over to see what animal made the track. I still say that it was a direct command.

I drove over, and turned parallel to the shore about ten feet from the edge. Then two cracks appeared in the ice. They started from the shore, one went to the front of the sno-cat and one to the rear. We both sat there and waited, as the sno-cat slowly sank. Thank the Lord it settled in about three and a half feet of water. We were on the bottom. After dropping off sharply, the bank shelved to more gradual descent. The engine continued to run. I then tried to dial the repeater station on Mt. Elden to no avail. It was then we realized that channel one on the radio had gone bad. We then tried to call Jack Woousley, manager at Raymond Buffalo Ranch, on channel two, but got no reply.

Levi's next plan had some merit. He took off his coat and shirts and put on a pair of chest waders, that were in the storage compartment, and pulled out the infamous come-along and a chain. Hooking the come-along to a stump was easy, but he had to reach down in freezing water to wrap the chain around the front axle of the sno-cat. I sat at the controls as he directed me to put the power to it as he cranked on the come-along and tried to pull the sno-cat forward and at an angle to the bank. As I sat there and he was cranking, I could see his face light up as he thought he was making progress. I did not apply the power to the tracks and he yelled at me to do so. I pointed behind him and when he looked, he could see he had pulled the stump out of the ground. All this time I was calling on the radio trying to tell someone of our trouble. While we tried to free the sno-cat from the water the sno-cat engine continued to run. It ran for forty minutes before it finally quit.

The reason the ice cracked was due to shelving of the ice because of the prevailing southwest winds, and probably because of this, the ice was only about four inches thick. The subsequent vibrations of the sno-cat caused the ice to crack.

While Levi was using his fertile imagination, after donning warm clothing again, I tramped HELP in the snow hoping a low flying airplane might see us. I also tried signaling high flying jets with reflections off my badge. That didn't work either. We tried to come up with a solution, but had no ideas, so we made plans for the night. We had some food, a tarp, a Coleman lantern, a single burner stove and plenty of firewood. But we didn't particularly want to spend the night out.

Fortunately for us, there was one small cabin on the other side of the lake near the boat launch area. Loading up all we could carry we trudged across the ice and snow to the cabin. Levi used a dime as a screw driver to remove the shutters from one window, and I jiggled the window up and down until the side latches released and it opened. In our "stash," besides the lantern and stove, we had a small portable Motorola radio that used the car-to-car frequency, but we were unable to get anyone to respond to our calls.

The owner of the cabin had firewood cut which we brought in and started a fire in the metal wood stove in the kitchen. There was some canned food in the refrigerator, which had not frozen. The crackers that had been left out had been well worked over by mice. It was bad enough to have the crackers eaten, but there were also several bottles of Jim Beam, totally empty! Levi mumbled something about the mice getting to the booze.

Near sundown, after cooking dinner and melting snow for coffee, we heard Wildlife Managers Jimmy Allen, and Ross Manes, talking about us on our portable Motorola radio. No one was sure where we were, but Jimmy was going down the Happy Jack road to find where we had parked. To get a little elevation while trying to answer Jimmy on the radio, Levi climbed up on the cabin roof, taking the portable radio with him. After Jimmy located our parked vehicle and trailer, he went south calling us on the radio. We could hear Jimmy on our radio and Levi kept answering him, but got no reply. Then we heard Jimmy say, "Levi, if that's you, break squelsh twice."

Then I crawled out the window, and practically ran up the ladder, breaking the bottom rung. Being taller than Levi, I grabbed the radio, climbed up on the chimney and holding the radio as high as I could, I yelled over and over again, "Long Lake, Long Lake,—".

Jimmy then got to an area where he could hear us on the radio and we could talk with him. We told him what had happened. Arrangements were made to get help from the Forest Service. They would come in via Meteor Crater with a Dodge Power Wagon because of the snow depth.

After that, we tried to make ourselves as comfortable as possible. In the cabin's kitchen were two stuffed chairs, the wood stove, a Coleman lantern and cook stove. We were to take turns getting up to refill the wood stove to keep warm and keep the Coleman latern going. The only problem was that I woke up first time around, did what was necessary, sat back down and was ready to drift off. Then Levi would wake up within five or ten minutes and take his turn. I would tell him that I just did it, and he would say he'd get the next time, but he never did. We repeated that process all night.

Anyway, the next morning here came Jimmy Allen and Doug Morrison, Range and Wildlife Staff Officer of the U. S. Forest Service, to rescue us. They told us the temperature in Flagstaff dropped to 19 below that morning. We were very thankful for the cabin.

The next day we hired a "Cat" that was doing juniper pushing in the area to come pull out the sno-cat. The only damage was that the clutch plate had rusted a little and, of course, every grease fitting needed to be lubed.

Like I said, it's not dull around Levi Packard. By the way, I don't remember if we ever bothered to find out what made the tracks we went to look for.

The following account of this event was written in the August 1966 edition of the Department's "Quail Calls". It is as follows:

Now it can be told! After several months of warming up to it, someone finally sent in the story of Region II's wayward cat — snowcat that is. Braving the winter's biting cold, two Department personnel, whose initials are Levi Packard and Wayne Anderson, eased the snowcat across the frozen surface of Long Lake. The purpose was to take water samples. Near the middle of the lake they had some rotten luck — rotten ice, and they would have been delighted to trade their expensive snowcat for a cheap boat. Fortunately, they escaped from their sinking craft, but our alert reporter failed to tell us if they recovered the snowcat. He did, however, uncover the following poem about the incident.

Listen all you people to what I would relate,

The story of a snowcat and the fleet commander's fate.

"Take her down the middle" was the order that he gave,

And Lieutenant Wayne obeyed him though his countenance was grave.

As they neared the distant shore and safe harbor could be seen,
The fleet commander ordered, "Dive this big orange submarine!"
Lieutenant Wayne looked and said "Sir, I have one fear,"
"We can't operate for long without our snorkle gear."
Again the order came to dive, and though it wasn't nice,
The Lieutenant took her down, through a foot of solid ice.
Now friends I'm here to tell you that recent surveys show,
snowcats run much better on solid earth and snow.

The Black Hills Snake & the Ranger

by Henry Stotts and Henry Stotts Jr.

Halfway up the hill, I paused for a few short moments to catch my breath. Anxiety was building within me. Perhaps it was fear, born from my reluctance to revisit a place with so many unwelcome memories. Fear and realization that no matter how confident an individual may be of his abilities, the desert is very unforgiving of even the smallest mistake.

The source of my apprehension lay just over the hill, a short distance from where I now stood. My upward progress was becoming more difficult as I neared the top of the hill, for I was loosing the mobility in my right leg.

Finally I gained the summit where again I was forced to stop, as each breath was now coming in rapid succession. A large granite boulder shadowed by a palo verde tree offered me a place to rest as I surveyed the country surrounding me.

To the northeast, the desert floor rose as if to challenge the mountains near the old mining town of Kearny, while southwest some thirty miles or more, lay the State Prison and the town of Florence.

I allowed my thoughts to focus on my immediate surroundings. The slope was a litter of sand, broken rock, cactus and low-growing brush. It was on this slope, six months ago that my story began.

I was one of a group of select Game Rangers in the Department. We were called "Rangers at Large," and our districts encompassed the entire state. In November 1967, I decided to patrol the area northeast of Florence, now known as Unit 37B. My sixteen-year-old son came along since it was the fall deer hunt and we both had deer permits.

I had driven the dirt road from Florence many times and the washboard condition of the road exhibited its usual teeth chattering annoyance. My son and I talked about desert mule deer and how nice it would be if we could bag one of the old moss backs.

It was afternoon when we reached the turnoff. We would try our luck with an evening hunt. The two track road I took appeared to ghost away only to reappear again winding down one of the many washes or up some distant slope. I drove this road for the better part of an hour, avoiding drop-offs and rocks.

Parking the patrol car at the top of the hill I decided to scope the surrounding country for deer. With my field glasses I stepped from the vehicle scanning the slopes around me. After searching for a period of several minutes, I was convinced no deer were in the vicinity and we would have to look elsewhere. I called my son who was extracting a desert whiptail lizard from underneath a rock. I cautioned him to be careful and make sure there were no snakes under the rock, even though I felt sure no snakes would be out this time of the year.

We had only a few short hours of daylight remaining. The road crossed a large wash and made an extreme upward turn that only a four wheel drive should attempt. This was the end of the road. Turning into the wash I felt the back tires slip in the sand. Perhaps I was too anxious knowing that we had a limited time to hunt until dark, for I accelerated and the back wheels became buried. We left the car where it was and started to hunt a low ridge to the west.

We had climbed several hundred yards when I spotted fresh deer tracks. Cautiously my son and I proceeded up the slope, expecting at any moment to jump the deer. I suppose it was out of habit, that I turned and whispered to my son not to drag his feet.

Turning back to continue up the hill I felt a sharp sting in my right leg just above my ankle. I mentally cursed myself for apparently stepping into one of the many cholla cactus that covered the hill. As I looked down, my heart suddenly stopped and then went into an accelerated pace, for I was straddling a large Mohave rattlesnake, not a cholla cactus. This was the source of my pain. I managed to tell my son to stop as I stood frozen in my tracks for I feared another strike was forthcoming.

I knew if I moved the rattler would strike again, for he was coiled between my legs in a tight spiral with his head cocked back like a compressed spring ready to be released. Everything seemed to move in high speed for me, I could clearly see the red forked tongue protruding from the mouth, then disappearing again as it tasted the air for scent. Many thoughts passed through my mind. Getting help. The car stuck in the wash. My son. Would I make it out of here?

I knew there was only one thing to do, my son must shoot the snake that lay coiled between my legs. It would strike again at any time, and any movement on my part would invite that strike.

I was not concerned with this decision, as my son was an excellent shot. He placed first in a shoot off with the Arizona National Guard rifle team four year earlier. My son was apprehensive about shooting between my legs, not for fear of hitting me, but concerned about fragments of gravel, rock or bullet casings. This possibility existed, but the alternative was more severe. My son fired one round from his 30-06 rifle. The concussion from the shot rang in my ears as I looked down and saw the snakes head severed from his body.

Now that I was out of immediate danger, my whole body seemed to turn to gel. My legs started shaking and I lost the strength to remain standing. My son grabbed my arm and helped me to the ground where I could inspect the snake bite on my leg. The bite was about three inches above my right inside ankle and blood was slowly oozing from the two incision marks left by the rattler's fangs. Several things ran through my mind. Was the strike a warning, meaning little or no venom had been injected, or a substantial amount?

I had to assume the worse. My son removed his belt and placed it just below my knee as a tourniquet. Both my son and I had heard about the cut and suck method of treating snake bites. A tourniquet and quick medical attention seemed like a better decision.

After applying the tourniquet my son took the rifles to the car while I made my way slowly down the hill. I would have preferred to have my son stay with me but a more important problem awaited us. I would be in real trouble if my son could not get the patrol car out of the sand by the time I got there. I had confidence in my son's ability to free the car even though this wasn't something he was used to doing.

Moving slowly so as not to increase my heart rate, I had covered about half the distance when I stopped to rest. My son ran up the hill, yelling that he had freed the car and it was ready to go. I knew then that the worst was over and with luck I would make it out. Together we went down the hill to the patrol car. My ankle had started to swell and I had to stop several times to loosen the tourniquet.

I sat in the rear seat as my son started the car and began calling the radio dispatcher at the Phoenix office. Repeatedly he called with no response. I could tell he was getting frustrated and I told him how to dial the microwave tower on Ord Mountain. We were traveling in a low ravine area between two large hills which prevented the radio signal from reaching Phoenix.

My entire body was beginning to swell. Touching my right leg I realized it was twice its normal size. I lit a cigarette to relax and was immediately chastised by my son saying that smoking would increase the heart rate and cause the poison to circulate quicker. Sometimes kids think they know it all but at this point I wasn't taking any chances so I put the cigarette out.

My son was driving the patrol car as if he were in a race, and I feared he would misjudge the terrain and possibly wreck or damage the vehicle. Being stranded out here could have a devastating effect on my condition.

All at once there was a clear response on the radio. A Sheriff's Office dispatcher from Flagstaff had heard us calling repeatedly for Phoenix Control. Hearing no response he decided to answer. He heard our story and said he would call Phoenix by phone. After what seemed like endless minutes, the radio suddenly came alive with activity. It seemed that every Game Ranger and law enforcement officer in the state had heard what was happening and wanted to help.

Phoenix Control came on the radio and told us an ambulance would be sent to take me to the Florence hospital. We had made it to the graded Florence-Kearny road and could go faster. Just west of the Box O wash the ambulance came in view. My son flashed the patrol car lights and pulled over. The paramedics talked with us as I was transferred.

Upon arriving at the Florence hospital emergency room, I was treated by an intern. He was from Mexico City and had little experience with snake bites. He made several phones calls and then I was injected with anti-venom. In addition to the injection, the intern instructed the staff to pack my lower body in ice to retard the blood flow. This proved not only painful, but caused more damage than the snake bite itself.

The ice bath continued for several hours, including the ambulance ride to Mesa Southside Hospital where my family doctor met me. He was distressed by the ice treatment and immediately instructed the staff to warm me up. I later discovered that by packing me in ice, my lower body temperature and blood circulation had been reduced to the point that my body tissue had begun to deteriorate. Essentially, I now had frost bite.

I underwent several weeks of physical therapy and was kept under close observation for signs of gangrene infection. I was visited numerous times by individuals I had never met, but had heard of my experience on that Sunday. Most were law enforcement personnel who had monitored the event on their radio that day and wanted to extend their get-well wishes, and hear first hand about my experience.

I was very fortunate that the only damage from the ice bath was localized gangrene about the size of a fifty cent piece on my ankle. It would take several months before I returned to full duty status and could perform at the level I had before the encounter with the snake.

As my thoughts returned to the present, I became aware of the slope around me. I was looking for something that was not easily seen. After searching an hour I was about to leave and return to the car. The sun glinted off an object and I felt a rush of adrenalin and a strange tingling sensation down my back. Lying among the grass clumps was the spent casing of the shot my son had fired six months ago. As I fondled the casing, my mind returned to the events of that day and I realized how fortunate I was. As I turned to leave I spotted something I had not expected to find. The dried skin of the Mohave rattlesnake was entwined among the bushes. I reached down and took the buttons (rattles) and parts of the skin and placed them in my shirt pocket.

The skin is gone, lost to some house cleaning chore or hidden between sheets of paper long discarded. However, the rattles from the snake are still in my possession. Every so often, when the grandchildren are over, I'll show them the rattles and tell them the story of the Black Hills Snake and the Ranger.

The Accountant's Fishing Trip

by Randle R. King

Sometime after I came to work for Game and Fish, I discovered most of the employees were Nimrods and Waltons. I was neither. It's a wonder they let me in the door. I had never hunted in my entire life and I had gone fishing once, with my father years ago. If I remember correctly, I caught one little minnow-sized blue gill. My Dad was from a Texas farm and liked the backwood sports, but it wasn't in my blood. I remember once when a Department Director wrote of a primordial lust carrying down in a man's DNA which impels men to the hunt to this day. To me, that was just more bologna coming from that office.

What I loved was accounting. My prior experience had been as a legislative fiscal researcher for the Post Auditor (predecessor to the Auditor General) and a year for a CPA firm. I held a Master's Degree in accounting. To me accounting is both an art and a science, and most certainly a profession. To the wildlife and fisheries biologists in the Department the word "professional" was applied exclusively to their fields and all other personnel were non-professionals. This was something else I learned after coming to work for the Department.

I have two Department-related fishing stories to tell. One successful and the other, well, you'll see. Actually, the laughter elicited from my fishing buddies upon my first big catch caused me to wonder how successful it really was.

As was usually the case, even other administrative types in the Department were fond of fishing and such. For this fishing trip, our leader was Roger Gruenewald, Assistant Director, who was loved by all who knew him and a professional turned administrator. If I remember correctly there were four of us on this fishing expedition. There was Roger, Data Processing Manager Pete Edgar, Supply Branch Supervisor Wil Nowinski and yours truly. We decided that it was absolutely necessary to conduct an administrative field investigation of Region III in northwest Arizona. Were the reports true that fishing was never better on Lake Mead? If we were going to save the Department from financial ruin, we had to find out for ourselves by personal inspection. Was Wes Martin, Region III Supervisor, really the best host for politicians and other low life? We had to know. Why did they want me on the fishing trip? I don't know, but probably they wanted my complicity.

Wes had a reputation as a good host, and with reason. He took us on a big boat to the best fishing spot on Lake Mead. By the way, we all had the proper fishing licenses. Wes even had extra fishing tackle for me. But, when it was time to fish, they ignored me and with gleeful delight began to fish. After some delay and frustration, I got my line ready and from observing the professionals, decided it was time to throw my lure into the water. I believe I am a quick learner, so after watching the others I was confident in my fishing capabilities. My cast went out as far as my inexperience could carry it and upon the lure touching the water it was grabbed hard by a fish. They were excited for me and very complimentary of the big crappie I just caught (I think that's what it was). Roger said it was near record size.

"What did you use?" they asked.

"I don't know but here it is" I answered, as I pulled the thing out.

"A river lug! You gotta be kidding!" was Wes Martin's reply. And there was wild laughter as only a gaggle of outdoor sportsmen can enjoy. To this day I don't know what my gaffe was. What is a river lug, anyway?

In later years, after having had such great luck at Lake Mead, I attempted fishing a few more times, but with my six children. We needed a way to supplement the food budget because in those days we didn't get paid as much as the professionals did. However, angling was frustrating and embarrassing, for the children and I did very poorly catching fish. And it cost a lot for the lures, flies, hooks, lines and sinkers we lost when getting stuck in old trees and weeds under water. I finally gave up.

A few more years went by. The Department built another dam on the Mogollon Rim and called the new reservoir Willow Springs Lake. I knew about that because of the capital accounting entries coming through and it looked as if it was about to be finished. At a Special Services Division staff meeting I learned that the lake was filled but that no signage had been done. No signs on the highway, none anywhere! Also, the access road needed a little work. I waited another week or two and asked again about Willow Springs Lake. No change. Good.

I went home and told the wife and children we could catch some fish, since we had what amounted to our own private lake. With keen anticipation we headed for the hills the next weekend. We made camp at my brother-in-law's rundown cabin and took off for Willow Springs

Lake. I wasn't even sure we could find the lake, but we did. We looked around and the place was deserted. No people! And a lake full of starving fish! Or so we thought, but we began to have doubts as an hour, then two, went agonizingly by. Not one nibble. Not even a snag. Just sunburns. We went home and I was never able to vindicate myself with my children.

At work on Monday morning a professional asked me about my sunburn and general malaise. So I told him what happened to me over the weekend. Once again, laughter.

"What's so funny?" I glumly asked. He replied that the Department had yet to stock the lake and that it did not have a single fish in it. I never picked up a fishing pole again!

Surprisingly, the fishing bug bit one of my sons. He is now an avid fly fisherman and even ties his own flies.

Remember When?

from Quail Calls

The following short stories are from the Department's internal publication called "Quail Calls." *This newsletter was produced by the Information and Education Division in the 1960s and told stories about things that happened to Department employees. Birthdays, events, new babies, items for sale and so on were included in this newsletter. What follows are some of those stories.*

Mike Yeager, Wildlife Manager for the Santa Rita Mountains and Ron Anderson, Wildlife Manager from Nogales were conducting deer surveys in Sycamore Canyon in Unit 36 in the Coronado National Forest. While out, the guys got a little hungry. Ron had just killed a coati-mundi for the pelt, it looked so good after skinning it out that Mike and Ron ate it. Mike's dog wouldn't touch it. Smart dog! April 1967.

* * *

If you've never been around home raised Canada geese goslings, you've missed something. Wes Flemming's fledglings are "too much." Under the watchful eyes of Charlie Copley, the birds grew, and looked on him as their mother. It was unbelievable to watch the way he could make them perform. The whole bunch do approximately the same thing at the same time. Charlie would say, "Everybody up," and they would all get up. The last time they heard his siren song was when he said, "Let's go everybody," and they followed him into a pen. He and Wes then caught them and put them into cages. Their new home is the cool White Mountains, but we bet they miss Charlie and going First Class. July 1966.

* * *

Back in the history flavored pages of the Old West, it was written that the Cheyenne Indians could outrun a horse. By this, it was meant that the Cheyenne, through rigorous training, could actually go into sort of a dog trot and wear down, or outdistance, a horse.

Unfortunately, it appears that neither modern Indian nor white man has that capability today, but at least one man has been known to try.

C'est La Vie for Steve Gallizioli. He put his feet in his mouth — both of them — when he bet Bob Kirkpatrick that he could outrun his horse for a short distance. The horse must not have read the book on the Cheyenne and won the race. Kirkpatrick is now five dollars richer. Incidentally, Steve is looking for a chance to try again. Any takers? January 1966.

* * *

Riney Maxwell and Harvey Palmer won the team tying roping at the Department's in-service training school in Prescott. Don Wingfield and Tom Waddell took second. The first prize was six dollars. The cost of using the livestock for the event had to be deducted from the entry fee of $2.00 each. The livestock owner made fifty bucks on the deal. Question: Who is the guy with the most? August 1966.

* * *

The Department's annual in-service training school in Prescott was under the direction of Cliff Sorrells ... and the first day brought discussion of P - Orders, the 1965 - 1966 budget, uniforms and gun holsters .... Phil Cosper was called on to speak and as he stood before the group remarked, "I don't really have much to say at this time." Before he could say anything else, a voice from the audience quickly replied, "Why don't you sit down then?" The voice was most likely Terry Starner, but we have no proof. The group went to pieces and Phil smiled, thanked the speaker and sat down. September 1964.

* * *

Buck Wallace and his horse "Pard" had a disagreement on the first day of deer season and Buck came out the loser. He's now at Good Samaritan Hospital with a broken collar bone and a couple of fractured ribs, but is doing OK. Buck passed up a chance to be worked on by Jerry Andrews. Said he'd just wait for the doctor, and it took a couple of rough hours of riding over back country roads to prove it. October 1964.

* * *

Barney Borneman had a tragic accident on December 8. Barney was busy in his jewelry workshop when the engine that operated his lapidary equipment exploded and spewed the shop with burning kerosene. In a matter of moments the shop became a holocaust and Barney ran out with his clothes on fire.

First Aid Instructor Dan Schadle rushed him to the hospital, but before arrival, Barney went into a state of shock. An examination revealed he was severely burned on the face, lower arms and legs, and he was hospitalized until January 16th — well over a month!

Barney's little jewelry workshop was consumed so quickly that Department employees at Deer Valley could do nothing to save it. In addition, the fire damaged his house trailer extensively.

To help Barney, Gabby Blaser has been taking contributions for him. Contributors should send their donations to Gabby in Law Enforcement. Everyone in the Department is happy to have Barney back again and hopes he can get everything squared away soon. January 1965.

(Barney was a long time trapper for the Department, see story on Pop Arrington Field Notes, he was retired at the time of the fire and lived in back of the shop area at the Deer Valley Office complex. After retirement Barney worked with animals at the Wildlife Building at the State Fair. Dan Schadle was the head of the Development Branch and Gabby Blaser was the radio dispatcher.)

* * *

From the old gold mine of Commission Minutes: April 5, 1948. Thomas L. Kimball was elevated from his position as assistant director of the Game and Fish Department (salary, $350 per month) to director of the Department ... After a trial run with the FM short-wave radio in Carl Jones' car, Commissioners Connor, Beach and Faver authorized the installation of radios in five enforcement vehicles. November 1965.

Attention meat hunters. If you're out to fill the freezer, the guys to take with you are Ron Smith, Paul Webb, Bob Jantzen, Charles Jordan and Ron Kufeld. On a recent chukar hunt, about twenty birds took to the wing in front of these safari greats and they got **one** of them. It only took thirteen shots, but they got him. November 1965.

* * *

Everytime the words Three Bar appear, certain AGFers wince. There have been numerous complaints concerning the rough work to be found there, and three people have been injured on the place. Just recently it was learned that these complaints were not unfounded. A burro being used by Dean Mace and the development crew couldn't take the strain and suffered a heart attack! Dean said the last he heard, the burro was convalescing in an amethyst mine. July 1965.

Ranger at Large Carl Jones and Wildlife Manager Jim Higgs listen to Howard "Barney" Borneman explain the wildlife exhibit at the Yavapai County Fair. (Old Arizona Game and Fish file photo)

Ear Plugs

by Dave Daughtry

The young Wildlife Manager finished his trainee program in the early 1960s, and was now a full fledged Commissioned law enforcement officer for the Arizona Game and Fish Department. His first assignment was in Lake Havasu City on the Colorado River. This was a brand new community, built by a developer hoping for big profits from people that liked fishing, water based recreation, a clean new town and warm winters. To support the town, the developer also built a chain saw manufacturing plant. The area had been known as Site Six, a remote World War II training center with a military runway. Later there was a small bait store and a boat dock. In the early days it was only visited by a few fishermen and game wardens on major holidays. Now Lake Havasu City is a busy place swarming with many California and Arizona recreationalists.

The new Wildlife Manager was Rich Beaudry, and it was his goal to “clean up Dodge.” Rich did his job well and developed a reputation for issuing citations quite freely for all types of violations, especially boating infractions on Lake Havasu. The population of this new community was less than 3,000 when he first arrived, but it was popular and grew in astronomical proportions. The Colorado River lakes attracted boaters and fishermen equally fast. This area became a favorite place for college students during Spring Break and other holiday weekends. As time passed each holiday attracted more and more people for sun, fun and alcohol. Fast boats were the game and it seemed all were imbibing great quantities of booze. Many of these people had no regard for public safety, the law, or those who enforced the rules.

Beaudry and other enforcement officers patrolled group after group of post-pubescent fun goers, issuing citations for boating and safety violations during holiday weekends. Patrols during these busy weekends in the 60s and 70s were usually not much fun. The hoards of boaters, skiers and outlaws came to the river and lakes to “by god, recreate” and no one was going to interfere. Law enforcement personnel were often surrounded by throngs of kids posturing and shouting insulting remarks, making their duties next to impossible. It was a time of caution for peace officers, and their patience was taxed.

During one of these busy weekends, a pair of officers approached a loud group of youths. Beaudry had observed one of their boats committing several infractions. They beached the patrol boat and proceeded ashore to talk with the boat operator. They were greeted with jeers, sneers and tough talk from the group who had obviously over-indulged in both sun and beer. Quickly, the group surrounded the officers. They identified the boat owner and approached him. Beaudry let the other officer issue the earned citation. The crowd tightened and grew more vocal. The tension gained intensity with threats toward the officers. Beaudry then stepped back, reached into his pocket and pulled out a pair of ear plugs. He made sure everyone saw him insert the plugs into his ears.

The leader of this loud and obnoxious group noticed what Beaudry had done and questioned the officer writing the citation. "What the hell is he sticking those things in his ear for?"

Not looking up from writing the citation the officer replied in a voice loud enough for all to hear, "Oh, he just can't stand to hear the sound of his gun goin' off!"

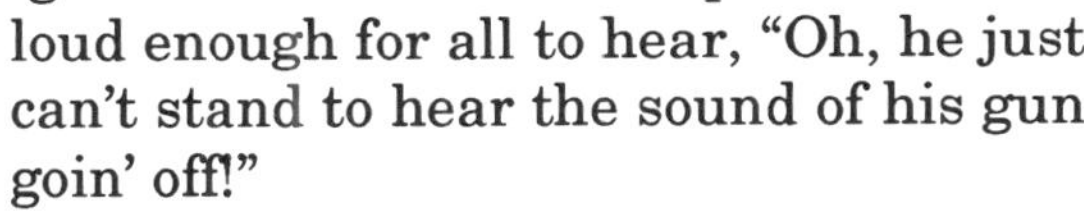

The crowd dispersed, quite quickly, and the boater only asked where to sign the citation.

A Call For Help

by Pat O'Brien

After considerable effort, I was finally able to coerce San Carlos Indian Reservation Game Warden Charles Aday to patrol with me on San Carlos Lake. My plan was to correct the ills that plagued society on this tranquil bass production factory. Charles did not like boats and he liked water even less. But he agreed to join me and we had a good day.

Inspired by our daytime success, we continued to patrol on into the encroaching hours of darkness. Our bounty consisted of some thirty or more citations and a dozen or so seized rods and reels. Following a few more contacts, we decided to work on trying to tag one elusive violator that continued to evade us — a boater operating without running lights.

After turning the boat motor off, the coal black darkness of night enveloped us and even the brilliance of a million distant stars provided little respite — in fact, we couldn't see our hands in front of our faces. Out of the silence we heard the high pitched whine of an outboard motor. The motor's whine changed to a loud roar as the boat passed by, close enough to rock our boat with it's wake. Without comment, we uniformly agreed that a person could get hurt sitting out here like a lame duck. We decided to call it a night.

We headed for the boat dock at full throttle with the aid of a million candle power light and my confidence of knowing the lake. Charles mounted the bow like a vigilant bird dog on point seeking any obstacles that might pose a threat to us.

"Look out!" Charles shouted.

Looming before us, with the defiance of an off-shore oil rig lay a U. S. Geological Survey weather barge. Firmly constructed of angle iron and floated by 55 gallon drums, the barge grew in size as we approached.

With the confidence of an Indy 500 race car driver, I spun the wheel to avoid hitting the barge. It was like being on an icy surface as the boat's bow changed direction, but our movement did not. It was only a split second before fiberglass and metal met! With the motor stalled and refusing to respond to re-start, gallons of aqueous liquid poured into the boats interior via the four foot long gash in the side.

"Row, Pat, Row!" Charles shouted frantically.

After grabbing an oar, I realized the futility of such an effort since we were probably a mile from shore. As the water level inside topped my boots, Charles collected all available life preservers, put them on, and abandoned ship. Obviously, he was not the Captain.

As the boat filled with water, it gradually submerged beneath the dark surface and I realized for the first time in my career that I could not walk on water. I swam over to the barge and climbed aboard.

As Charles pleaded for help, I tried to coax him toward the barge. "I can't swim!" was his only reply. "Well, kick your legs and paddle, get over here!" I yelled at him. Charles finally made it to the barge. Now we needed help.

"Help! Help!" Charles shouted loudly.

"Help! Help!" I joined in.

"Help!" Some distant shoreline resident added.

For what seemed like hours we continued to chorus in repetitive unison until the obvious shoreline drunks decided to give up, or they passed out.

In response to our continuous pleas for "Help!" over the lake's placid surface, we finally observed distant lanterns being lit and heard boat motors being cranked up. After a period of searching, the first rescue boat approached our location. Charles and I stood there dripping wet astride the barge in our full Game Ranger regalia.

"Oh my gosh! It's the Game Warden!" one of the boaters remarked. "And we don't have running lights!" another added.

"Never mind that!" I shouted. "Get over here, we need your help."

Charles and I had finally trapped our elusive quarry — only to turn the other cheek until another time and place.

The Boston Whaler & the Rapids

told by Howard McDonald

All of us knew our Boston Whaler was not designed to go up rapids, but we had to try. The trip started because Bud Bassett, Chief of Fisheries was interested in knowing what kinds of fish were in the Colorado River tributaries and Levi Packard, Region II Supervisor wanted to look for bighorn sheep in the lower end of the Grand Canyon. So, we set off on this doomed expedition in April 1968. The party consisted of Bud, Levi, Wildlife Managers Hal Wenthe from Prescott and Jimmy Allen from Williams, Fisheries Assistant Riney Maxwell and me. Harold Pratt, Wildlife Manager from Fredonia, was participating in the bighorn sheep helicopter survey. He arrived at our camp after we started upriver and was not part of the boating trip.

We trailered two boats down the road from Peach Springs, setting up our base camp at the confluence of Diamond Creek and the Colorado River, about fifty miles upstream from Lake Mead. This site is used as a takeout area by commercial river runners because it provides the first vehicle access to the Colorado River, 226 miles downstream from Lee's Ferry. After lunch we were ready to begin our survey. We loaded the equipment needed for fish surveys, put on life jackets and took off upstream in the two boats. The Boston Whaler led the way with all the fisheries survey equipment. Riney was driving, and Bud and I were passengers. Levi was driving the second boat, a larger fiberglass hulled outboard. Hal and Jimmy were with him. We had good luck and no difficulty running the rapids at Mile 224, Granite Springs and Mile 217. At Three Springs Rapid we ran into trouble.

This rapid is not described as difficult but the rating system is for downstream travel. When we got into white water the bow of the Boston Whaler went under a wave and the boat submerged, dumping the three of us went into the cold, chocolate milk colored water. Everything that floated was going down river. I saw one of the gas tanks floating by, swam over and hung on to it. Riney was pushed over against the river bank and got caught in a whirlpool. I saw something that looked better than the gas tank I was clutching so I let go and grabbed the seat cushion as it floated by. As I looked around I spotted the top of Bud's head. He looked like he was in trouble. Just then the Boston Whaler came up underneath me and I grabbed on. Since I had the boat to hold on to, I threw my life jacket to Bud.

Levi could do nothing to help us until he went up though the rapids and turned around. As he came back down I yelled at him to look for Riney because the last time I saw him, he was caught in the whirlpool. As Levi went after Riney he went past Bud, who let go of the life preserver I had thrown him and grabbed the side of the boat. One rescued. Levi didn't want to drive into the whirlpool so he threw Riney a rope and it promptly got caught in the prop. Levi was able to jockey

The Colorado River rapid runners talk about their great adventure. From left to right are, Riney Maxwell, Harold Pratt, Hal Wenthe, Levi Packard (back to camera), Bud Bassett, and Jimmy Allen. (Photo by Howard McDonald)

the boat around and cut the rope. Riney caught the second throw and was pulled out of the whirlpool and along side the boat. Two rescued. I'm still holding onto the sinking Boston Whaler with no life preserver, but my rescue was uneventful, since by now I had drifted into calmer water. Levi took us to shore and then went to rescue our equipment floating in the river. All he could find was a gas tank, an oar and a cushion. And the Boston Whaler.

Levi picked us up off the rocky shore and took us to a sandy beach. Jimmy and Hal gathered a big pile of driftwood and built a fire. We undressed and dried ourselves and our clothes around this nice big fire. I felt really lucky, through all of this my Stetson hat never left my head. While we were drying out, Levi, Jimmy and Hal worked on the Boston Whaler, getting it upright and starting the motor. Heading back to our base camp, Riney and Bud were in the Whaler, but I decided it would be better, at least for me, to ride with Levi in the bigger boat.

By the time we got back to camp Harold was there. He was just about ready to call for help because he noticed our equipment floating down the river and he knew something was wrong. We built another big fire, dried some more, cooked a good meal and talked about our adventure. We knew we were lucky. We also admitted that we would have continued up the river until something like this happened. Who knows, we might have tried to go up the big one, Lava Falls.

Shadow

by Wayne Anderson

After the big snow of December 1967, my wife Connie and I inherited a two year old female black lab. Her name was Shadow. Shadow loved women; they were cool. Shadow did not like men; they were to be shunned. She was the perfect watch dog for my wife. Until I started taking her along on some of my patrol trips, Shadow just tolerated me. She loved to ride in the back of the pickup. After a few years Shadow became as well known as Levi Packard, my Supervisor, and developed a reputation as a great law dog.

Once when stopped at the Flagstaff Trading Company on Highway 89, the manager commented to me that Shadow was a really well trained dog. I asked what he meant. He said several people told him that when I was on patrol I would let the dog sniff around camps while

I talked to the hunters. He added that Shadow would find a deer or elk hanging out of sight. According to him, the word around Flagstaff was that Shadow should be given credit for many of the tickets I wrote. My comment was, "Drats, the cat's out of the bag!" or something like that. It was a great story and I did not tell him the truth. Actually, the only thing that Shadow did was retrieve waterfowl for hunters hunting the lakes and stock tanks around Flagstaff. Of course, sometimes these ducks were illegal, ones that the hunter did not want retrieved.

One of these retrieves occurred during waterfowl season at Ashurst Lake south and east of Flagstaff. Ashurst Lake is now closed to waterfowl hunting. It was opening day, and very cold and windy, with a mixture of snow and rain. On the north end of the lake, a hunter had downed a bird that fell into the offshore weeds. I threw a rock in the general direction and Shadow took off after it. Swimming through the weeds, over fair sized waves, Shadow was performing beautifully when she grabbed the bird. On her return Shadow was having difficulty fighting the weeds and waves. I began to doubt my judgment for sending her after the bird in this nasty cold weather. But she made it back OK and the hunter was impressed and happy. He praised Shadow for her efforts and was grateful for not losing his bird. Then he asked me what kind of bird he had shot. I looked at it and said, "It's a grebe and it's illegal." A grebe is a waterbird similar to a coot, but the season has never been open for them. The hunter's admiration for Shadow plummeted. In the cold and wind my hands were shaking as I wrote the citation.

Later, I filed the case in Judge James Brierly's Justice of the Peace Court in Flagstaff. When I went to check on the disposition of several cases I discovered that this grebe killer had been fined $50.00. Before a grebe had always resulted in a $25.00 fine. I asked Judge Brierly why this one was $50.00. "A grebe?" he said. "It looked to me as if you wrote one goose during closed season." Sure enough, I had been shaking so bad in the cold and wind that even I could hardly read if it was "grebe" or "goose" I wrote on the citation.

In the eleven years we had Shadow, she probably made three to five cases a year for the Department. I know these were her cases because my co-workers and I would never have gone wading or swimming for any birds hung up in cold water and weeds. After she died it took a few years before people in the field finally quit asking me where Shadow was.

Whenever I went to the Regional Office, Shadow jumped out of the truck and went to the back of Levi and Donna's house. Even though Shadow loved to hunt and was a good retriever she never bothered Donna's ground squirrels. It's probably because she always hung around at Donna's back door waiting for a "goodie" and I know she was never disappointed. When I was ready to leave, I always found Shadow at Donna's back door.

Shadow embarrassed me once. It was when Connie and I took her sister and husband to show them some property we had purchased east of Flagstaff. Shadow, being the retriever she was, took out after a neighbor's chickens. She zeroed in on one, grabbed it and brought it to me. Unfortunately, it was dead. It was a pretty retrieve to watch, but I was embarrassed as Shadow and I turned ourselves in to the neighbor. He was a good sport and was not too upset after I bought the chicken.

A Shot in the Night

by Paul Webb

It was September, and preparations were being made to get fall elk surveys underway. A group of Levi Packard's Region II Wildlife Managers were gathering at a cabin above the Mogollon Rim just north of the small town of Pine. Surveys were to start the next morning. Headed toward the cabin were three Phoenix office biologists who were glad to shake the bonds of office life for a few days of surveys in the field. The trio included Dean Carrier, Jim Wegge and myself.

The cabin was in a heavily wooded area and could not be seen from the highway. Near the highway was a meadow frequented by elk. The combination of elk, the meadow and the highway was a poachers delight!

It was dark and as the three Phoenix biologists neared the rendezvous cabin, a plan was hatched which would add a little excitement for the survey crew. The plan was to use a cigarette as a slow fuse and attach it to an M-80 firecracker. The device would be lighted and planted in a tree next to the meadow a few hundred yards from the cabin. The three activated the plan just before reaching the cabin.

Since they were the last to reach the cabin, everyone was in place for the ensuing action. Some of the wildlife managers were cooking dinner, some were just talking, telling stories. Others had their boots and shirts off with their gun belts hanging on hooks. It was an atmosphere of calmness and relaxation that only a cool, quiet night in the mountains can generate. The three greeted their old friends and tried to become part of this calmness, but kept looking at each other wondering when the big bang was going to come. After ten or more minutes, they began to think the device was a dud.

Suddenly, "BANG!" the silence of the night was broken. Everyone, including the Phoenix trio, froze for an instant before being galvanized into action. The M-80 produced a most realistic rifle shot.

Someone yelled, "Let's go get 'em!" Shirts were grabbed and buttoned, boots pulled on or laced, guns strapped on and a mass exodus erupted through the cabin door. Trucks roared out of the yard, through the meadow, and onto the highway. Half went north and the others went south. Radios were alive with chatter on how to surround the poacher. Some wildlife managers were chasing each other on logging roads through the forest. This went on for over an hour before the chase wound down and everyone gave up looking for the poacher and returned to the cabin. Here the discussion turned to the poachers. Who were they? What should be done the next time this happens? Everyone was really disturbed that they could not catch an elk poacher who was so close. How in the hell had they escaped?

The unholy three, of course, participated in the chase but because of a total lack of valor decided not to tell anyone what actually occurred. Now it can be told. The elk survey was accomplished without any other disturbance from phantom poachers.

Unforgettable Characters

by John N. Carr

As Wildlife Managers we often meet some very interesting characters. When I was a Wildlife Manager in the Sonoita and Patagonia area in the 1960s I met my share of these characters. It was part of my job to stop and meet the people that lived in the country, the ranchers, the miners, and so on. Some of them I really liked and talked with them everytime I had the chance, and others I only stopped to visit once.

There was Henry Van Horn, a miner and prospector in the Huachuca Mountains who even though he had lived alone at his camp since the end of World War I, was a knowledgeable man, full of interesting information. When ever I stopped to see Henry I had to plan on staying at least three hours, because he had few visitors and he liked to talk and talk and talk! His one room cabin was as clean as a pin. I took my wife Sally to visit him once. She enjoyed her visit and was amazed that this hermit's cabin was cleaner than her home! For years he worked for the U. S. Forest Service as a summer fire lookout on Miller Peak. He never learned to drive a car and lived in the Bear Canyon area of the Huachuca Mountains, a long way from the nearest store. When he was younger he used to walk the 40 miles to Bisbee if he could not find a ride. He had an arrangement with the mailman to deliver groceries to his mail box which was two miles from his cabin. He survived on his veteran's disability pension and his summer Forest Service job as I doubt he ever shipped more than a few hundred pounds of ore from his mines.

* * * *

Then there was Old Man Anderson. I never knew his first name. He was a miner too. He lived near the West Gate of Fort Huachuca and always believed his mine would become another Bisbee. He didn't like people and he did not like to wear clothes. In the summer or even in the winter, if it was warm enough, he ran around naked. It was quite a sight to see this shriveled up old man of ninety plus years working his mine without any clothes on. When someone came by his camp he would just lie down on the ground, stare up at the sky, and not move. Every year deer hunters would report finding him dead, but he was just trying to avoid having a conversation with a stranger. But he was old enough to die and Deputy Sheriff Joe Hill would sometimes take me along to check and see if he was still alive. He always was. He was still alive when I moved to Phoenix in 1968, but died a short time later.

* * * *

Then there is the story about a former employee of the Game and Fish Department. Philip Welles worked for the Department in the 1940s as a biologist. He worked all over the state, from Flagstaff to Tucson. When I knew him he was Superintendent of the U. S. Park Service's Coronado National Memorial on the southeast end of the Huachuca Mountains. Phil loved to hunt even though he was crippled by some terrible disease. He wore steel braces on both legs and could only walk with the aid of his walker. He killed a whitetail deer every year I knew him. Early in the morning he would drive up the Montezuma Pass road to a switchback that turned just outside the

Park boundary. He would sit and wait and watch for a buck to shoot. Then he would drive back to the Park Headquarters getting someone to recover his deer.

I used to spend hours at the Memorial Office drinking coffee and listening to Phil's stories. He grew up in Chihuahua, Mexico and knew the country south of the border well. He told me that he once worked for the U. S. Military Intelligence in Mexico, but got in trouble and had to leave. After he graduated from an eastern college he went back to Mexico to guide hunters for big game, including bighorn sheep. He was able to get permits to hunt sheep when very few others could. All it took was knowing the right person and a few extra pesos. Probably all of the sheep hunts Phil guided were illegal, but they were profitable. He once told me about a night hunting trip in Mexico where the hunter swore he could tell the difference between the light shining from a deer's eyes and those of a burro. Phil said he was hesitant but the hunter insisted he knew the difference. He was wrong, and they wound up buying three dead burros.

I remember Phil telling me about one experience while he was doing survey work on bighorn sheep and whitetail deer for the Department. He was camped in the Santa Catalina Mountains north of Tucson, somewhere near Pusch Ridge, and stayed there for several weeks at a time. He was up there during the deer season and met two wealthy hunters that asked for his help in locating a nice whitetail buck. He helped the hunters and they each killed a nice buck. They wanted to pay Phil for his help, but he refused. These two hunters hung around Phil's camp for a while drinking coffee and telling hunting stories before heading back to town with their deer. According to Phil, about a week later, when he was breaking camp, he found a hundred dollar bill stuffed in the pocket of his clean pants. That was a hell of lot of money in those days, probably more than two weeks pay. Phil knew that it wasn't his money, but he knew where it came from.

The Cookout

by Jim Whitham

While serving my six month Wildlife Manager training period during the summer and fall of 1968, I was assigned to work the antelope hunt in Region III in northwestern Arizona. Although I rode with several officers during the four day hunt, I elected to camp with Wes Martin, the Regional Supervisor. We were in Unit 18A and it was Saturday night.

We both brought top of the line steaks for dinner. Wes built the fire to generate some good coals for our steaks. After we stoked up the good hot fire for an hour or so, we were ready to cook. Going to the truck for my grill Wes said, "Oh you won't need that, we'll just cook them directly on the coals, it works great!"

As I watched in disbelief, he took our two prime steaks and threw them directly on the coals. He continued to assure me that they would be OK and were going to taste great.

The results! It took longer for me to scrape all the ashes and charcoal off my steak than it did to eat it. Needless to say, the next night I used my grill! Wes still cooks his steaks this way, but I don't!

To Build a Road

by Louis Carufel

Sometimes when you need help it isn't available. Early one morning in late February or early March, 1968, I left Phoenix to check water levels in Apache and Roosevelt Reservoirs. I also wanted to see if there was any fishing activity taking place. After lunch I decided to check out the Four Peaks area before heading back to Phoenix. I was driving a two wheel drive pickup.

As I traveled up the road to Four Peaks, I encountered patches of ice and snow in the areas shaded by cut banks and north facing slopes. I kept going because it wasn't too bad and there were no places to turn around on this single track road. It didn't get any better the further I went. I was quite concerned when I was going up a pretty steep grade, because it was several hundred feet down the slope. I was looking for a place to turn around. Nearing a section of the road where it began to widen out, I hit a heavy patch of ice and the rear of the pickup just slipped sideways toward the outside steep edge of the road. I thought it was going to go all the way over, and I could do nothing to stop the truck's movement. Lucky for me, it did stop, but the left rear wheel dropped off the road and the truck came to rest on the axle. I was lucky, but now what? Somehow I had to get the pickup back on the road.

My first instinct was to use the radio for help. I tried for an hour, but no luck. I was in a blind spot. I was going to have to do this myself. Luckily, I had a shovel, a handyman jack, and tire chains. I knew I had to build a road under my left rear tire, which was hanging out in space. I worked on that for four or five hours. I put tire chains on the wheels and started to build a platform to support the rear left tire. In building the road, I used everything available, rocks, brush, dirt, ground cover, and sticks. I thought I had it once and tried to drive off but just became stuck in more mud. I had to jack the truck up and start again, with more rock and brush.

A couple more tries and I finally got the truck back on the road. I still had to go up the road, but I finally found a place to turn around. Putting the pickup in creepy crawly low gear I made my way down the road over the bad parts with the snow and ice patches. I finally got home, but it was really late. It was a long day, but not as long as it could have been. I fully expected to spend the night on the side of the mountain hoping someone would come by and find me.

I wished I'd had a four wheel drive. It might have kept me out of this predicament. But then again, a four wheel drive can only get you to the end of the road where you get stuck even worse!

The Rating System

by Phil Cosper

A lot of things changed for the Department when the Legislature gave the us the boating enforcement and registration responsibilities. In order to personally experience some of these changes, I joined the Region IV staff to patrol the Easter invasion of California boaters and party goers along the Colorado River in the Parker Strip section.

I worked with quite a few of the Region IV fellows. This was a new experience for me, and I never, ever before saw so many obnoxious, drunk, and stupid people gathered in one place. We spent a very busy weekend checking boats and hauling these obnoxious guys and a few girls to shore. I'm sure we saved some lives from their stupid actions. We hauled many of them to shore and the Department of Public Safety took them to the Parker jail. What a weekend!

On the last afternoon I was working with Ranger at Large Buck Wallace. Buck liked to work on the water and loved his boat. He knew he and his boat were one of the best. We had decided to head back to the dock and get ready to go back to Phoenix when this big, fast, hog boat from California came roaring past us. The guy in the boat flipped us the finger.

Buck looked over to me, patted his boat, and with a smile said, "Well, we're still number one on the river!"

Old Grandpa

by Wes Fleming

We called him Old Grandpa, an old loner buffalo bull that we seldom saw and never could round up for any of the hunts. He lived at the Department's House Rock Buffalo Ranch and had been there as long as anyone could remember. He always avoided the main herds and usually hid out in the juniper.

Jimmy Wilson, Ranch Manager, moved the buffalo herds from pasture to pasture by manipulating the availability of water, but even this failed to move Old Grandpa. Jimmy had been forcing the buffalo to another pasture by shutting off waters. When I arrived on one of my inspection visits to House Rock, Jimmy came out and said, "I've seen Old Grandpa and I know where he is!" Then he added, "He has a terrible abscess on his sternum, he's lying down in the junipers near North Buck Farm Canyon." There were a couple of pools of water in the bedrock of this canyon that no one knew about, except Old Grandpa. Jimmy had finally figured out where he stayed all these years.

As Jimmy had described, the abscess was bad. If we didn't treat it soon it would kill him and no one wanted that to happen. We knew there was no way in the world to get Old Grandpa to the ranch and into a squeeze chute to treat him. We would have to do it in North Buck Farm Canyon, just the two of us. We knew the abscess had to be drained. There was only one way. One of us, I can't remember who, said that we could put a hole through the abscess by shooting it. That way we didn't have to get too close to this big buffalo bull. We decided

House Rock Buffalo Ranch Manager Jimmy Wilson displays the skull of a large buffalo we called "Old Grandpa". (Photo from the January/February 1971 issue of Wildlife Views. Photo by John Theobald.)

to try. We snuck within several yards of Old Grandpa, and when he stood up and I got the right angle, I shot the 30-30 and punched a drain hole in the abscess. We then ran like hell! Old Grandpa survived the treatment!

A couple of years later Jimmy found Old Grandpa dead. The skull was massive, with huge horns, but needed some cleaning up. I happened to tell the Director that Old Grandpa had died and Jimmy had the skull. The Director said the skull belonged to the state and he wanted it cleaned up and delivered to his office. He also wanted a large juniper stump cut "just so" and polished to display Old Grandpa's skull. Jimmy thought it was finders keepers and he wanted a written opinion from the Attorney General.

In the meantime Jimmy had put the skull on an ant hill near the ranch house to let the ants do all the cleaning work. Lo and behold, someone stole Old Grandpa's skull. End of story.

Handling a Road Kill

by Jim Whitham

It's always fun to get out of your district for awhile and see new country. I always enjoyed the opportunity to get into the cool pine country and out of my hot desert Wickenburg district. I was glad when I was assigned to patrol the 1969 spring turkey hunt around Payson. I was to work with Harold Van Sickle, Wildlife Manager for Unit 21.

It was Sunday morning, the weather was bad, and the hunter activity was light. I was riding with Harold in his sedan along the main highway just above Kohls Ranch, when we happened on a road kill deer. We had to do something. We could not leave it there on the road.

The deer had been there too long and was too beat up to salvage. Most of the time we would have dragged it off the road twenty or thirty yards so it was out of sight and leave it for the coyotes and ravens to eat. But there were a number of occupied houses in the area so we could not drag the carcass off the road. Harold did not want to put this beat up deer carcass in his sedan and haul it off. We got out the tow chain and hooked the deer to the back of the sedan and took off towing this carcass down the highway. We dragged that deer for several miles before we found a suitable place to discard it. Needless to say, we attracted a few strange looks and quite a bit of attention from passing motorists as we did our duty handling that road kill deer.

The Desert Fox Incident

by Harley Shaw

This is a brief account of the incident in Chino Valley that led to the death of Highway Patrolman Paul Marston, the wounding of me and Yavapai Sheriff Jack Finley, and ultimately the death of escaped convict Danny Eckert. I wrote this for the Arizona Game Ranger Association News Letter and passed it on for this book. It's the only time I've written about this happening. I probably never will again.

Things happened awfully fast that day, and I could see only a narrow part of the action, so I cannot give the full story. Most of the newspaper articles I have read about the incident seem inaccurate, but no one at the scene was taking notes at the time. It happened in early June 1969.

Don Neff, Miles Rodda and I had traveled from Flagstaff to Chino to buy hay for the tame deer Don used in his food habit study. We were all working in research, but like all field people at the time, we carried Game Ranger commissions. This made us State Peace Officers, subject to call on any law enforcement situation.

At that time, there was no Arizona Law Enforcement Training Academy, no Department enforcement training program, and no handgun qualification, at least for G & F officers. Wildlife Managers and Game Rangers carried handguns most of the time. Those of us in the gray area were allowed to carry a handgun, but we seldom did. It wasn't becoming to a research biologist. Nonetheless, we were required to wear uniforms identical to the enforcement people (including our badges). This was kind of a schizy situation that developed because some early research people wanted to collect a uniform allowance. Most of us wanted out of the uniform.

We had a mid-morning break at the old Chino Valley Truck Stop for coffee and pie and had just got the first bite down when Officer Gilpin of Yavapai County Sheriff's Office walked in and beckoned us to follow him. He had been sitting across the road from the cafe and had seen a pickup with an APB out on it go by. They were looking for Eckert who had tied up a couple in Groom Creek and stolen their pickup. His name had been in the paper off and on for the past couple of years, because of his escapes from Florence and cat and mouse games with the police. Although he had military experience, he was considered by many to be harmless. He was in on a rape conviction, some said trumped up.

Rodda and I joined Gilpin in his S. O. sedan. The only gun we had between the three of us was a S & W .38 with target wadcutters. As we headed north out of Chino, attempting to regain sight of the pickup, Gilpin told us he thought we were chasing Eckert. Because of his past actions, we assumed he would either escape again or, if cornered, would give up.

We regained sight of the pickup just south of Paulden. By this time, of course, Gil was on the radio directing in other police units. We had Department of Public Safety or Sheriff units moving along all possible highways and arterials to head Eckert off. Although Gil held back about a quarter mile from the pickup, Eckert identified the squad car and turned off on the old highway around Sullivan Lake. I'm sure he was testing to see if we were following. When we turned, he hit the gas. We headed back toward Chino at about 100 miles per hour. I was wondering if the subject was worth the effort.

As we hit the north end of town, the DPS car with Paul Marston and Ron Mays appeared Code 3, from the south. Eckert turned east on the Perkinsville Road, and the DPS car turned right behind him. We were one car back now. We learned later that Marston, the local patrolman, was pushing to get to Eckert first. He felt he could talk him into surrendering and prevent bloodshed. Mays was a new patrolman, assigned to replace Marston in the Chino area. Marston was being transferred to Phoenix, a move he thought would benefit his career.

Eckert turned into the 4-Winds Ranch at the edge of Chino, with Marston and Mays on his bumper. I think the convict thought he was turning onto another side road and realized too late that he was dead-ended in a ranch yard. Whatever the case, he left the truck and started to run. Marston pursued afoot. About this time, Eckert fired the first shot, hitting Marston, I believe, in the side of his buttock. Marston had seen him point the gun and dodged sideways, I imagine, hence the point of impact.

We arrived about this time and things were pretty chaotic. Several ranch hands were diving for cover in the barn. As it turned out, so was Eckert. He was dressed in a t-shirt and levis, amd was wearing leather gloves. In the turmoil, you couldn't tell him from the ranch hands.

I remember Marston was still on his feet, behind a post of the porch. I didn't know at this time that he had been hit, but we had heard the shots as we pulled in the drive. Mays waved Gilpin to the back of the barn, and I dropped out of the passenger side of the car into a low ditch to cover a part of the side and front of the barn. About this time, Eckert started shooting from inside the barn, and I made a dash across the driveway to the DPS car. Mays was behind the car talking on the radio to other units moving in. He glanced up at me and said, "Paul's hit." The shooting from the barn continued.

I moved briefly to the back of the DPS car so that I could see into the barn. I wasn't willing to shoot. I'd seen several people disappear into the building, and the last thing I wanted was to have my bullet identified in the body of a citizen. I remember thinking this clearly. I'll admit that I wasn't too excited about drawing fire, either. Lack of training and attitude were big factors governing my actions. As a biologist who happened to carry a badge, I didn't feel like a "real cop." Shooting someone was on my mind, but I sure didn't want to do it. I could plug a gap or help someone who was wounded. Becoming cannon fodder, as it were, was a serious concern of mine also.

About this time, I realized that Marston was no longer standing behind the post on the porch. I didn't know that he had been hit again, but I moved in that direction. Shooting had started at the back of the barn, where Gilpin had gone, and I wanted to be able to see down the west side of that building. I ran to a ranch pickup that was parked a short distance ahead of the DPS car, planning to use it for cover while I located Marston and watched the off side of the barn.

When I raised up to look over the pickup hood, Marston was lying near the post on the porch where I last saw him, and I was face to face with a civilian with a shotgun. I was pretty sure it was Eckert, but hesitated nonetheless. As I said, shooting was for the real cops who knew how to make these decisions. I ducked behind the truck, trying to gather my wits. Eckert must have stood as high as he could and aimed downward over the pickup hood to shoot at me. I felt a heavy impact over my right eye, like someone had hit me hard with their fist. I think I was knocked down. I remember realizing that I was hit in the head and wondering if it was fatal. I also ran down a quick list of things I still wanted to do in life. I scrambled for the back of the pickup and was just turning around the rear bumper when Eckert fired at me again around the front of the truck. The .38 in my hand exploded, and my right arm kind of went limp. I don't remember real pain from either shot.

I dove into the passenger side of the DPS car. Mays was still on the radio, trying to direct other units to the site. He looked up and saw my bloody face and asked where Eckert was. By this time, Eckert was pursuing me and was right off of the hood of the DPS car. I'm not sure what I screamed, but Mays came alive just as Eckert pointed the shotgun in the driver's side window. I assume Eckert pulled the trigger, but he'd used up all of his shells shooting at me and Jack Findley. Mays fired two shots, I believe, through the driver's window of the car, and Eckert dropped and dodged like a cat. He ran back around the front of the car and toward the open passenger-side door where I was sitting. I remember wondering what I could find to use as a weapon. I don't know if I actually looked for anything. I doubt that there was time. Mays fired three more shots as Eckert rounded the front of the vehicle. Then as I remember it, Eckert froze facing Mays, standing just forward of the passenger window, perhaps five or six feet from me. He seemed to be confused, like he hadn't realized the car held two officers. He still had a handgun tucked in his levis. Mays fired the sixth shot from his revolver, and Eckert went down.

I lose track of time here, but I remember finally standing up outside the car and looking down on Eckert. A large pool of thick blood had already gathered under his head. Other officers had arrived and were moving up from the driveway. Mays once again grabbed the radio, as I remember, and announced that the subject was down. Someone, perhaps a dispatcher, called back, "cover him." I was looking at the hole in Eckert's head when I heard that remark. I remember mumbling, "bullshit," and walking away toward a Yavapai S. O. car parked in the driveway.

About that time, Prescott Police Chief Lindley arrived (all units in the area had moved in), scanned the scene, decided the action was over, looked at me and said, "this one can ride sitting up." He and Rodda herded me into the Prescott City car and we went Code 3 to the Yavapai Community Hospital. At this time, I still didn't know that Marston was dead. I was aware that sometime during the action a Sheriff had been hit. It turned out to be Jack Findley from Camp Verde.

I won't give the details covered in the reconstruction. That's a matter of record if you want more detail. For my part, I had taken impacts resulting from two shotgun blasts. The first was a rifled slug. Eckert had jacked out one loaded round, buckshot, from Marston's riot gun, when he picked it up beside Marston's body. I'm not sure whether the slug itself actually gouged my forehead or whether a large chunk of metal from the pickup side mirror hit me. The slug had ricocheted off of the mirror. I think it was the slug because of the kind of groove over my eye, and because of the size of the hole in the brim of my hat right over the place where I was hit. I still have the hat.

The second round that hit me was buckshot. Two pellets passed directly through my right thumb and hit the frame of the .38 I was carrying. That gun exploded in my hand, and I still have metal fragments scattered up and down my right side and right arm. Every time I get an X-ray, the technician gets excited. One piece of metal, probably the cylinder release button from my handgun (it's about the right size, and the piece was never recovered) lodged against my right radial nerve just above the elbow. It's still there. My right hand was partially paralyzed for several months after the incident—radial paralysis it was called. I could grasp things, but couldn't extend my fingers. The hand specialist told me it would cure itself, and it did, finally. My right thumb has no joints left, it's solid bone, but it functions pretty well. I fumble a little when working on small projects; probably cuss a little extra when working in tight places on cars.

I can't say that I can give any advice from this experience as far as how to react in such a situation. Obviously you can't predict when these things will happen. I can give advice regarding the aftermath. Get an attorney and cover yourself personally. Don't depend on the agency. With few exceptions, those higher than you are going to worry more about their own careers, and the lawsuits that might reach them, than they will about your plight.

I learned sometime after I left the hospital that Cliff Sorrells, then Chief of Enforcement for the Department, had quietly bought me a membership in the Game Ranger's Legal Fund the instant he learned I'd been involved in this situation. I think Levi Packard, Region II Supervisor, had a hand in that decision also. Cliff wasn't my boss; he wasn't even particularly fond of research people, but he always worried about personnel first and the agency second. There haven't been many like him, from that standpoint. For the record, I did not fall under the Public Safety Retirement Plan, and retired under the regular state retirement system.

This all happened over 20 years ago, and probably even some of the things told above have become distorted with time. Since then, I have spent one day on a lion hunt with Ron Mays. We never talked about the incident. I met Marston's widow a few years back at a historic preservation meeting. When we realized our connection, we avoided the subject. Patrolman Brian Marston, an infant in arms when his father was killed, lives next to our horse property in Chino Valley. We wave; we've never talked.

All of you in enforcement are better trained now than we were then. I would hope that any of you would react better than I did. I hope even more, that you never have to.

My Dog? . . . . . Your Dog?

by Rich Beaudry

Just after I was assigned to the Lake Havasu district as Wildlife Manager, I went to the Regional Office in Kingman on business. I took my black Labrador puppy along for the ride. I wanted him to get used to traveling because I expected him to be a good companion for some of those lonesome days when I worked alone.

When I got to the office I noticed Wes Martin, Regional Supervisor had brought one of his dogs to the office and it was running around the conference room. I figured, what the hell, I'll let my puppy come into the building and meet some of the people there. After a little sniffing, stares and other dog gestures the two dogs began to play together. I left the two dogs in the conference room and went to talk with Wes about the business at hand. After several minutes we headed back to the conference room to check on the dogs. There on the floor was a piddle puddle. Wes looked at me and said, "Your dog pissed on my floor, clean it up!" I looked at Wes and stupidly said, "Wait a minute Wes, how do you know my dog made the mess?"

"I'm your boss and it's my job to know these things," he replied.

I took my dog outside, tied it up and cleaned up the mess. At the same time Wes took his dog in his office and closed the door. With the mess cleaned up and the dogs taken care of we went to lunch.

When we returned I checked my dog and went inside to continue my work. I found Wes standing at his office door scolding his dog with a string of expletives. Looking in, I could see his office was a mess. There was dog crap on the floor, piddle puddles, paper scattered around and worst of all, feathers all over the place. His dog had attacked one of the mounted ducks in his office.

I looked at Wes and said, "You're right, boss, the other mess was my dog!" I then quickly finished my work, picked up my dog and headed home before Wes could use his supervisor logic to blame the destruction of his office on my dog.

I Don't Ride Horses

by Pat O'Brien

I checked to see if my seat belt and shoulder straps were secure as Department Pilot Jim Bickel lifted off from the Willcox airport in the Department's Super Cub, an airplane not known for its comfort. It is an in-line, two seater, known for its ability to fly low and slow, and a great plane for wildlife surveys. We were on our way to count deer and javelina.

Skirting the eastern edge of the Winchester Mountains, we sighted a few deer and javelina enroute to our next destination. Riley Butte was an isolated malapai mountain near Bonita and known for hosting good numbers of mule deer, javelina and occasional antelope. My previous horseback surveys in these rugged mountains were always time consuming and slow, due to the steep and rocky terrain. This airplane survey would be quick and should produce a good number of sightings.

Our first pass across the mountain's highest peaks revealed a large mule deer herd perched precariously along one of its many vertical rock faces. A second pass proved inadequate to count and classify the herd into bucks, does and fawns. Lining up our third approach on the unmoving deer herd, I was confident about finalizing the classification count. As we flew near the peak, there was plenty of air between us and the valley below, but we wanted to be close to the mountain top to get a good look at the deer.

Twisting for a better look at the deer and fighting the tight shoulder and seat belt straps I became aware of the familiar sound of the plane's stall buzzer, indicating that our air speed was too slow. During wildlife surveys the stall buzzer comes on a lot, ignoring this warning I continued to count the deer. It was only Jim's abrupt utterance of a few choice words that took my attention from the deer. The ground was close, — too close for comfort, in fact. As we plowed into the uneven rocky terrain and teetered on the plane's nose, it felt like we were going over, but I was concentrating on the deer.

Between this point and in the brief seconds that passed, I found myself some seventy-five yards away from the plane glassing the puzzled deer. It was only then that I realized that we had crashed. Looking back towards the plane I noticed that Jim was still in his seat.

"Are you hurt?" I shouted.

Flying wildlife surveys is fun for some and scary for others. Unfortunately airplane crases, such as this one occur far too frequently in wildlife work. Pilot Jim Bickel and Wildlife Manager Pat O'Brien walked away from this one near the Winchester Mountails west of Willcox. (Photo courtesy of Arizona Game and Fish.)

Jim's only reply was his fist pounding on the plane's dashboard. No one hurt, good.

Jim crawled out of the plane and we surveyed the damage and wondered how we could get the plane off the mountain without drawing attention to ourselves. No such luck. I noticed a horseback rider watching us from a distant hill. With my binoculars, I recognized the rider as the resident cowpoke.

Beckoning him forward, he seemed reluctant to approach. It was only later that he explained his hesitancy. He felt there was a strong possibility that we were drug haulers. If that was the case, he didn't want anything to do with us. After an evaluation of our situation we made radio contact with the Region VII office in Pima to tell them we needed someone to come to Riley Butte and pick us up.

"What are you doing on Riley Butte?" was Don Wingfield's curious reply. "I thought you were flying deer surveys."

"We were, but ... !!!"

After some conversation the cowboy offered to ride to the ranch headquarters and return with a couple of horses. Then we could ride horseback to the ranch and wait for the truck to take us back to Willcox.

"No thanks, I don't ride horses, " replied Jim, "A guy could get hurt on one of those things."

Compulsive Behavior

by Don Neff

The Department's tame deer feeding study was begun by Charlie Wallmo in 1963, as a means of assessing the habitat changes caused by the Beaver Creek Watershed Project near Stoneman Lake. This watershed study was a forest tree thinning program to see if more water runoff could be produced for the water users of the Salt River Valley. When Charlie went on to the U. S. Forest Service in Fort Collins, Colorado, I took over his job and continued the work from 1965 to 1970.

The idea of the study was to get deer fawns and let them grow up with humans so they would not be wild. We could then follow them around to watch them eat and record what they fed on. Only two of the fawns we raised grew up to work well with us in the field, but they were champs. Miles Rodda, Wildlife Research Assistant, and I did all the field work because the fawns imprinted on us. As they fed, we tried to identify every food item taken, the species of plant and the parts taken. We counted and recorded the number of bites for each and every plant they ate. The early training was a bit wild and very unpredictable, but later it smoothed out and became quite routine. Keeping a deer on a leash while it ate and following it around was not always an easy task. While we tried to identify the plant and the parts just eaten the deer wanted to move along at its usual fast rate, sometimes dragging us along in the process.

This was fun, and interesting and we learned a lot. Such work takes intense concentration and we found ourselves reacting compulsively to the deer's behavior. Sometimes we chewed along with them, salivating when they found a highly palatable item. I don't know who was training who, us training the deer or the deer training us, so they would not be hindered with their feeding habits.

We suffered compulsive reactions due to the intensity of our work at other times, also. After sitting in a small tent blind for two days, waiting for turkeys to come on bait at a cannon net trap, Miles told me

Lucy heads for a "picnic" in the woods with Biologist Charlie Walmo. (Photo from the November/December 1964 issue of Quail Calls.)

he drove all the way home at twenty miles per hour because he felt trapped and just couldn't go any faster. Another time, after a week of walking long transects and counting paces between sample plots, I once found myself driving home down the road slowly and still counting. When I realized what I was doing I had no idea what I was counting.

A Bad Day

by Dave Daughtry

Some people violate wildlife laws out of ignorance, and others out of contempt for the law and those who enforce it. Some violators are caught through exhaustive investigations and some through stealth and cunning. Once and awhile, violators are entangled in their own lies and are caught through careful interrogation. Others are apprehended by coincidence and blind luck.

During one of Arizona's first archery elk hunts Wildlife Manager Terry Landrith was lucky to have been drawn for an elk permit in his own district. Through an agreement with his boss, Region II Supervisor Levi Packard, he would hunt elk in the morning and evening and carry out his law enforcement responsibilities during the day. That was an acceptable arrangement as both recreational and professional obligations could be served.

Terry started off in the pre-dawn morning with his bow and arrow in hand, wearing camouflage coveralls over his game ranger uniform. His quarry was a bull elk or a mule deer buck as both were legal during this archery season.

The distant bugle of a bull elk quickly riveted Terry's attention. It was coming from a nearby hill. He started slowly up the slope toward the sound of the bugle, but quickly became distracted by two gun shots followed by another single report. By the sound of the shots the shooter was not far away. This was archery season and therefore no firearms were permitted afield. A game law violation must be in progress. Terry quickly forgot about the bugling bull elk and struck a quick pace in the direction of the shots.

After about ten minutes, an opening in the forest exposed a small aspen rimmed park ahead. He slowed his pace, carefully examining the area for signs of the shooter. His stealth and caution was soon interrupted by a startling "Howdy." It came from behind a large ponderosa pine just out of his peripheral vision. He quickly turned to see a man leaning against the tree, holding an old pump shotgun.

"Hi, whatcha doing?" the Ranger blurted in response.

"Oh, just shooting some bandtails," the man said as the bow packing Ranger approached.

"Hell, I thought pigeon season didn't start for another month or so!"

Terry coyly retorted.

"Hey, it doesn't, but what the hell, those damn stupid game wardens couldn't catch me if their lives depended on it!" the violator said as he raised his shotgun on an incoming flock of pigeons. The gunner stepped forward from the tree line, killing a double in the presence of the camo clad Ranger and then quickly running into the meadow to retrieve his poached birds. Dropping his archery tackle, Terry followed the shooter, each step writhing and wriggling to remove his camo coveralls. The gunner bent over to pick up the pair of birds he had dropped, then straightened up and turned around proudly displaying the two bandtail pigeons.

The life and color seemed to drain out of his body as he turned to see a fully uniformed Game Ranger standing in front of him ready with his citation book. Terry then smugly stated, "Pardner, this just ain't your day!"

The Mexican Connection

by John N. Carr

In February 1971, I was fortunate to participate in an aerial survey for wildlife in northern Mexico. At the time I was working in the Game Management Division for Paul Webb. My primary responsibility was to conduct the hunter questionnaire program which consisted of mailing thousands of questionnaires to small game and big game hunters and from the responses received determine the number of hunters, how many days they hunted and what kind of success they had. It was a boring job that confined me to the office crunching numbers and pushing paper.

However, I did have another job, which I really enjoyed, as it got me out of the office and into some new and different country. I was conducting surveys looking for the Sonoran pronghorn. This desert pronghorn lived in the Cabeza Prieta Game Range and the Luke Air Force Gunnery Range, the area between Ajo and Yuma along the Arizona-Sonora border. I had been poking around this hot dry desert off and on for about three years looking for pronghorn. I had even made a few trips to Mexico on my own time looking for pronghorns around Caborca and the Pinacate Mountains.

At the same time Dick Todd, the Department's Non-Game Biologist, was working on the Yuma clapper rail. The Yuma clapper rail and the Sonoran pronghorn both have a major portion of their habitat in Mexico. Somehow we were able to talk Director Bob Jantzen and the Governor of Arizona into making this aerial survey in order to expand our knowledge of these critters. Roy Tomlinson, a research biologist with the Fish and Wildlife Service also came along on the trip. He was the Service's Endangered Species Biologist and was working on the re-introduction program for the masked bobwhite quail. These quail were once native to Arizona, but at this time were found only in remote areas of Sonora. We were in the Department's Cessna 206 and Jim Bickel was our trusty pilot. I always liked flying with Jim because he was so steady.

We left Phoenix early in the morning on February 8th, picking up Roy in Tucson, and going on to Nogales where we met with Ron Anderson, the local Wildlife Manager. After lunch we flew to the Nogales, Sonora airport to get visas and travel papers for the airplane. After getting these papers in order and stamped by the officials, we traveled south along Mexican Highway 15 to Rancho El Carriso near Benjamin Hill, looking at known masked bobwhite habitat. We then flew west along the Del Pacifico Railroad past Pitiquito and Caborca and into the sand dune habitat of the Sonoran pronghorn. We spent about an hour zigzagging across this desert area between the little town of San Luisito on Highway 2 and the railroad near the Gulf. We saw 19 pronghorn before returning to Nogales for the night.

The next morning Roy stayed at the hotel while Jim flew Ron, Dick and me east of Nogales. We flew south along the Santa Cruz River to the town of San Lazaro and then turned east to Cananea and then to the head waters of Rio Sonora. We then flew around the Sierra de los Ajos before returning to Nogales. We were looking for the riparian habitats and places where the Mexican turkey still might be found.

Back in Nogales, we dropped Ron off, and picked up Roy and proceeded west to Yuma, flying over the Buenos Aries and Santa Margarita Ranches of Altar Valley, the proposed masked bobwhite transplant area. We then few into Mexico, going south of the Baboquivari Mountains and near the Sierra Cubabi and the Pinacate Mountains of Sonora. We saw eleven pronghorn before landing in Yuma for lunch. After lunch we flew the Colorado River delta area and along the west coast of the Gulf looking for coastal marshes. We saw the first mangrove swamps near Punta Sargento. After landing at the Hermosillo Airport we took a cab to town for the night. We stayed in a nice hotel and had a good Mexican seafood dinner.

The next morning we flew south along the coast past Guaymas to Bahia de Santa Barbara, just south of Huatabampo. On our return we looked for fresh water marshes along the coast. We re-fueled at a small airport north of Guaymas. We watched with some concern when the barrel of gas was rolled to the Cessna and the fueler hand pumped gas into a five gallon bucket. With the fueler standing on a ladder, gas was poured through a filter into the wing tanks. We began to wonder why we hadn't landed at the larger commercial airport on the south side of Guaymas to top the tanks off. We then flew northwest toward Kino Bay. While flying about 500 feet over a forest of ironwood and palo verde trees, cardons and organ pipe cactus, our trusty Cessna 206 coughed and sputtered. Bad fuel! Jim Bickel, usually pretty calm and laid back while flying, reacted quickly to switch fuel tanks. Thankfully, the normal purr of the engine returned. Now we knew we should have refueled at the main Guaymas airport. We still had a long way to go.

We continued our surveys along the coast and flew around Tiburon Island, returning to Hermosillo for the night. After parking and securing the plane, we got a taxi to go to town to get a place to stay. No problem! The night before we had no trouble getting a room. Not today! It was the first day of a Rotary convention and every room in town was full. I'll give credit to our cab driver, he worked really hard trying to find a place for us to stay. We were ready to return to the airport and spend the night in or under the plane. But the cab driver said he knew of one more place to check. When we got there, none of us really wanted to go inside. It looked pretty sleazy. But they had two rooms. We decided it would be better than spending the night in the Cessna. Our concern became even greater after we checked in. Each room was $1.25. The place we stayed at the night before cost 12 or 15 dollars. What were we going to get for a buck and a quarter? We were all ready to sleep on the floor, but instead we were amazed at how clean the rooms at the Hotel Kino were. There were clean sheets on the beds and even running water in the bathrooms. Wow, what a deal!

Since it was to be our last day we canceled our visas and travel papers at the Hermosillo Airport and then traveled north along the coast and then inland looking for pronghorn. We found a group of ten north and east of Puerto Lobos. We continued north towards Yuma and decided to take one more look around the Pinacate Mountains just south of the Cabeza Prieta Game Range. In the Pinacate area there are several large craters. These are really calderas which form when the ground collapses and falls into a void caused by volcanic activities. One of these is called Crater Elegante and is more than a mile across and several hundred feet deep. They look a lot like Meteor Crater east of Flagstaff. We talked Jim Bickel into flying over these craters at a pretty low elevation so we could get a good look and photographs. As we flew over the last crater, a down draft caught the Cessna and we dropped real fast. I thought we were going to go all the way to the bottom of the crater and never come out. Jim and I had our seat belts on but Dick and Roy in the back, did not. They went up and hit the roof. They both were taking photographs and somehow exchanged cameras returning to their seat. When Dick came off the roof he also opened the airplane door. There was a lot of stuff flying around in the back. Well, that was enough for Jim. He said, "That's it, the surveys over!" He took the Cessna up to 8,000 feet and we stayed there till we got to Yuma.

More Flapjacks for Breakfast?

by James R. Wegge

This story about Research Biologist Clay McCullough needs to be told because to look at him, the truth isn't obvious. Clay is a tall lanky quiet fellow with large feet.

Near as I can remember, the year was 1971, and the usual crew of about ten men were working the North Kaibab deer checking station. We were staying in the old TSI Forest Service cabins and I was doing the cooking.

In those days the checking station opened at 6:00 am, so at 4:30 am I went to the cook shack to start coffee and turn on the grill of the beautiful old Garland gas stove. It had six large burners and a large grill that could cook a dozen eight inch pancakes at once.

Clay was always the first one in for breakfast. When he walked in I'd say, "Good morning," and hand him a plate of pancakes, a side of bacon and a large milk. Clay would get right down to his eating business, not being one for much "chit chat." Clay had emptied the grill twice when there was a knock on the door.

No one ever knocked on the cook shack door! Surprised, I said, "Come on in." The door creaked open and a huge fellow ducked as he walked in through the door and stomped the snow off his size 14 pacs. He said the Jacob Lake Lodge wasn't serving breakfast yet, but he had been told the checking station crew cook would probably feed him. He had been driving all night and was very hungry. We talked briefly and I motioned for him to sit down. He sipped a cup of coffee and I soon gave him a plate of cakes and bacon and also filled Clay's plate for the third time.

He was an impressive man as he sat there putting away the grub. He was wearing a red plaid wool shirt, dark heavy wool pants, snow pacs and had hung up a old time black loggers cap before he sat down to eat. I kept frying pancakes as fast as I could, trying to keep up with the two hearty eaters. The stranger said that where he came from they called these cakes "flapjacks" and I became suspicious that he might have lived in Minnesota at one time.

Well, the frying and eating went on until the stranger said he was "as full as a tick after a two week ride on a blue ox" and he got up to say his good-byes. As he thanked us and put on his cap I said he looked familiar and asked what his name might be. He looked surprised and said, "Well, it's Paul Bunyan!" and stepped out into the cold.

I turned back to Clay and said, "Hey, Clay, he was a pretty good flapjack eater, wouldn't you say?" Not seeing Clay at the table I turned around to the grill and there stood Clay, empty plate in hand.

With the same hungry look on his face he said, "Yes, he was a pretty good eater Jim, pretty good!" And then he said, "Jim, can I have some more?"

Blackpowder and Wes Don't Mix

by Rich Beaudry

You could hear a pin drop that afternoon when Wildlife Manager George Welsh gave his mule deer hunt recommendation to John Russo, Game Management Division Chief and Paul Webb, Big Game Supervisor. George recommended the first blackpowder hunt for Arizona. But wait a minute, I'm getting ahead of my story.

In 1970, if my memory serves me correctly, the Department recommended and the Commission agreed to change from a state-wide general deer season to issuing permits by hunt units. This was a big change, as it placed greater restrictions on the hunter. The wildlife managers felt it was needed because hunt pressure and range conditions combined had lowered deer populations in many areas of the state.

One hunt unit that had experienced a sharp decline in deer numbers was 15A, northwest of Kingman. George felt that he needed to cutback on the deer harvest, but he did not want to close the unit completely to all deer hunting. In the morning, Region III staff met to discuss proposals prior to meeting with the Phoenix Game Management Division staff. George wanted his Unit 15A deer hunt open only to blackpowder muzzleloader hunters.

Wes Martin, Regional Supervisor, opposed the recommendation and began to play devil's advocate with George's proposal. As the discussion progressed, voices got louder and it appeared that neither would give up their opinion. After what seemed like hours, probably only twenty minutes, Wes could see he was not getting anywhere with George, so he turned to the rest of the Regional staff for support. He got none. We all thought George had a good idea, it was a unique solution which still allowed hunting and would result in a reduced harvest. Besides, it got Wes's goat and we kind of enjoyed that.

Wes finally agreed to let George present his recommendation that afternoon to the Game Management staff. But, Wes let it be known he was positive the Phoenix people would not agree to such an off-the-wall proposal.

At the afternoon meeting John Russo and Paul Webb were in rare form. They questioned almost every hunt recommendation. They felt the Region was proposing too few permits for antelope and bighorn sheep. When the proposed deer hunts came up for discussion, John and Paul continued to question the wisdom of the Wildlife Managers and made us justify every recommendation. It was not an easy meeting as we had to battle for every one of our recommendations.

We all knew that George was going to be in for a real fight when he recommended his muzzleloader hunt. Because the Regional Supervisor did not support it, and because of the way John and Paul were questioning our hunt recommendations, we felt George would fall flat on his face.

Finally, it was George's turn. He stood to begin his presentation. Looking at Wes and without any explanation he said, "I recommend 50 muzzleloader only deer permits for Unit 15A."

Silently we waited, all eyes shifting between Wes and John. John looked up from his papers, jotted a few notes and said, "OK, I'll accept that, what are your other recommendations?"

We all looked on in disbelief. Wes' jaw seemed to hit the floor. He was speechless. Well, almost!

George is no dummy. He had done his home work well by pre-selling his innovative idea to John and Paul long before this meeting, and they agreed to keep his secret. And so, the State's first muzzleloader hunt was proposed, and the rest became part of Arizona's wildlife management history. It was an event all of us in attendance will remember.

Don Taylor, the Story Teller

by Jerry Day

Don Taylor, a Development Crew Leader, loved to tell stories about his observations and field exploits. Most of us felt he exaggerated a bit. I remember the time he told me about the many javelina herds he found north of Mammoth, the largest of which numbered fifty to seventy-five animals. Since I had spent many years studying javelina and the largest herd I ever tallied was thirty-seven, I naturally concluded that Don was exaggerating or pulling my leg. One time on the Three Bar, his creditability declined even more. He told me about the bear he saw running around me while I was trying to capture a javelina with a capture gun. I explained that it was a javelina and not a bear, but Don was not convinced and insisted it was a bear.

Don's fishy stories were probably the most difficult to believe. He liked to tell about catching brown and rainbow trout that were always more than twenty inches long. I simply dismissed these stories as stretching the size a wee bit, like he did with javelina herd counts. However, I had to rethink my evaluation of Don's fish stories after I observed him in action. This took place on Big Lake during one summer in the 1970s. We were staying at the Big Lake Cabin, now removed, while conducting turkey surveys. One evening, while trying my luck with a fly rod, Don walked up with a spinning rod and a very big bass lure. He muttered something about trying for some big ones. I laughed, since a twelve inch trout was the longest any of us had caught in Big Lake. I watched him make one cast, and then on the second his rod almost doubled over. At the same time he yelled, "I got one." He began reeling madly and asked for my help when the fish got tangled in the weeds. Not having a net I waded into the water to help land it. The large rainbow trout flopped near me, but it broke free before I could grab it.

On Don's next cast his pole doubled over and he shouted, "I have another big one." He began horsing the fish in rapidly, past the weeds and on the shore. This beautiful rainbow trout, as I recall, measured twenty-one inches and weighed over three pounds. Fishing nearby, Research Assistant Norm Woolsey saw what happened and ran to his tackle box for a similar bass lure. Others followed.

After witnessing Don's fishing exploits first hand, I began to realize that I might have been too critical of Don's other stories.

So Don, please forgive me for not believing your fishy stories. However, I am still not ready to accept your javelina herd counts.

A Driving Lesson

by Jim Whitham

I was a Wildlife Manager assigned to the Wickenburg District in the early 1970s. My patrol area included the Peeples Valley area just north of Yarnell. During hunting seasons other Wildlife Managers and Officers in Region V were often available to assist with patrol efforts within the Region. On one particular weekend during the deer season in 1970, Howard McDonald, the Region V Wildlife Assistant, was assigned to help me patrol in Unit 20B, the Yarnell and Peeples Valley area.

I felt really good as I had recently been assigned a brand new 1970 Chevy four wheel drive pickup to replace my old beat up two wheel drive Ford pickup. Howard and I met on the main highway in Peeples Valley to discuss patrol strategies. We decided that I would follow him into an area where there was always a good concentration of deer hunters. Howard left first on the dusty road with me in hot pursuit. It was really dusty as it hadn't rained in a long time. I was running between 35 and 45 miles per hour, and the dust was so heavy I could only catch occasional glimpses of Howard's truck.

As we approached a fork in the road, Howard elected to go left. I followed the dust. All of a sudden, I entered a huge boiling cloud of dust. Unfortunately for me, Howard was stopped in the dust cloud and right in the middle of the road. The dust obscured everything. It was then that the front bumper on my new truck met the old and very sturdy bumper of Howard's truck. I hardly had time to hit my brakes. Fortunately, neither of us were injured. Howard got out of his truck to survey the damage. Then with a big ear to ear grin, he looked at my pretty new truck and commented, "What did you do that for?"

The Big One That Got Away

by Don Vance

On a summer weekend in the late 1960s, I was working with Harold Van Sickle, Wildlife Manager for the north half of Unit 21. We wanted to check fishermen at some isolated locations along the Verde River, areas that are not frequently patrolled. One of these areas was down Houston Creek.

I had never been on the Houston Creek road before, and I haven't been back since, so I really can't say the road was worse than usual on that particular trip, but it compared with some of the roughest roads I was familiar with in the Superstition Mountains. At one place on this road I had to decide to drop the truck wheels off the right side of the road or to scrape up the left side of the truck. I asked Van if he had been down Houston Creek before. He said he had, but swore he would never go down it again. When I asked him why he had decided to go down this nasty road with me, he just chuckled and said it was because I was driving.

When we finally got to the confluence of Houston Creek and the Verde River, we found a camp. It looked like all the occupants were asleep in the shade. We drove on past their camp to the edge of the Verde River. We could see where several people had been fishing during the night, and judging from the number of forked sticks stuck in the mud along the bank, there were more fishing poles than fishermen. Walking up the river bank Van found a stringer anchored to the shore and pulled it out of the water to look at the fish. On it were several small fish and one really nice channel catfish, it weighed about ten pounds. As Van held up the stringer to get a good look, the clip opened and the big fish fell off and swam away. All of a sudden that fish seemed even bigger.

Van put the stringer of fish back in the water and we got into the truck. As we drove by the fishermen's camp Van asked me if I wanted to stop and wake them up to check licenses. Thinking of the big catfish that got away, I said, "No, not this time." And we started the long haul back out Houston Creek.

I'm a Jerk

by John N. Carr

When I worked in the Game Management Division I helped with the North Kaibab deer hunt checking station. That was nothing unusual, every one in the Division did. We also got help from others in the Department. Sometimes we were able to get wildlife management students from Arizona State University to help. The students really enjoyed their time at these checking stations. They got to meet people they hoped to work with and they got to see some of the famous big Kaibab bucks. The usual North Kaibab checking crew from the Game Division included Bob Weaver, Paul Webb, John Russo, Jim Evans, Charlie Jordan and Jim Wegge. They were a good crew to work with. This story happened in 1971 or 1972.

One night during the week, I think it was Thursday, I had the late shift. Weeknights are usually not very busy, and I was there alone except for a young ASU student volunteer. It was getting close to quitting time and we had not had any hunters check in or out for about an hour. The two of us were just killing time talking, while waiting for the 10 pm closing time. He was asking questions about working for the Department and I was answering them the best I could. It was a cold night and there was six or eight inches of snow on the ground. Just before closing time, a pickup with a big camper rig pulled in. There were two hunters in the truck. They wanted to check out and had two pretty nice bucks. But they were in a hurry. In fact they were in a real big hurry. They said they needed to get back to Phoenix, now!

That year we were weighing every buck. It was part of the checking out procedure. No weigh in, no check out. These two hunters had everything in order. They had checked in before they went hunting and their licenses and permits were valid, so every thing was OK. Now I had to weigh the two bucks.

One of the hunters said. "No way, as far as I'm concerned we have checked out! We don't have time and we are leaving!"

I told them they could leave if they wanted, but if they did, as far as I was concerned, they had failed to check out. I also told them this would result in a citation and they could expect a visit from a Game Ranger in the near future. Well, that really pissed them off. One of the hunters really got on my case. He stomped around in the snow, threw down his hat and wanted my name and badge number and shouted, "By God, I'm going to report your ass to the Governor!"

When he threw his hat down I could see his face clearly and I recognized him as a person I had met the past summer in Phoenix. He had called the Department and asked someone to identify some horns he had found in the Vermillion Cliffs. John Russo, the Division Chief, asked me to check them out. Russo had worked for a number of years as a biologist on the North Kaibab and knew the country well. He also spent a lot of time working with bighorn sheep and he did not believe there were any sheep in that area. But, to be sure and to satisfy his curiosity I went to look at the sheep horns. I went to the address near the Capitol and was invited inside. The horns were light weight, in a tight full curl and a half, and came from a domestic sheep. They would look good as a lawn ornament. The two of us talked about hunting and fishing, the usual stuff, over several cups of coffee and had a good visit. I was in his house for at least an hour.

The second hunter realized that getting the bucks weighed was better than getting a citation. So he got his buddy calmed down and told me to go ahead and weigh the bucks so they could get checked out and on the road. But they both said they would be damned if they would help and we had better be real careful not to scratch up the inside of the camper! The two deer were laying on their backs stuffed in the isle of the camper. They were frozen stiff, with legs sticking out everywhere. Getting two bucks out and then back in without dinging up the cabinet work of the camper was quite a chore, but we did it. After all the arguing and carefully moving and weighing the deer, it was now well after ten. We were lucky no other hunters came into the checking station while we were arguing with these two hunters. That would have complicated matters.

The hunter that I had recognized was still mad as hell and was pouting off to the side. After doing all the necessary paper work I went up to him and told him about the time he invited me into his home this past summer to look at his "sheep horns". He looked shocked! I took off my hat and he looked at me hard and said, "I thought I had seen you before, but couldn't remember when. By golly, I guess I've been a real jerk." Well, I had to agree with him. We exchanged a few more pleasant words and then he stuck out his jaw and said to me, "Just give me your best shot, hit me in the jaw as hard as you can, I've got it coming." It was a tempting invitation, but I passed it up.

I think the two hunters left happy. At least they had something to talk about on the way home. I left happy, I still laugh about it. The ASU student was dumbfounded about the whole incident. He could not understand how I kept my cool while taking so much BS from these two hunters. I told him that after he had worked for a few years with hunters he would be able to do the same, because you will meet a lot of jerks and you must "at least pretend to be nice," to all of them.

Rosary Beads

by Wes Fleming

The Pacific Flyway meeting was in Boise, Idaho. Waterfowl Biologist Don Berlinski and I flew with the Department's pilot, Jim Bickel. We headed north, stopping in Elko, Nevada for gas. We were flying along a black top highway toward Boise, when the weather conditions changed for the worse. As the ceiling got lower and lower the ground elevation was getting higher and higher. Bickel and I glanced at one another when we flew under a powerline spooking a herd of antelope in front of us. As we banked to get the hell out of there and into a safer area I caught a glimpse of Berlinski in the back seat counting his rosary beads. I have no doubt that Berlinski saved our lives that day.

The Lost Girl

by Phil Cosper

In the early 1970s, I was involved in a hunt for a lost young girl that I will never forget. I was in the Pinetop area to help patrol during the late elk hunt. It was very, very cold; the nights were dipping close to zero. There was also about six inches of snow on the ground. Perfect for elk hunting, but very dangerous for a six year old girl to be out overnight without protection.

Late in the afternoon, we got word through the radio that there was a lost child in our patrol area. The Apache County Sheriff was asking for help. The Sheriff had his men out in the woods, as did the Forest Service. Bob White, Regional Supervisor, mobilized his forces. A lot of Game and Fish people helped. I remember Rex Hansen, Harvey Palmer, Allen Severson, and Bob White being involved in the search. There were others, but my memory has failed me. Everyone felt we had to find the little girl soon, or she would surely perish during the cold night.

The girl had wandered away from camp. Someone had wisely put up some signs on pine trees that said, "Lost girl last seen here, 3 pm." Everyone spread out from that starting point. We drove roads, walked into the woods shouting the girl's name, but no one found any sign of her. We were getting really worried.

At midnight we came upon a camp that had their lanterns still on. We stopped to ask questions and to advise them about the lost girl. We also wanted them to keep the lanterns on all night so the lost girl could see them. It was an elk hunter's camp. They had heard about the lost girl, and that was why their lantern were still on. They asked us if we wanted coffee. After a cup of good hot coffee we continued our search. We looked all night without luck. We knew the girl was in trouble.

At daylight we went back to the place where the "Lost girl" signs had been posted. They were gone, but new ones were in their place. The new signs read, "Hope you had a good night, there wasn't any lost girl." What a hoax! There were a lot of upset people who had spent the night in the forest looking for nothing. We spent more time trying to find out who put up the signs than we did looking for the "lost girl." We never found out who did it.

Me and the Javelina

by Jerry Day

For many years I conducted research on javelina, Arizona's little desert pig. I was bitten twice by javelina over the years and this story is about the most serious episode which occurred in the early 1970s at the University of Arizona Farm. This facility consisted of five pens housing deer and javelina used to test safe drug dosages during field captures. The chainlink pens were seven feet high with doors opening into a narrow, covered, sixty foot runway.

One day, I noticed a sick deer which had to be isolated. To make room, I had to move a former pet javelina, a known biter. No problem,

I had moved this animal many times with the help of a wire barrier for protection. The javelina did not have to be encouraged to follow me, because it charged and bit at the barrier as I moved toward the middle of the runway. I took my eyes off the animal to open the gate latch when I suddenly felt a sharp pain as his teeth sank into my right leg. I dropped the barrier and began kicking the javelina with my left leg. At the same time I tried to climb the chainlink fencing to get out over the top. Unfortunately, I was wearing leather soled shoes and I slipped, and the javelina grabbed my leg again. I finally made it to the top as the mad javelina snapped below. I soon found out the screened roof was securely fastened and I could not escape out the top. Managing to get one leg through to hold me up, I hung upside down like a monkey, with the javelina trying to bite my rear end. No one was around to hear me yell for help. It was midday, no one would come to check the other animals till dark. While I waited, I looked at my injured leg. My jeans were shredded from the knee down and blood flowed from the bites. After hanging there a short time, my wallet fell out of my pocket. The javelina grabbed it, ran to the end of the runway and began chewing on it. This was my chance, I looked for the barrier and it was right below me. I got my hooked leg free, but the javelina saw my movement and came charging back, snapping its teeth. Fortunately, it soon went back to the wallet. At that moment, I dropped to the ground, picked up the barrier, stopping the charge of the javelina and then directed it into a pen.

I drove to the closest hospital to get treatment. It took about twenty stitches to close the wounds. Unfortunately, I developed an infection which required daily soaking in salt water and extra time to heal.

The only visible scars from my 35 years with the Department came from this javelina. After reading this story and those of other Department employees, some of you may think we were lucky to survive our adventures. We were; I believe my guardian angel was looking after me.

The Buffalo Cowboys

by Wes Fleming

Gathering buffalo at House Rock Buffalo Ranch for the hunts was a real chore. Usually the herd was scattered on South Canyon Point and up the slope into the junipers. It took several days of hard riding to get the buffalo to the hunting corrals. In the 1950s, 60s, and 70s, buffalo were gathered and placed in corrals and then released in small groups to be "hunted." Gathering the buffalo was a real picnic for the Department's buffalo cowboys as they yelled and whooped, killed horses, broke vehicles, fought, drank, broke bones, crippled and killed buffalo, tore down fences, and generally had a good time. Compared to the buffalo roundups, Sherman's march to the sea was child's play!

The Game and Fish Department's "Buffalo Cowboys" prepare for a buffalo roundup at House Rock Buffalo Ranch. From left to right are: Jerry Andrews, Cliffy Bennett, Jack Bennett, Bob White, Cliffy Sorrells, Jack Woousley, Harvey Palmer, Gary Beasley, Buck Wallace and Howard McDonald. (Photo courtesy of Howard McDonald.)

One year was different. Thanks to the U. S. Forest Service, the developed grazing plan and Department grunts, including myself, Ranch Manager Jimmy Wilson, Robbins Butte Wildlife Area Manager Charlie Copley, and others, we devised a system of fences, triggers, water hole exclusion corrals, pipelines, water manipulation, and baiting. When all this was in place and timed correctly, the herd was coerced into a small holding trap next to the main cutting corral near the Ranch headquarters.

When it came time to gather the buffalo, many pickups and horse trailers drove over the twenty miles of dusty road to House Rock Ranch for two or three days of being buffalo cowboys and participating in the traditions of the hunt. The cowboys anticipated a great chance to let off steam and prove their manhood to themselves and to one another. When they arrived the first question always was, "Where the hell is the buffalo herd?"

This time Jimmy Wilson was feeling very pleased with himself. With a cold beer in his hand, he pointed to the placid herd in the small holding pasture and said, "Boys, they are right there waiting for you to nudge them into the corral. Glad you came, I can use your help!"

Superstition Salmon

by Don Vance

When I first moved into my district at Apache Junction, I heard all kinds of stories about the strange goings-on in the Superstition Mountains. Most were about lost gold mines. Some, however, were about the wildlife that called the Superstitions home. Stories about who killed the last bighorn sheep or wild turkey on the mountain or about the miniature deer that supposedly lived in seclusion there.

Although just about all the stories were interesting, I discounted most of them, especially after I got to know the people who told me the stories. Some I filed away for future reference. What would have been one of the most unbelievable stories was about the spring run of silver salmon in LaBarge Canyon. If I had heard this story when I first came to Apache Junction I would have discounted it immediately. But it did happen, there really was a silver salmon run in the Superstitions. It was no great mystery and really didn't do anything to perpetuate the many myths surrounding the Superstitions. It may become a myth in the future.

For several years in the early seventies the Department experimented with stocking silver salmon in Canyon Lake. Winter stockings of these fish made the snow birds from Apache Junction happy. The results of the 1973 winter stocking were a little different. Heavy rains came shortly after the fish were stocked, and the runoff turned the lake chocolate brown. The rains kept coming and the lake stayed turbid most of the spring. Several of the tributaries draining the Superstitions Mountains ran fresh, clear water into muddy Canyon Lake for several weeks after the heavy rains had quit. The salmon found the fresh water inviting and most of them headed upstream. They went up Tortilla Creek as far as State Route 88 where they were blocked by the elevated road crossing. When I discovered them, I asked for assistance from the Fisheries Division, and we seined several hundred of the silvers and returned them to Canyon Lake.

A short time later I decided to check out Boulder Creek to see if any of the fish had headed upstream. Sure enough, I found a good number had gone up Boulder Creek and into LaBarge Canyon. They were stranded in pools scattered among the boulders. The pools were deep, and the water coming into them was still cool and fresh. I decided to return in about a week to check on the fish and perhaps catch one just so I could say I had caught a salmon in the Superstition Mountains. When I returned, there was no sign of fish in any of the pools. None. There was sign, however, that some well fed raccoons were in the vicinity. There was also more than a little evidence that some of the flower children living in the area might have had a good salmon meal or two.

But What are Friends For?

by Bud Bassett

Bob White was Regional Supervisor at Pinetop from 1960 until 1977. He could usually observe the inexplicable machinery of bureaucracy with detached good humor. Occasionally, when things got a little too hectic around the office, Bob liked to get away from it all by going on a horseback deer survey "down on the Blue," a wilderness area.

In the summer of 1974, the hectic bureaucracy apparently found its way to Bob's desk and mine simultaneously. Strange as it seems, I found myself riding with Bob on one of those deer surveys "down on the Blue." We stayed at Winter Cabin and worked the surrounding country for a few days. I was riding my sorrel horse named Eutah. Eutah could go forever but was not the fastest walker in the world. Bob's horse had a good gait and liked to go fast, so Eutah and I usually ended up a ways behind.

On one such occasion Bob, ahead as usual, got off his horse and sat on the ground waiting for me to catch up. After a bit I came riding up and Bob waved his arm out to his side and said, "Get on down and sit awhile." I looked at the spot where Bob motioned and replied, "I don't think I want to sit just right there!" When Bob looked, he saw his hand waving over a rattlesnake who was coiled, but being quiet. The snake was nevertheless paying close attention. At that moment Bob revealed that his horse was not the only one that could move pretty fast. We sat in a different location and watched the snake crawl under a hollow stump and then we moved along.

Back at camp, Bob suddenly announced rather emphatically, "Bas, if you'd have gone ahead and sat there, you probably would have gone ahead and died, 'cause I sure wouldn't have been caught sucking venom out of that bite site!" This deflating comment was of course followed by the famous Bob White laugh. I knew, I think, he was just kidding.

The next day going down the trail Eutah threw a shoe. Bob had nails and a hammer with him so he went to work tacking the shoe back on. Without any warning, Eutah sat on Bob. It knocked Bob over, rolling him down the hill and chipping a chunk out of his front tooth. Could be that Eutah knew something that I didn't.

Firearms Training

by Jim Whitham

In the mid-seventies Wes Martin, Region III Supervisor, and I put together a basic firearms training program for the enforcement officers in the Region. At the time I was the Regional Enforcement Specialist. Enforcement training was becoming more and more important as new training standards were being established for all peace officers in Arizona and the Game and Fish officers had to comply with these new qualifications. Our program was quite successful and well received by those who went through the course.

Bud Bassett, Chief of Regions, asked us to conduct our training program for the personnel in the Phoenix Office. There were a number of Commissioned Officers working in various administrative positions that found it difficult to attend training programs held in one of the six Regions.

The first morning was devoted to procedures and lectures on safety. Prior to the lunch break, Wes and I instructed everyone to bring their weapons and leather for the afternoon session, but under no circumstances were they to bring any live ammunition to the classroom. The classroom we were using was the main conference room in the Phoenix Office Headquarters. Known as the Roadrunner Room, it is always busy and is often used for the public Game and Fish Commission meetings.

The afternoon session was for reloading drills and practice shooting. This practice would make officers more efficient on the firing range when shooting for score and certification. Everyone was issued twelve dummy rounds. They lined up facing the south wall of the conference room. They were to load six dummy rounds, draw and fire the six rounds and then reload and fire six more rounds. This exercise must be completed in fourteen seconds. We gave the command, "Draw, fire six rounds, reload and fire six rounds."

Everyone fired their first six dummy rounds, reloaded, and commenced to dry fire the second six. All of a sudden there was a loud bang! Someone had placed a live round in their gun and it went off! A deadly silence filled the room. The bullet had hit the wall, waist high in a direct path to the Director's Office. It knocked a chuck out of the slump block.

Almost immediately, Assistant Director Roger Gruenewald responded to the gun shot. It took him only a minute and a half to come across the walk from the Director's Office to the Roadrunner Room. He was visibly agitated and for once, almost at a loss for words as were the rest of us.

Robbins Butte Wildlife Area Manager, Charlie Copely, a participant in the class had unloaded his weapon en-route to the afternoon session. He forgot about the live rounds in his front pocket, the same pocket where he put the dummy rounds used for the reloading drill. Charlie was the most scared and shook of all of us. All us will remember his gun shot!

Safety is always important even when using dummy rounds. No one was hurt. The mark on the wall is still there. The Roadrunner Room was never used again for firearm training!

The Life List

by Russell Haughey

Ron Engel-Wilson is a Department biologist with a very broad range of skills. He is probably most famous among his co-workers for his cooking. He is always trying new recipes using strange things. For example, while working a buffalo hunt he served some unsuspecting cohorts fried bison spleen. That was the last time Ron cooked for that crew.

In addition to his cooking skills Ron is a very knowledgeable ornithologist. In fact, while in graduate school he distinguished himself while studying birds of the Colorado and Rio Grande Rivers.

Once, an avid birder was bragging to Ron about his life list. Many serious bird watchers keep a list of all the different birds they have ever seen. This birder said his life list included over 455 species of birds. He asked Ron if he kept a life list. Ron replied, "Yes, I have about 165 or so."

The birder haughtily responded, "Only 165? That isn't very many."

Ron cooly replied, "Well, those are just the birds I've eaten!" The birder was speechless, awed and disgusted.

You see, part of Ron's research on birds involved collecting and mounting them as museum specimens. Not being one to waste anything edible he took it upon himself to eat whatever he collected. Ron has high moral standards!

Yes Sir, We'll be Ready

by John N. Carr

I was the Wildlife Manager in Sonoita the first time I worked with Orville Townsend, Development Crew Leader and heavy equipment operator. With his equipment he dragged a surplus airplane wing-tip fuel tank up the nasty road to Guajalote Flat in the Patagonia Mountains, to add capacity to a rain water catchment. This catchment always went dry in early summer because of high use, and the extra tank would provide enough water to last through the dry spell. It had not been easy getting the wing-tip tank up the narrow, two-track mountain road, but Orville was a hard worker. I admired his tenacity and determination.

No one called him Orville; to everyone in the Department he was known as Major. Major was not a big man, about five feet five and weighing no more than 125 pounds. But, pound for pound no one was stronger, no one worked harder, and no one was tougher. He was like a piece of barbed wire.

I remember an incident in 1968, when he helped move my furniture and belongings from Sonoita to Phoenix. We were loading everything into a Department stake bed truck. Major and I were carrying a hide-a-bed couch and as we tipped it to get it out the door, it unfolded. I didn't know it at the time but it mashed Major's hand. He never said a word. After we got it loaded, I noticed his hand. Blood was dripping from his finger tips and although he showed no visible signs of pain, he must have been hurting. He only asked for some bandages and we finished loading my things. That's when I knew Major Townsend was some kind of tough guy.

I got to know Major better when I was Supervisor of the Planning and Evaluation Branch and shared the office complex with Dan Schadle's Development Branch. I was able to share stories when crew members came to the office for assignments or to turn in their paper work.

Sometime in the 1970s, the Department went on a military surplus acquisition mission. Will Nowinski, Supply Manager, and Warner Poppleton, Funds Coordinator, went to military bases all over the west. They acquired everything from bulldozers to canteen corks. A lot of useful equipment was added to the Department's inventory. There was also a lot of junk which was sold at the Department's auction and turned to cash.

At Luke Air Force Base, west of Phoenix, Nowinski was able to find a surplus roadgrader. Major Townsend was sent with his lowboy tractor trailer rig to pick it up. This should have been no problem as he had loaded and moved this type of equipment many times. But somehow, when loading the grader, it ran over Major's foot and broke it. As tough as Major was, he needed medical attention. The Luke Hospital was called and was advised that a patient with a broken foot was coming in. The usual information was given; name, age, sex and rank. When told that the patient was Major Townsend, the voice on the phone said, "Yes, sir, we'll be ready!"

A large group of officers and medical personnel, including the Chief Flight Surgeon, waited at the emergency room for "Major" Townsend.

They were sure surprised when a small skinny man in dirty overalls limped in and said, "I'm Major Townsend, and my foot is broken."

12 Birthday Cakes

told by Joy Schantz

Walt Morris was the Department's mailman. His job was to sort and deliver the mail, and most everyone thought he read it as well. If you wanted to know what was going on in the Department, you asked Walt. He knew. Or at least he acted like he knew. He usually only got half the story when he read the mail, and so he was the beginning of many office rumors. His job got him into all corners of the Phoenix Office and he knew everyone, especially the female employees. He thought of himself as a ladies man. He always talked and joked with the girls. Some of his jokes were on the questionable side of respectability, at least as far as todays standards go. Walt retired just before new office policies went into effect and "sexual harassment" became the buzz word. But he liked the girls, and the girls must have liked him. One birthday he got twelve birthday cakes. It seemed there was a birthday party and a coffee break for Walt in every office complex.

Walt's wife, Jane, even got along with him. On celebrating their 40th wedding anniversary she was asked about the longevity of their marriage. Her response was, "I don't know, do you think it'll last another day?"

From his mail room Walt liked to watch the ladies walk up and down the hall at Deer Valley South. His favorite expression is remembered by many. "Boy, I wish I had that swing in my back yard!"

Don's Dark Glasses

by Wes Fleming

We were flying annual waterfowl surveys in the Fort McDowell Indian Reservation area of the Verde River. Jim Bickel, the Department's able pilot, Waterfowl Biologist Don Berlinski, and I were in the plane. Berlinski had a brand new pair of expensive Air Force type dark glasses. We saw a bunch of mallards on a pool. Somehow he got his head too close to the open window and the glasses were sucked out. There was a piercing scream followed by a paragraph of Polish street language that turned even Bickel's face red.

As we turned right to count the mallards I noticed a flashing light flipping its way toward the ground and stopping in the upper branches of a mesquite tree. I turned and told Don, "You can find your fancy dark glasses in the top of that mesquite next to the big saguaro."

He got a good fix on where his glasses landed and the next day he left the office for a field inspection of the mallard ponds on the Verde River. When he returned to the office he was wearing his new glasses and a big smile.

The Top Hat

by Don Vance

I received a call from the Phoenix College campus police that I can't forget. It was 1975, and the campus cops were holding a student for possession of live wildlife they thought was illegal. When I arrived at the campus security office, I was escorted to a small room and introduced to the violator.

He was, by my standards, a strange individual. He had not shaved for several days and probably had not washed for a longer period. He wore a long black rumpled trench coat similar to the one Lt. Columbo wore on television. He also wore a black top hat. A security officer told the student to remove his hat. What a surprise! A screech owl perched calmly on the guy's head.

After a short interrogation, I learned that our violator did not have a permit to possess the owl. He had captured the bird near Carefree. The owl was apparently blind. I wrote the student a ticket and seized the owl. As I prepared to leave, I asked him why he brought the owl to school.

He replied, "He's my only friend."

It Was a Clod

by John N. Carr

In order to complete some of my law enforcement requirements, I was assigned to patrol in the Florence Junction - Queen Creek area during opening weekend of the 1976 dove season. This was a change from my normal duties in the Phoenix office and I enjoyed the chance to be in the field. I invited one of my long time hunting friends along for the ride, thinking that Harvey would be interested in what I did during a law enforcement patrol. The first day was routine with nothing out of the ordinary happening. We had checked some of the fields in the Queen Creek area and some stock tanks near Florence Junction. We found quite a few hunters and checked a lot of dead doves.

On the second day I was watching some hunters with my binoculars and saw them shooting out of the back of their pickup. Nothing unusual here, that's a common practice, but there were some tickets to write. They had not seen me and started to leave the area. I had to get in front of them to make them stop and I was still quite far away. The patrol car was a big Ford LTD sedan from the Department's motor pool. It had plenty of power and could move pretty fast. Taking off at a good clip I intended to cut off the hunters "escape" route. Harvey was getting a little nervous about what I was doing and he wasn't prepared for what happened next. Going along on the dirt road in a cloud of dust, I got the Ford LTD in front of the pickup and slammed on the brakes. Everyone stopped, real fast. Everyone, that is except Harvey! He continued forward and slammed his head into the windshield, creating a big starburst fracture on the passenger side. (If he had buckled up, there wouldn't have been a story!) Fortunately, Harvey is a hard headed guy and he wasn't hurt; he didn't even get a good welt on his head. It must have been the hat he was wearing.

I wrote a bunch of tickets. They saw the busted windshield, but didn't say anything about it. They must have figured that Harvey was one of us and he wasn't in any mood for joking around.

On Tuesday morning I returned the Ford LTD to the motor pool. I knew that Art Reynolds would be upset about the broken windshield. He reminded me of the supply sergeants I knew when I was in the Army. He took personal pride in "his vehicles" and thought every one of them belonged to him, especially these Ford LTDs. When I told him the windshield was broken, he did exactly what I thought he would.

He got a terrible look on his face and said, "Let's go look at it".

When he saw it, he asked, "What happened?"

I had not thought about what I was going to tell Art. These words just came out of my mouth, "Well, Art, a big old clod hit it." I guess he must have accepted that because he didn't fuss as much as I expected him to.

The Director's Secretary Remembers

by Trudy Hurley

I was surprised when I was asked to contribute to this story book and that I was remembered after retiring seventeen years ago. The last day or two I've been reliving those long ago days with the Department. Most of my memories are of little things and the many people who were so kind to me during my nineteen happy years as a secretary for the Department.

Before I was hired, most of the Department people I knew were in law enforcement, such as Cliff Sorrells, Chief of Law Enforcement, and Game Rangers Jack Bennett and Bob Beasley. We had met at Department Bar-B-ques. But I still felt strange going into the old Capitol Annex building, looking for a job. I bounced around in various sections, starting in Administration and filling in on the alternate half days we used to work on Saturdays. I remember motherly Sue Flake, of the pioneer Arizona family, and how nice she was to me — and what wonderful lemon meringue pies she brought to the office celebrations.

Before long I settled in at the desk between the offices of Cliff Sorrells, Law Enforcement and A. W. "Dud" Yoder, Fisheries. I often helped O. N. "Pop" Arrington, who seemed to like the way I typed his long and complicated letters, for what was then known as Special Services. It was when I was on duty for Larry Powell, Chief of Game Management, that the rather austere appearing Director Bob Smith came to my desk and asked me to go back to his office with him. I was searching my mind for what I could have done wrong to merit his visit, when he asked if I'd like to be the Director's Secretary. So I bid Larry Powell adieu and took up the front desk for Bob Smith's office, and that of Wendell Swank, Assistant Director.

I remember visitors such as Governor Sam Goddard and Jordan Green of the Attorney General's office (who loved to raid my candy jar).

When Bob Smith left to work for the Feds, Wendell took over as Director, with amiable Phil Cosper moving up to Assistant Director.

One of the most difficult duties for me was the taking of minutes at the occasional meetings of the Commission. Most of that august body were too awe-inspiring for me to get to know them, or even have much contact with, aside from seeing that the minutes were given to them for approval, and all the Commission Orders were written up and recorded.

When Dr. Swank left to pursue a research project in Africa, my new boss was Bob Jantzen, promoted from the Wildlife Management Division. He become my third Director. When we moved to the Greenway Road offices, I shared the reception area with Virginia Yates, who became my lifelong friend. She was secretary to the two Assistant Directors, Phil Cosper and Roger Gruenewald, while I continued as Director's Secretary until my retirement in August 1976.

About the only Divisions I didn't work for were Research and Information and Education, although I remember a lot of good guys from their offices. The late Bill Lewis, for instance, passed along some lovely outgrown children's clothes for my brood, and Bill Sizer lent a hand when I was involved in a play about the Irish Republic Army and he agreed to become a "terrorist." (Some of his effectiveness was lost in one scene, though, when he entered brandishing a handgun, only to have it fall open, to a lot of laughs.) I must say I always enjoyed Sizer's contributions of humor to the *Wildlife Views* and I miss them, even though the current staff produces some really wonderful photography.

I still feel very lucky to have been able to work with so many wonderful people, and I felt very appreciated when the Commission presented me with my retirement gift, a plane ticket to New York City to visit my daughter.

I've Seen It All

by Rich Beaudry

Patrolling Lake Havasu is always an adventure. I remember once when Jim Warnecke, Wildlife Manager in Bullhead City, and I were finishing up a late night patrol. We were sitting in my patrol boat in the London Bridge Channel and there were no other boats in sight. I was telling Jim some of my London Bridge stories from years past. I told of citing the first skier in the channel's "no wake zone," being pulled by a truck driving along the channel's construction road. I told him about the person that jumped off the bridge and how I cited him for interference with navigation. I used that statute because at the time there was no regulation about jumping from London Bridge. I even told Jim about using the navigation statute to cite a seaplane pilot cruising his plane under the bridge. And the stories went on and on, for I had been the Lake Havasu area Wildlife Manager for almost ten years. I knew I'd seen and done it all.

It was quiet so we decided to head back to the boat ramp and call it a night. As I reached for the key to start the motor, we heard a strange and eerie noise coming from the channel. We waited to see what this strange noise was. As it got louder and closer we could see the outline of a sailboat coming our way. The noise coming from the sailboat was beginning to sound more and more like music.

Looking at the sailboat we were able to make out three men standing on the bow, playing bagpipes. Bagpipes, wow!

I learned a lesson that night. Never, ever think you've seen it all. Over the next dozen years on Lake Havasu, I saw many new indescribable things.

The "76" Special

by John N. Carr

In 1976 I was Supervisor of the Planning and Evaluation Branch and worked for Bob Curtis, Chief of Special Services Division. Bob came to the Department about 1963 by way of the Michigan Department of Natural Resources. There he had been a research biologist working on deer. In Arizona, he was first assigned as a Wildlife Manager in the Safford area and worked for the infamous Pat Kelly, Region VII Supervisor, headquartered at Cluff Ranch. Bob was a quick thinker and a good talker. He moved up in the ranks quickly and became the Chief of Special Services Division. I first started working for Bob when I became the Department's wildlife planner in 1972. I worked for him for twelve years and we went to a lot of meetings together; the Governor's Commission on the Environment, Colorado River Work Group, Department Commission meetings and more. I got to know Bob pretty well as we spent a lot of time together.

There were some employees in the Department who didn't like Bob. He often boasted about his accomplishments and at times could be arrogant. He often quoted dates and legal terminology and his know-it-all attitude rubbed some people the wrong way. He was also an ex-Marine and let people know. One thing was for sure, Bob was never at a loss for words. Some times his act did get to me, but we got along pretty well. It was real hard to get one up on Bob because he was smart and quick.

In 1976 we were at a three day meeting in Las Vegas, discussing water and wildlife issues of the Colorado River. We were staying at the meeting site, the Union Plaza Hotel, one of the really fancy hotels on the Strip. Like many Las Vegas hotels, they had a meal special at the restaurant. The hotel was celebrating the 200th year of the United States with a *"76 Breakfast Special"*. Entering the restaurant I saw the sign advertising the "Special:" two eggs any style, hash browns, ham, bacon or sausage, toast, orange juice and coffee. When the waitress came for our order, I asked for the "Special," eggs over easy, sausage links and all the trimmings. Bob ordered coffee, toast and orange juice.

The waitress asked him, "Are you sure that's what you want, why not the Special?"

Bob, in his own way, said, "I'm not very hungry and I know what I want!"

The waitress shrugged her shoulders and said, "OK, if that's what you want, that's what I'll bring you."

I said nothing.

After finishing our breakfast and a few cups of coffee, the waitress brought the check. I saw Bob's jaw drop. My bill was 76 cents, his was $5.95. He wasn't speechless; he had plenty to say, most was directed at me and the waitress. I chuckled, and still do when I think about it, since it was one of the few times I ever got one up on Bob Curtis.

The Infamous Native Trout Robbery

by Al Essbach

When I was Chief of Fisheries during the mid 1970s, the Division was engaged in a very ambitious program to propagate Arizona Native Trout, *Salmo Apache*, in our hatchery system. Over a period of ten or more years, we were very successful in capturing wild native trout, primarily from streams in the White Mountains and moving them to our Sterling Springs Rearing Station in the upper end of Oak Creek Canyon, north of Sedona. These fish ranged from six to ten inches in length. They were taken using electrofishing and hook and line. Because of their restricted habitat, many of these trout were sexually mature at this small size.

Over the years, utilizing specific culture methods, we were able to produce native trout up to five pounds and twenty or more inches in length. Eggs were taken annually, fertilized, and hatched, adding to a sizable hatchery population. Restocking selected streams began as part of the newly instituted "Arizona Native Trout Recovery Plan." It aimed at eventually removing the fish from the endangered species list established by the U. S. Fish and Wildlife Service.

Things were moving along quite well - UNTIL! The exact date escapes me, but it was in late 1978 or early 1979 that an incident of monumental proportions hit our native trout program.

We had moved approximately three hundred of our prime size, three to five pound, native trout from Sterling Springs Hatchery to Page Springs Hatchery for holding and sorting prior to fish selection for spawning and or restocking into certain waters. This was truly a beautiful group of natives, representing the culmination of years of culture effort. They were held in a large concrete raceway on the west side of Page Springs Hatchery in a purposely selected, somewhat remote area. After all, fish of this size and quality do offer a temptation to people of the "poacher mentality." And, unfortunately, that's exactly what happened! They were "poached" or "stolen," each and every one of them!

Apparently, the perpetrators slipped in under cover of darkness, pulled the drain plug on the raceway, shut off the water and went to work. Since there was at least half a ton of native trout in that lot, it meant that several people were involved. They must have used small seine nets and dip nets to catch the fish and had a heavy duty pickup to haul them away.

A lot of enforcement people became involved in finding out who took the native trout. The Yavapai County Sheriff, the Department of Public Safety and the Department's own enforcement people were used in the investigation. Game and Fish officers even went under cover to try to ferret out the culprits. Even the Federal Bureau of Investigation became involved because of the endangered species status of the fish. Unfortunately, even all the hatchery personnel had to undertake lie-detection tests and we were pleased when all passed. The undercover work involved bars, restaurants, butcher shops and fish markets in the Verde Valley as well as in Phoenix, Flagstaff and a few other cities. The city and county dumps were searched, as were other locations that could have been used to get rid of half a ton of fish. Not a shred of evidence was ever found about these stolen native trout. Due the prevailing price of meat and fish at that time, it is very possible that the fish were immediately transported to a fish wholesaler in Los Angeles, San Francisco or some other large city. The value of the fish at market price was at least $4,500, and probably higher due to the size of the fish.

Of course, the case remains open and if anyone reading this happens to have any information in reference to this theft, please contact the Department in Phoenix. A reward may still be available. One "Infamous Native Trout Robbery" is one too many.

Jumping Into the Bear's Den

by James R. Wegge

I was finishing the radio tracking for the day, but it was later in the afternoon than I'd planned. We were conducting a black bear research project and had radio collared several bears in the Mazatzal Mountains between Apache Lake and Mount Ord. Study objectives included finding specific locations of bears of different sex and age classes at different times of the day and seasons of the year. Another objective was to identify preferred denning habitat and to document specific den characteristics: size, exposure, and so on. During the winter denning period, the dens of radio tracked bears were visited, radio collars were changed on sleeping bears if necessary, cubs were identified and the location of dens were mapped. In the summer months, the dens were revisited to take specific measurements and photographs.

Well, anyway, late in the afternoon I was headed into Bull Basin to measure the previous winter den of a bear we called "the Boulder Mountain male." It was October and usually by this time we had completed our summer den visits, but it was still prior to denning and this was the last one to inspect. Ron Horejsi, Research Biologist, and I had been to this den site the previous winter and I had the aerial photographs that Bill Carrel, Wildlife Specialist, had taken from his radio tracking flights. The fall days were getting noticeably shorter so I wasted no time. I had no trouble finding the den. It was getting close to dark when I saw the hole and a pile of excavated dirt, a tell tale sign of a bear den. The den was among massive boulders at the head of a steep canyon. There were two ways of getting to the den. I could circle lower into the canyon and come up from the bottom or I could jump down the ten feet or so and land on the soft dirt the bear had scrapped from the den. The dirt pile looked soft and it would save time so I jumped.

As soon as I was airborne a very large bear's head emerged from the den over the pile of dirt — my intended landing site. This bear had heard the soft whispers of human voices when we snared him and attached a radio collar, but believe me, what he heard as I descended were not soft whispers! If you had asked Mr. Bear, he would say that every word he heard had four letters and it was loud. I would not dispute that.

It seemed I was airborne for an eternity, and believed it to be my final destination, but as I was about to land, the bear's head disappeared into the den. I hit the ground running, or rather rock climbing and in seconds found myself ten feet up a white oak tree 100 feet from the den.

I had caught and handled many bears and did not consider them aggressive under most circumstances, but then I had never ever jumped into the lap of an unrestrained large male bear. This bear scared the bejeezus out of me. And I was by myself. While in the tree, I wasn't sure if the bear had come out and left or if he was still in the den. I only knew he hadn't followed me down the canyon. Looking toward the den I saw only darkness. Using my binoculars I looked into the den and sure enough, there he was, backed up as far as he could go. He was staring out as wide eyed as a bear can be.

At this point I had no intention of running him out of his den to take measurements. I waited in the tree until full darkness before I left.

When I jumped, I didn't notice a radio collar on the bear. I only saw a very large bear! Back at my truck I hooked up my telemetry receiver and sure enough, the frequency indicated it was the Boulder Mountain male in that den.

I spent the night at the Three Bar Cabin and the next morning returned to Bull Basin to measure the den. But this time I took the telemetry receiver with me. This told me the bear had moved down below Rock Tanks in Balentine Canyon. It was safe. I measured the den without any problems this time.

I learned a good lesson that day. Look! Take a very, very long look before you leap!

Strange Bedfellows

by Don Vance

I supervised the Metro Branch that was created when the old Region V was disbanded. It dealt with Phoenix urban wildlife problems. The Metro Branch lasted only two years. There were the normal problems to take care of with both live and dead wildlife. Some were not normal problems.

In late 1978 or early 1979, I got a call from the Phoenix Police Department regarding a deer at a motel on I-17 and Camelback Road. This type of call wasn't particularly unusual, so I sent Wildlife Assistant Bill Frantz to check it out. Bill had dealt with a lot of strange wildlife situations in the Phoenix area and also when he worked for the Fisheries Division. This time, however, he found something very strange and unexpected.

For several days the motel maid had noticed a foul odor in one of the rooms. It finally got so bad that she investigated and decided the odor was coming from under the bed. The bed was typical for motels, built on a solid frame. The hotel management called the police and an officer responded, removing the mattress and box springs. The stench about knocked him over.

Whatever caused the stink was wrapped in a blanket and as the officer poked around he saw a hoof. That was enough for him. He ran out of the room gagging and advised his dispatcher to notify Game and Fish. It was, thank goodness, out of their jurisdiction.

When Bill got to the motel he did indeed find a very ripe deer carcass inside the bed frame. Bill had to remove the carcass and recognizing a violation may have occurred, he saved it for evidence. I really don't know how he did that, and I'm not sure I want to know. I am sure he got no help from the police officer or the motel staff. It wasn't just a matter of dragging the deer out of the room to his truck; the room was on the third floor.

Bill brought the ripe carcass back to the office and after nearly loosing my lunch trying to photograph it, I told Bill to take the deer to the dump. We never made a case. We didn't know how the deer died, we could not get close enough to find out. We never found out who took the deer to the motel, why they carried it to the third floor or why they put it under the bed. Or when. Maybe they were mad at the hotel staff, or maybe they had some reason to get back at Game and Fish. Or maybe they had a sick sense of humor. Or maybe they got scared and just left it there. Maybe they will read this and laugh. They will be the only ones who think it's funny.

In Her Bathroom

by Richard Ockenfels

When I stepped into her house on that September day in 1981, Sarah Gorby looked at me and ordered, "Go to the bathroom, just go to the bathroom!" I didn't have to go and I wondered what in the world was happening. I was with Jerry Day, the Department's Research Biologist, and he just chuckled. I was new to the Department and had never met the lady whose house we were in. Jerry knew her well, knew her habits and didn't help me by laughing as Sarah bossed me around.

Sarah's house was beyond repair; it was the classic pigsty, but she was a great old lady. She was an animal rehabilitator in the Tucson area and took in a wide variety of wild animals that needed a little help or time before being released back into the wild. The wild animals Sarah cared for often had free rein in her home. Everyone in the Tucson area having anything to do with wildlife knew Sarah. Being from Phoenix, I had never met her and did not know about her odd habits.

Why should I go to the bathroom because this weird lady commanded me to? All I could do as Jerry's new Research Assistant was to look to him for help in dealing with this strange lady. Jerry offered no help, so I gave in and hustled to the bathroom, even though I still didn't have to go. Looking around this pigsty I wondered about the cleanliness of the bathroom.

As I shut the door behind me, the room suddenly came alive with flying fur-balls bouncing off the walls and me. Bobcats, bobcats everywhere! Three kittens were careening off everything in sight. Sarah and Jerry laughed, enjoying the fun. Opening the door I asked Sarah if I was allowed to come out.

"I couldn't go!" was my only comment.

A Toy Crescent Wrench

by Don Neff

I've had pretty good luck with the vehicles the Department assigned to me. Some of the other employees have not. I've known of breakdowns that left people in bad situations and bad places. I was with Harley Shaw and Ron Horesji once when we thought the truck was going to blow up, or at least it sounded like it.

We were on the North Kaibab in 1980, working on the fall pellet group count surveys. Ron and I were riding with Harley in his four wheel drive pickup when it seem like all hell broke loose. The rear drive shaft had broken loose at the front u-joint and dropped to the ground. We were on a graded logging haul road with a low windrow of loose gravel down the center. The end of the drive shaft hit the gravel and rebounded to strike the bed of the truck like a big sledge hammer blow. It struck more than a half a dozen times before Harley got the truck stopped. We were lucky the shaft didn't dig into something solid in the road. I think if that had happened it would have totaled us and the truck too. For some reason Harley had no tools in the truck. Pretty unusual for Harley, or any of us. He did, however, have a toy crescent wrench on his key chain. I never would have thought that little wrench would turn a nut. However, it was a good wrench because it was big enough and strong enough to remove the nuts from the rear u-joint which then released the drive shaft. Thanks to that toy crescent wrench we were able to get back to camp on the front half of the four wheel drive.

Tommy and Tadpole

by Glen Dickens

At one time or another we all get called out to take care of wildlife that someone has kept as a pet. Usually these calls are routine. This one was far from that. It is one I will never forget, and has to be one of the strangest.

By now, I expect that Tommy is dead. He was a bum living on the streets or near the railroad in Flagstaff. He had a wild skunk he picked up that he named Tadpole. I don't know which one abused the other more.

In 1981, I was the Habitat Specialist in Flagstaff. Don Randall, a new Wildlife Manager trainee, and I responded to a call from the city's animal-control people about someone with a skunk. Since it was a wild animal, and especially a wild skunk, they did not want anything to do with the problem. When I saw Tommy, I understood why the city folks wanted no part of this man and his pet skunk.

I would guess Tommy was 55 or 60, but he might have been 40. He looked like he had lived a long, rough life. He was small, only about five feet tall, and probably weighed less than a 100 pounds. When I walked up to him, he glared at me with small, sunken blue eyes and told me, "You ain't gonna take Tadpole away from me. I ain't gonna let you. It's not right."

He looked and acted like he had been drinking a lot of cheap wine. He could not stand up very well and swayed back and forth. He wore dirty, greasy clothes. I could not see his pet skunk until he pulled on a chain. The chain looked like it came off a swing set. Out from under his coat came Tadpole. The skunk hung by the neck from the chain. The skunk fought the chain and raised its tail to spray. I could see the muscles under her tail working as she tried to spray. But she was empty. Tadpole has used up all her scent on Tommy over the past few weeks. He reeked. The smell was so bad it was hard for us to stay near.

Tommy and the skunk were chained together. One end was around the skunks neck and the other around Tommy's waist. The two lived like that for three weeks. The skunk lived under Tommy's coat and under his armpit. Every time Tommy wanted to show off his pet he would yank Tadpole out from under his armpit and dangle her in the air for people to see. The chain around the skunks neck had rubbed the neck raw with open wounds. Tommy must have dragged the skunk around also because the claws on her feet were worn to the quick.

Tommy had paid a price for keeping Tadpole. The skunk had bitten him many times. His hand was swollen to twice its normal size and his middle finger was about the size of his wrist. His fingers were all infected with pus draining from them. It looked like Tadpole had been eating Tommy's hands. But Tommy was drunk, and felt nothing.

Skunks are known rabies carriers and there was a good chance that Tommy might be infected. He had to go to the hospital to be treated for his infected hand and checked for rabies. Tadpole had to be checked for rabies too. The trick was to separate the two.

Don and I tried to explain the situation to Tommy. I don't know if Tommy was too drunk to understand or if he was too attached to his new pet. But he would have none of it. "It ain't right, it just ain't right," he said, "she's the only friend I've got in the world and nobody is gonna take her away from me." Then big tears would fall from his eyes.

I don't know if the tears were because of his attachment to Tadpole or from the reeking odor of his pet. I know that I was about to get tears in my eyes, but I knew they were from the aroma that Tadpole had left. I did feel bad for Tommy. I'm sure he had no friends or family and he felt a bond to this skunk. We kept talking to Tommy about how serious the problem was and that he needed to go to the hospital to get treated. We finally convinced him and we even got him to put the skunk into a burlap sack.

Tommy was really sad about losing his pet. He knew what was going to happen. "They are gonna kill poor Tadpole, I know it," he said crying. He even went over to the truck and patted the box Tadpole was in and said good-bye. It was really emotional. We all felt bad for Tommy.

We took Tadpole to get checked. Tommy was right; she was killed for the rabies examination. It proved negative.

Tommy went to the hospital and was treated for his infected hand and was released. He must have left Flagstaff, as no one ever saw him again.

Don and I were glad it was over. We went home for some clean clothes and a shower.

At the Front Counter

by Charlyne O'Connor

My first day with the Department was deadline day for javelina hunt applications. What a day to start a job at the information counter for a hunting and fishing agency! This was the last year the Department manually selected hunters by pulling applications out of a barrel. Now the drawing is done by computer. But deadline day didn't change when the Department went to computer hunt drawings. The gals at the front counter called the application envelopes by their color "passionate pink." Deadline for hunt applications was 5:00 pm sharp! No applications were accepted after that. Louie Melendez, Maintenance Supervisor, would lock the wrought iron gates leading into the office complex and the main door to the front counter. When the gals left the office at five they watched hunters throwing their pink hunt applications through the gates or stuffing them under the door. The late arrivals always had an excuse or a reason why we should accept their envelope. Often wives of hunters would be delivering the applications and the late ones would say, "My husband will kill me if you don't take this application." Others would say, "If I'm not drawn for my big game permit I'm calling my lawyer." Or, "I got caught in traffic and could not get here before five." The morning after deadline day there were always pink envelopes scattered all around the office front door.

Then, as the years passed and the state grew, more hunters applied for permits. It became more and more hectic. The front lobby would be packed with customers and traffic backed up in both directions on Greenway Road. To help solve the traffic problem the Department hired a Phoenix policeman to direct cars in and out of the office. Once during these hectic times, a woman called the office and said she had no idea what Game and Fish did but she had just driven by and knew we were giving something away and whatever it was she wanted her share. After we explained what was happening she changed her mind.

On another deadline day, the policeman was directing traffic into the office parking lot. A woman driving by followed his direction, drove in and parked. She followed the crowd into the lobby and got in the line of waiting customers. When she got to the counter she asked what she should do next. Obviously, she didn't know why she was there and it was really difficult keeping a straight face as I explained the hunt application process to her. I don't know what she was thinking, and I am not sure she ever understood why there was a crowd of people at the office.

The day after the deadline for hunt applications many hunters would call the office asking if they had been drawn for a big game permit. It's hard to believe, but many people thought the Department could do the permit drawing overnight. I guess they thought we just put their application, money and all, in a magic box, or a computer, and out popped a hunt permit.

After the drawing, when the permits had been mailed we began to get calls about replacing missing permits. There are provisions for issuing duplicates for lost or destroyed permits. Some of the reasons the hunters gave were pretty funny. "I'm going through a divorce and my wife cut it up in little pieces." Or, "My dog chewed it up." Or, "My wife put it in the garbage disposal." and "My wife doesn't want me to go hunting so she dumped it in the trash." and "I thought it was bulk mail advertisement so I tossed it." and "My baby got a hold of it and slobbered all over it." Or, "My mother-in-law took it from me."

Another time a gentleman came in for a duplicate tag because he had placed it on the dash of his car, rolled down the window and it flew out. Half an hour later he came back because it happened again on his way home.

When the big game hunts started we got a lot of calls from girlfriends, wives and even employers who wanted to verify if boyfriends, husbands and employees really did have a hunting permit. I guess some people use hunting as an excuse to get out of the house and go somewhere else. I have also heard of lost hunters being found in Las Vegas.

One time a lady called the office and informed us she knew we manufactured "games" for children of all ages, but she wanted to know how the "fish" fit in.

Another lady called and asked if we could get her a copy of her divorce papers. She had forgotten the name of her lawyer and knew that Game and Fish could help her.

We girls at the front counter were usually referred to as, "you guys." Customers would start their conversation by saying: "Did you guys receive my application?" Or, "When are you guys going to stock the lake?" Or, "When are you guys going to fill up the lake?" Or, "When are you guys going to mail the hunt permits?" Or, " I gave you guys my name and address for some info, have you guys mailed it yet?"

At one time, not too many years ago, there was a restaurant located in the south part of Phoenix which oddly enough was named Game and Fish Restaurant. Every morning about eleven we got calls requesting table reservations for four or six. At first we didn't know the restaurant existed and we would explain the hunt drawing process and that no more than four could apply in one application and be sure to use the pink envelope. It didn't take long to figure out it was a restaurant they were calling and they wanted reservations. Unfortunately, the restaurant didn't stay in business long, or maybe they changed their name. The people calling us must have thought we had a strange menu when we explained about elk, bighorn sheep, and javelina applications.

Once I got a call from a gentleman who told me he was blind and could not read. He asked me to read the fishing regulations to him. I began reading to him. After a paragraph or so I heard this soft voice in the phone reading along with me. I stopped and the "blind man" kept on reading. Realizing he was the only one reading the regulations, he stopped and said to me, "Well, I just wanted to see if you would be willing to help me and how much you knew." With that I heard the dial tone in my ear. I guess it takes all kinds, doesn't it?

Hold That Puppy Up!

by Rich Beaudry

Jim Hinkle was the new young Boating Safety Officer working in the Parker area. He spent a lot of time checking boaters and fishermen on the Colorado River. Jim is a long and lanky guy, and in spite of his long arms he quickly learned that you don't bring your patrol boat gunwale to gunwale with another boat, especially in rough water.

Approaching a boat Jim would politely identify himself and ask the boat operator to hold up their fire extinguisher, lifejackets and other safety equipment. If fishermen were onboard he'd take time to check their fishing licence and pass along a couple of fishing tips. Sometimes as Jim pulled along side a boat the operator would not hold the safety equipment up high enough to see. When that happened Jim's favorite expression was, "Hold that puppy up so I can see it."

Once after telling a particular boater a couple of times to hold the safety equipment up high enough for him to see, Jim became a little frustrated. He asked to see a fire extinguisher and the boater kept it too low. "Hold that puppy up!" Jim commanded. The boater bent over, and much to Jim's surprise up came a small fuzzy puppy.

Soon after that incident, Jim changed jobs and became Wildlife Manager in Bagdad, far from any navigable water where he no longer had to ask boaters to "hold that puppy up!"

The Biological Urge

told by anonymous (to protect both parties)

She was one of the Departments first female Wildlife Managers. Sometime in the early 1980s, she was assigned to a desert district in western Arizona . One day she had to drive to a local ranch in response to a radio call from the Department dispatcher. On the way she felt one of those common biological urges. As we all know, out in the desert there are no bathrooms, so she just pulled off the back road and stopped. Taking her gun belt off and leaving it on the truck seat she headed for the bushes. Finding a suitable place she lowered her Levi's and prepared to relieve herself. Just then she noticed a large diamondback rattlesnake only inches from her exposed rear end. Well, this new Wildlife Manager knew enough about snakes to know that any movement could result in a strike from that snake. She also knew that any quick movement with her pants around her ankles was next to impossible. So she froze, remaining perfectly still hoping the snake would go away. It didn't. It stayed for what seemed an eternity. That big diamondback must have liked what it saw because all it did was look. Finally, after a long, long look, it moved on and a "relieved" Wildlife Manager was able to respond to the radio call.

Under the Mule's Belly

by Richard Ockenfels

To be a wildlife research biologist for the Arizona Game and Fish Department requires a Master's Degree from an accredited university, but the work often requires some common sense not learned in college courses. I was a Research Assistant for Al LeCount, the Department's expert bear biologist, during his bear study in the Four Peaks area. I also worked with Jim Wegge, another Research Assistant, who is a consummate field man, a knowledgeable horseman and a person with a dry sense of humor.

On January 10, 1983, Al sent Jim and I into the Four Peaks area to retrieve a radio collar from Lucky, a big old boar bear. Lucky's den was high up on the mountain, so we rode horseback, or rather muleback. Jim was riding his mule Timber and I was mounted on Grady, a mule belonging to Al. Retrieving the radio collar from the bear was no problem. On the return trip, Jim and Timber who were ahead, disappeared from my view. This did not concern me, but it upset Grady.

When my mule lost sight of his buddy, he panicked and bolted down the trail. As he ran, the loose saddle I had been fighting all day rotated under Grady's belly, with my feet still in the stirrups and me in the saddle. Around the bend Grady met Timber and stopped. Hanging upside down I was still with my mule.

As I dropped head first to the ground, Jim asked, "What happened?"

"I guess the saddle was too loose," I replied.

"I could have told you that" was Jim's wry response, knowing something I didn't about checking your cinch before you ride. I learned something that day from a veteran. Smart-aleck college kids don't learn everything about wildlife and the outdoors from books.

One Really Big Dove

by Larry Riley

Shortly after joining the Department in 1983, I got my first taste of working at a dove checking station. I couldn't quite figure out why they wanted a fish squeezer to work at a dove checking station, but being new at the job I was eager to please.

They sent me to the old Hassayampa check station west of Buckeye. I arrived early on opening morning and after a little training by Ron Engle-Wilson, Small Game Supervisor, we began to check the hunters' birds.

A few individuals came through the station with over-limits, and an occasional hunter with an Arizona hunting license and California license plates on their vehicle, and even a bus load of about thirty hunters with all of their birds mixed in a cooler (and one bird too many). But there was one fellow who really stood out in my mind. He came up to the station really proud of his birds. He'd shot a limit of mourning doves and white-wings. I can't remember seeing anyone smiling quite so broadly that morning. He and I set about separating the birds in his bag and counting out the white-wings and mourning doves. The count looked right, but he was particularly proud of one mourning dove - he proclaimed it to be largest mourning dove he'd ever seen, much less ever shot. This man was truly in celebration.

I had to feel a little sorry for him as I explained that it wasn't really a humongous dove but a fairly normal flicker. I even felt sorrier for him when the smile left his face as Law Enforcement Specialist, George Daniels led him aside to explain why he had to write him a citation. I expect, that when he got home, mama wasn't too impressed with his story of the big one that got away!

Who Says Deer are Scared!

by Ron Horejsi

In the winter of 1983/84 a new research project was initiated on the Three Bar Wildlife Area and adjacent Tonto Basin areas. This study was to evaluate mule deer habitat use and the effects of hunting. As part of this study we needed to radio collar 50 individual deer and track them. In order to radio collar deer you must first capture them — naturally! Our capture technique involved a relatively new system using a three barreled net gun to shoot a capture net over the animal from a helicopter. This was our first full fledged attempt and emotions ran from pessimistic to complete confidence in the technique.

Chris Issacs, from Mesa, was our contracted capture technician (gunner), while I rode shotgun up front with the pilot. The first day had gone fairly well and we had captured and collared five or six deer. The second day, however, really clicked and we had just finished collaring our tenth deer. During this time we had observed a large mule deer buck on a ridge top and feeling "Froggy," we decided to make this buck the last capture, a record eleven deer in one day.

We flew to the ridge and immediately spotted the animal and gave chase. Chris was sharp as a tack with the net gun and rapidly shot the net over the bucks head and front legs. At this point the helicopter dropped Chris and myself off to tackle the deer and collar it. The deer, however, had other ideas! The chase had pushed the deer down into a ravine and when Chris and I approached, the buck was still standing and not happy. His back legs were not entangled in the net and he was capable of walking. The buck backed into the brush and with a wild eyed look lowered his antlers to challenge his human tormentors. Brave souls that Chris and I are, we decided a frontal assault was not advisable so we backed off and allowed the buck room to move out of the ravine. At just the right moment I made a full body tackle on the buck with Chris closely behind. The buck was ours. We blindfolded the deer, ear tagged it and attached the radio collar and finally untangled the capture net. The buck was a nice mature deer with 25" spread and 4 point antlers. He was under our control, or so we thought. Having finished our marking we carefully released the deer, pointing him away from us. He regained his footing, and dipping his antlers hooked the capture net and ran up the hill dragging our expensive net. Our pilot, observing what had happened, immediately took flight to keep the deer confined in the brush thicket. Deer are naturally scared of vehicles. RIGHT? WRONG! As Chris and I ran after the buck, we watched as the deer decided enough was enough. With the chopper hovering low, the buck charged the landing skids twice with his antlers, and bowed up facing the helicopter with his hind end pushed into the turbinella oak brush. By this time Chris and I had gotten to the scene but couldn't get at the deer because of the thick brush. The deer was intently watching the chopper with hate in his eyes.

Anticipating the deer would escape with our expensive net, my rational thought dissolved. I made a full length dive over the brush onto the back of the deer with a death grip on each of his antlers. One problem, I only weighed 160 pounds, the buck about 200 pounds and my feet were stretched out behind me. According to the pilot, I resembled a flag waving in a strong wind as the buck proceeded to shake violently in order to rid himself of the large parasite attached to his antlers. Another problem, we were on a steep slope. In his efforts to dislodge me, the buck stumbled and I went through his antlers still keeping my death grip. We rolled about fifty feet down the hill finally coming to a halt. I still had my death grip on the antlers and was bear hugging the deer underneath me with my legs. To my amazement I saw a pair of boots, toes pointing up, protruding around the deers muzzle. Chris had gotten ahold of the deer on our tumble down the hill, and was laying underneath the deer while I was on top. We finally managed to remove the net and set the deer free.

I wish there had been a video camera on board the chopper; we put the National Football League tackles to shame. Some sore muscles, bruises and brush scratches were the only damages accrued by the human combatants. The buck eventually succumbed to a mountain lion about a year later.

Leave the Editing to the Editor

by Paul Webb

In the early days of a Game Department employee's career, making friends with a good editor is valuable, especially when your writing needs correction in grammar, punctuation and sentence structure. As time passes you may not need much editing; you might even be asked to assist others who need help. But, it never hurts to have someone review your work, no matter how good a writer you become.

Just such a valuable editor existed in the days when Game Department personnel started attending more and more regional and national meetings to present their research findings. This biologist gave freely of his editorial time and helped many to deliver a clearer, more lucid paper to their peers.

As time passed, the editor advanced to positions of greater and greater responsibility. And it seemed, his editing became more and more precise. From a simple editing job of crossing "t's" and dotting "i's" and suggestions on how to clarify sentences, he progressed to practically rewriting other's work, eliminating the style of the "editee." His comments in the margins became terse.

At the top of his career the editor took a position that directed the activities of several supervisors. On an annual basis, one of the supervisors had to present the Department's recommendations for new hunting regulations and hunt permit numbers to the Commission for their approval. Before the supervisor's presentation, however, the editor gave a synopsis of Department activities that led to the proposed recommendations.

The editor asked the supervisor to write the synopsis. The supervisor did so, getting the long manuscript typed neatly and double spaced before handing the copy to the editor. Several days would pass before the synopsis was returned. Completely astounded, the supervisor stared at the copy. Every sentence had been changed, words crossed out, and new punctuation entered. Oh well, the supervisor reasoned, it was the editor's synopsis, not his. He dutifully had it retyped and returned to the editor.

A year went by and preparations were being made for the annual Commission event. The editor again asked for a synopsis, which the supervisor wrote. The results were the same. The synopsis was returned completely changed, with every sentence altered, words crossed out and new punctuation entered.

The third year came. Again, preparations were made for the annual season setting Commission meeting. Again a request was made for a synopsis. But, by this time the supervisor was gun shy. He took last years edited synopsis and changed only the numbers, leaving the sentence structure and punctuation intact, and gave it to the editor.

Several days later the synopsis was returned to the supervisor. With considerable glee, the supervisor stared at the copy where every sentence had been changed, words crossed out and new punctuation entered. The editor had "mega-edited" his own words!

The Arizona Tuna

by Linn Montgomery

Upon returning from a trip early in the 1980s, I discovered that a gigantic, stuffed, bluefin tuna had been placed across my doorstep by a well-meaning student. Despite its dilapidated appearance and the fact that some unfeeling individual had painted it white, the tuna became a centerpiece for conversation. Unfortunately, as it was roughly seven feet long and weighed well over 100 pounds, it was soon placed out of sight and out of mind.

I had known Bruce Taubert, then the Chief of Fisheries, prior to my appointment to the Commission, but we became better friends during my Commission days. At one point, it became clear that Bruce really deserved to have the tuna, so I loaded it into my pickup and set off to a Commission meeting in Phoenix. My intent was to sneak to Taubert's house during the night and leave the fish for him as it had been left for me.

This plan was derailed when we discovered that following the Friday portion of the Commission meeting there was to be a reception at Director Bud Bristow's home in honor of his wedding. The event had been kept secret, in part because Bud had not wished to attract the usual collection of gifts and wished merely to share his happiness and good fortune with his friends. Fred Baker, another Commissioner, and I, with the general agreement of the Commission, felt that we could not let the event go unheralded, and we knew that Bud would surely appreciate receiving the tuna.

During the reception late that evening, when most participants were mildly stuporous, Baker and I snuck to my truck and hauled the tuna into Bud's back yard. Knowing that he would be embarrassed by such an obvious and valuable gift, we felt it best to sneak the treasure into his bedroom through the window, so that he and his bride could share the excitement of the gift as they retired for the night. Through much sneaking about, we finally managed to dissect the window which was too small for the tuna. We had to remove the screen and one pane of glass entirely before we could drag the fish inside. Not having wrapping paper, we simply tucked the lovely mount into Bud's waterbed.

The next day, Director Bristow appeared more than a little weary. As you might imagine, he thanked us profusely for the gift, noting that it had taken him and his wife roughly an hour to wrestle the tuna from the bed to the back yard so that they could finally retire, and remarked how fortunate we all were that the spines and other fish parts had not punctured his waterbed. The Commissioners were delighted that they could bring such happiness to the newlyweds, and it only took two to three weeks for our cuts, scrapes and Baker's aggravated vertebral disc pain to disappear.

Don't Kill the Collars

by Richard Ockenfels

It is well known that wildlife researchers pride themselves on attention to detail. Research Biologist Ron Horejsi was no exception to this rule. In 1984, Ron was conducting mule deer research at the Department's Three Bar Wildlife Area just west of Roosevelt Lake. In the study area, a one square mile deer and predator proof fenced enclosure was built by the Department in 1971 to determine the effects of predators on the mule deer population.

Ron's study involved deer population dynamics on the Three Bar and adjacent areas of the Tonto National Forest. It also included the square mile fenced area. Inside the enclosure the deer population had increased beyond what the area could support and Ron felt is was necessary to reduce the herd.

Ron developed a detailed plan to harvest seventeen deer within the enclosure. The deer were to be removed at random. The rules of this reduction are simple, as Ron explained: "First deer seen, first deer killed." However, there were two deer he did not want killed. One was a radio collared, three by three antlered buck that Ron and Research Assistant Norris Dodd captured for the enclosure in 1982. Ron explained that it had a radio collar and a red ear tag and should be easy to spot. The second deer was an old doe with a bell collar which had survived in the enclosure since its original capture in 1971. Biological samples would be collected for genetic testing and other factors of interest and the carcasses would be donated to charities in Payson and Phoenix.

Ron, a certified gun nut, assembled a crack team of Research Assistants. Jim Wegge, another gun nut, was riding his mule Timber and was armed with a .375 rifle. Hyper-active Norris Dodd, who wouldn't let himself be left out of anything, was riding a little Research Branch horse named Babe, and was armed with a 30-06 rifle. Ron was riding the Branch's big stout horse Buck, and was armed with his huge .458 Winchester. I was to ride if there was an extra horse or be on foot. Certainly, this team of excellent hunters and crack shots could slay the mighty beasts as detailed and save the genetics of the deer herd in the enclosure. Science and firepower is a strong combination!

The day came, January 25, Ron, Jim and I rode into Walnut Canyon. Jumping a herd of deer near Walnut Springs, I dropped a small buck at 300 yards. Out sprang a second buck across the canyon to the south, and Ron opened up with his big-bore rifle. The mighty .458 wasn't enough, and soon Wegge was galloping after the wounded deer. Jim finished it off and guess what? It was one of the deer Ron wanted saved. Ron had randomly shot his first deer, the radio collared deer with the red ear tag.

Now, you ask, did the old "belled doe" survive the carnage? Thirteen years in the enclosure and she too fell to the theory of randomness. For on the next day, Norris drove a herd of deer out of Spike Canyon into Capture Canyon, and I dropped the lead deer; first seen, first killed, the doe. For thirteen years she made a good leader.

Armed as if for a hunt in Africa, the crack team of hunters soon got the seventeen deer as planned, but we also had a radio collar, a red ear tag and an old rusty bell.

Oh No! It's My Wife!

by Rich Beaudry

Tim Wade's promotion to Boating Coordinator in the Law Enforcement Branch required him to patrol Lake Havasu during Easter weekend. This is the busiest weekend on the lake and the Department always provides extra help for the local officers. Being a family man, he took his wife and daughter along for a little rest and relaxation away from Phoenix. Some of his family friends also came along. They planned to visit the many stores along the London Bridge Channel and see the sights while Tim went on patrol with Game and Fish officers.

Tim was riding with me in my patrol boat. After a full day on the lake Tim asked me to take him to the infamous Copper Canyon cove of Lake Havasu. For people who have not been to Lake Havasu, Copper Canyon is the place to party and play. On holiday weekends, several hundred boats with a couple thousand occupants will crowd into this narrow bay to drink, play loud music, swim and jump off cliffs. Some sun worshippers get so in the spirit of things they jump right out of their swimsuits. Nudity is not uncommon and bare breasts seem to be the norm.

As we pulled into the northern edge of the cove we noticed a few members of the opposite sex who obviously were concealing nothing. This was a new experience for Tim and he was asking questions about Copper Canyon and making comments about what he was seeing. Our attention was drawn to a pontoon boat that was leaving the area and heading directly toward us. Tim began to make a comment about the boat having only women aboard. He stopped in mid-sentence and loudly exclaimed, "Oh no, that's my wife!"

It seems that Tim's wife and friends had heard the stories about Copper Canyon and they rented a boat to see for themselves if the stories were true. They are!

The Bullets

by Linn Montgomery

In retrospect, it is clear that the Commission on which I served caused many headaches for Department personnel, yet we all numbered many of the Department employees among our friends. Practical jokes were not rare. One, I remember, arose from the good natured ribbing that Deputy Director Roger Gruenewald took when he arrived at a hunting camp with other Department members, fully equipped except for a minor omission - he had forgotten the shells for his rifle.

During the next Commission meeting, with knowledge of most of the Commission, I told a sad tale of an unidentified member of the Department who had fallen on hard times. The story unfolded slowly, with the suggestion that we take up a collection for this poor individual to help him through this difficult period. Serious looks abounded among the Commissioners, Department personnel and the audience, with wallets and purses appearing from everywhere. Seeing that this would soon get out of hand, and moments before he dropped his own ample contribution into the hat we were passing, I finally announced that the gifts were to go to Roger, so that he might afford shells for his next hunting trip. The house came down, of course, with Roger laughing as loudly as anyone.

Actually, I have always been sorry for three aspects of that prank. First, I always wondered whether I had gone too far in embarrassing Roger in a public forum (I was not known for my care in thinking certain statements or practices through before acting ...). Second, since the meeting was heavily attended by animal rights folks and many of these had dug into their wallets for contributions, I wonder whether I should not have let the hat go a bit further before exposing the ruse (the Department has always found it hard to obtain financial support from the not-consumptive public, despite the many services provided for them). And last, I wonder what the animal rights folks would have done had they known the money was to buy bullets for Roger's rifle.

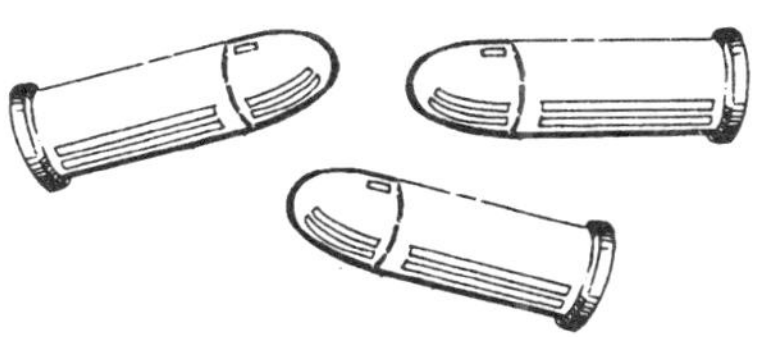

Headache Time

by Richard Ockenfels

Wildlife researchers are always looking for new ways to make their jobs better or easier. Capturing wild animals has always been difficult, and unfortunately, sometimes results in the death of the animal. In the mid-1980s, Cory Gray, an inventor, developed a new method of capturing animals with a net shot from a gun.

Trying to interest the Department in his new invention, Cory set up a demonstration of the new capture gun through Research Supervisor Ron Smith. The empty lot behind the office complex on Greenway Road was used for the demonstration. There were a number of people watching. Cory's invention was an unstocked, three barreled gun that fired a small net weighted at three corners. The corner weights were inserted into the three barrels and propelled when fired by a blank .308 cartridge.

I was the designated animal. Actually, I was throwing softballs and the shooter would try to catch them in the air with the net. Cory was the first shooter. He had a lot of practice and was fairly successful in catching the softballs while still in the air with the net.

Ron Smith soon stepped up to try. Unfortunately for Ron, a tall slender, gentle man of intellectual prowess, not known for his physical strength, I threw the ball too high. Ron instinctively followed like a good wing shooter and fired, but he failed to lock his left arm to hold down the recoil of the un-stocked net gun. This recoil from the .308 blank drove the barrels up and back, bouncing them off Ron's forehead. It was a clean between the eyes knockdown punch. I saw Ron's knees buckle as he fell to the ground.

We took time out for a quick trip down the road to the Greenway Emergency Medical Room for Ron's stitches. When we returned for more practice with the net gun I threw more softballs, but boss or no boss, we wouldn't let Ron take another shot!

Power of the Press

by Linn Montgomery

A few short months after I joined the Commission, we had a very long and difficult meeting in Pinetop. The meeting lasted two full days, and toward the end of the second day we had to deal with potential budget cuts. Central to this issue was the problem of possible layoffs of Department personnel, and we were seeking ways to avoid such actions. Parts of the discussion were heated and probably lengthened by the fact that both Larry Adams and I were new to the Commission. Hence, we were being educated while more knowledgeable Commissioners were dealing with the issues. Larry, as always, had some very strong feelings about what was going on, and he stated those feelings clearly and vigorously on several occasions.

As the evening wore on, virtually all attendees outside of the Commission and a few Department personnel departed. One who did not was Bob Thomas, the outdoor writer for a Phoenix newspaper, who sat directly in front of me. We were all very weary, hungry and a bit cranky, and Thomas slumped down in his chair and nodded off, not writing anything in his little notebook for well over an hour. At one point, Frances Werner took issue with one proposal for action, stating that the Legislature would probably not be happy with that action. I responded with a grumpy, "To hell with the Legislature, our job is to do the best we can for the Department!" Thomas immediately woke up and scribbled a short phrase in his notebook. I had little doubt about what he had written, but was naive enough at that time to believe that if he used the quote he would do so only in the context it was intended.

As you might expect, there were consequences for the freshman Commissioner. The next day, Thomas' column reported on the meeting and commented particularly on the two new Commissioners. Adams was described as a sensible individual who quietly stated his well-reasoned position on the issues. I was described as a quite different type of person who at one point hollered, "To hell with the Legislature!" A few weeks later, I had to try to explain to Senator John Hays, one of the Department's strongest supporters in the Legislature, what my outburst was all about. While that was uncomfortable, it didn't match the suggestion by a senior Northern Arizona University official the Monday after Thomas' article appeared. Knowing that I had been on the University faculty only a couple of years, he suggested that perhaps

I could look forward to a long career as the sole NAU faculty member assigned to a small Arizona town far from Flagstaff and somewhat distant from most amenities.

Wegge, the Cossack

by Ron Horejsi

In the mid 1980s, Jim Wegge was assisting Al LeCount on the black bear study in Unit 22, north of Payson, just below the Mogollon Rim. Larry Peterson and I were working with Jim one day riding horseback along a bear snare line from Tonto Creek Hatchery to the east Verde River. It was a warm lazy day, and the trapping had not been good. Jim was on his new mule, Timber, and I rode my horse, Buck, as we headed back toward the trucks. In our discussions as we rode, the subject of guns and horses was brought up. Nothing unusual here, guns and horses are a common topic. As we rested, Jim commented about how Timber would react to a gun being fired around him. I was carrying my .357 Smith & Wesson and handed it to Jim to let him fire off a round. We were dismounted and Jim, holding Timbers reins, shot my gun. Timber jumped a little but all-in-all handled the discharge rather well.

Jim mounted up and said, "I wonder how he will do if I shoot from the saddle?" WRONG! At the detonation, Timber reared up, spun and took off at full speed. In doing so Timber ran over my horse who also bolted and galloped off. Jim was still mounted, at least to some degree. Watching, I saw Timber heading down the trail with Jim impersonating a Cossack horseman who was trying to pick a white handkerchief off the ground with his teeth.

As Jim leaned farther and farther out of the saddle, I could tell this was not an intentional act. The horsemanship display ended abruptly in a large cloud of gray dust with the steeds continuing on. As I reached Jim, a slate gray figure emerged from the dust cloud; clothes, face and boots all dusted. "I guess Timber didn't like that!" or comments similar to this were uttered by the slate gray image. Larry had managed to control his steed and finally retrieved our mounts. I haven't tried shooting from a horse since then. Have you, Jim?

Bow Ties and Jock Straps

by Larry Riley

Once upon a time, not too terribly long ago, I was a Planner (read — untouchable - and to some others - the scum of the earth). It was not the best of times; it was not the worst of times. It was the time we got a new Director — Temp Reynolds was his name.

Just prior to Director Reynolds beginning his tenure, the planners started working on planning for the agency instead of concentrating on species plans. We had just learned all there was to learn about comprehensive planning and MBO (an old Hopi word for Bull ——).

The planners were John Carr, Rick Miller and myself - an odd lot by anyone's standards. Odd though we were, we were a group to be reckoned with! We had laid elaborate plans for the future of Arizona Game and Fish at the behest of the outgoing Director and the Commission. Those folks were really serious about finding other ways to pay for wildlife management, and had sent us on a serious fishing expedition (I had to get fish in the story somehow).

By the time Temp arrived we were really in over our heads, and we had scrapped our old accounting system in favor of a brand new one under development. Things were serious because in the interim we really didn't have an accounting system - a very scary situation for accountants. We had to keep our chief accountant Randy King medicated most of the time! Between trying to keep Randy strapped into his white jacket and Data Branch Supervisor Pete Edgar from leaping off the roof at Deer Valley, we really had our hands full. Now we had a new Director to control.

Well, after Temp had been with us about a month or so we figured we ought to go in and explain to him what a great idea this comprehensive planning stuff was, and how it was all his idea. (For some reason, Directors feel better when they think things are their ideas). We scheduled a meeting through Roger Gruenewald, the Deputy Director. If you recollect Roger the ruthless, then you know that getting this meeting was no small feat! Roger came into the office and announced that we'd meet the next day at 10 in the morning, and that we'd better be there with "bow ties and jock straps." That was Roger's quaint way of suggesting we'd best be prepared.

Being a serious lot of planners, we arrived at the Director's office promptly at ten as Roger had requested, each one of us sporting a bow tie. They were left over from the time I was a first grader at Catholic school. We wouldn't let Roger check on the jock straps, though I'm sure he was suspicious!

Hoping that the bow tie chuckle would break the ice, we were escorted into Temp's office and seated before THE DESK - John, Rick and me.

We went through the process of explaining what the planners were doing for the Department, but there were only three things I remember about that fateful meeting:

1. Wearing a bow tie.

2. Being seated behind the god-awful feathered lamp that Temp's desk sported, and straining to see around it.

3. Temp's ironic and fateful admonition at the end of the meeting — "Well boys, I hope it works. In case it doesn't, don't invest in any major appliances."

Two Minutes, Two Minutes

by John N. Carr

The National Basketball Association and the National Football League have a two minute warning in their games. In basketball, the public address announcer gives the notice, "Two minutes, two minutes," and in football, there is a scheduled time out. This story is about our two minute warning.

When Temp Reynolds was Director of the Department in the late 1980s, he wanted to develop a Department plan with goals and objectives. While we did have Strategic Plans for various wildlife species, Temp wanted plans that were focused on the agency's activities. The task was assigned to the Planning and Evaluation Branch, which I supervised. I had two very capable wildlife planners working for me, Rick Miller and Larry Riley. With their hard work we completed the plan as desired by the Director.

It got quite complicated at times. We decided to start by creating a Department team composed of a wide variety of people who questioned and discussed future agency needs. This team was named "The

Prescott Ten" because we met for two days in the Prescott National Forest Service office. We did this to concentrate on the issues, away from Department telephones and interruptions. We followed up with a small pamphlet called "Wildlife for Tomorrow," that included a survey asking opinions about questions we had raised. This survey was sent to all Department employees, to conservation clubs, rod and gun clubs, livestock organizations and to a segment of the general public. We even hired a private professional polling organization to test and verify our questionnaire and the results.

When we got enough information together, we went on the road with our "dog and pony show" to talk with groups and get input from them. Rick, Larry and I probably talked with more than 40 organizations in Arizona, including the Arizona Wildlife Federation, various rod and gun clubs, Sierra Club, Audubon Society, four wheel drive clubs, and the Arizona Cattle Growers. We were well received by almost everyone. We told them the results of our surveys and wanted their input to complete our project. In the end, we established the goals and objectives that Director Reynolds wanted and which the Commission adopted.

One of our meetings had an unexpected ending. We were talking to a four wheel drive club at a meeting in a back room of Max's Sports Bar in Glendale. We usually took turns with the program. One of us would do the introduction, one would give the slide show with the data and discuss the details and take questions, and one would be the note taker. On this occasion, I gave the introduction, Rick was the note taker and Larry gave the presentation. Everything was going well until Larry got to the discussion about how the Department should react to environmental issues and what some of these issues were. Larry talked about gravel pit operators and their bad reputation for destroying valuable wildlife habitat along riparian water ways. At that moment, it became clear to everyone in the room that the president of the club was becoming agitated with our presentation. In short order he stood up and said, "Gentlemen, you have two minutes to complete your program, and then I want you out of here!"

The man sitting next to me leaned over and asked if I knew who the president was. I said, "No, who is he?" I was told he was vice-president of one of the largest sand and gravel operation in Arizona.

Well, we sure hit the wrong button at that meeting, and in two minutes we were out of there with all of our equipment. We did not get any of the feedback we were looking for except to know that at least one person did not agree with what Larry had said.

We packed all our equipment in the sedan and started to leave. But it was early, so we decided to go back in Max's, have a beer and watch a ball game on TV.

Climb the Burning Tree

by Larry Riley and Richard Ockenfels

There was the occasion of the big elk workshop at the U. S. Forest Service Chevelon Work Station. Elk management and elk depredation were becoming a really hot issue, and for some reason, some nut in the Director's Office thought Rick Miller and Larry ought to facilitate this workshop. Well, the two of them did the best they could and only made a few dozen enemies in the process, so I guess they were moderately successful. But this story isn't about the workshop, it's about the evening's festivities at the Department's Vincent Ranch.

It had been a particularly difficult day, and most of the participants were enjoying a few libations during the evening hours. I couldn't begin to list all of the faces around the campfire that night, but I do remember a few striking personalities who emerged from the crowd.

It seemed that there was a snag in the meadow that someone decided needed to be burned, so we commenced to build the evening's campfire around the base of this old tree. As the evening progressed and more and more libations were imbibed, some of the more rugged characters emerged to dominate the evening's entertainment.

Tim Baumgarten, Wildlife Manager from Tusayan, met the challenge to be King of the Hill climbing the snag above the flames and dared others to follow! Next was Lee Luedeker, a Wildlife Manager from Region II. Those who know Lee agree he's the strong silent type. To prove this Lee leapt from the crowd, grabbed ahold of the burning snag, and began climbing to the top. After the crowd demonstrated their admiration for Lee's skill and lack of common sense, he returned to earth.

Now Lee was bad enough, but there were others in the crowd that simply couldn't let the feat go unchallenged. Sam Lawry, a Wildlife Manager from Region I, had to demonstrate his bravado and leapt up to repeat the challenge. Again the crowd cheered their approval and Sam returned to earth unscathed.

Type A personalities couldn't just stand by, so Wildlife Management Division Chief Bruce Taubert, with proper encouragement jumped into the growing flames and pulled himself hand over hand to the top. By now flames were up high and wisdom was starting to overcome hormonal influence.

I was thinking that the exciting part of the evening's entertainment had come to an end, but apparently there was another in the crowd that needed to demonstrate his masculinity. The crowd parted as he approached the fire, obviously out of respect for the individual's courage and disregard for personal safety. He leapt over the flames, grabbed the snag, and climbed like a bear cub to the top of the burning tree. Bob Barsch, a new Wildlife Manager in Region II, was not as monkey-like as the doubled jointed Lee nor as strong as the ex-ASU footballer Tim, but the Texas Aggie was willing to prove his manhood. When Bob reached the apex, I am sure he expected to be greeted by the crowd's admiration. Unfortunately, his past job history with the Department; as a planner (read: untouchable, and to others, the scum of the earth), legislative liaison (read charlatan), and personnel manager (read son-of-a———) had caught up with him.

It's impressive how many sparks can fly when 40 or 50 boots kick smoldering logs in the fire. Even more impressive is the way old Bob clung to that burning pole as it began to sway back and forth through an arc of about 60 degrees!

I never knew exactly how Bob got down from the top of that snag. I think he may have still been there when I went off to bed, but by the next morning I knew he was safe when I heard that irritating, extended Texas drawl going 10-8 on the radio for the trip back home.

The Tiger

by Russell Haughey

At 4:30 pm, November, 5, 1990, I got a frantic call from the dispatcher, Janie Brown. Phoenix Police had called saying a tiger was loose at a resort hotel near South Mountain and it had bitten someone. I quickly headed there. On the radio, I heard that Wildlife Manager Kevin Bergersen was also heading that way. Because it was rush hour, traffic on the freeway was moving slowly. At one point traffic slowed to a standstill so I used my lights to travel down the shoulder and off the exit ramp.

As I approached the resort I was going over in my mind what to do. Should I shoot it? Would my .357 even stop a 400 pound Bengal tiger? Although I expected bedlam when I arrived, things were calm. Kevin arrived shortly after I did and we were disappointed we had missed the excitement. The tiger had indeed bitten someone, but it was now in its trailer cage. We started to piece together what had happened.

The resort was hosting a computer software trade show. One particular CEO was to be the subject of a roast at the evening banquet. This gentleman apparently was an aggressive, upwardly mobile executive who used a tiger symbol as his personal trademark. He thought he would make a grand entrance at the banquet by walking in with a tiger on a leash. He hired an animal trainer from Minnesota to bring "Sarang," a female tiger, to the resort.

For obvious reasons, possession of animals such as tigers is restricted in Arizona. However, Department rules make allowances for traveling entertainers like this tiger trainer. There are some restrictions, such as keeping the animal from direct public contact, and under control at all times. This trainer ignored these two rules.

Before the banquet, the trainer walked the tiger up and down the aisles of the banquet room to become familiar with the setting. Finishing the orientation the trainer had the tiger lay down in the patio among the executives who were sipping wine and drinks. The setting seemed oddly inappropriate for what was about to happen.

The guests were impressed with the beauty and size of the 400 pound Bengal tiger. A woman who loved cats, was especially fascinated by Sarang. She told the trainer he had a beautiful cat and asked if she could pet it. The trainer said yes. As she patted the tiger's head, it suddenly bit her lower leg. She screamed, and so did everyone in the patio area. People jumped from their seats and moved away from the tiger. The commotion scared the tiger, and it held tight to the woman's leg. The trainer tried to make the cat let go by hitting it on the head with the leash. Someone hit the cat on the head with a camera tripod, and someone else used a chair. This only scared the cat more. The woman yelled to stop hitting the tiger because that only made it bite harder. Two men grabbed the woman and tried to pull her from Sarang's jaws. Each time they pulled, the tiger clamped down tighter. The tiger was so scared, nothing seemed to work. It reverted to its innate predator instincts, holding on to its prey.

The cat began to back away from the people and commotion, dragging the now pale and petrified woman. There was no way the 175 pound trainer could control a scared 400 pound tiger with his leash. The tiger dragged the woman about 30 feet into a corner of the patio. Finally, a waitress had the presence of mind to jam a broom handle down the tiger's throat, making it release the woman's leg. Then the trainer was able to calm the tiger and put it in the cage. The woman was in shock. The resort employees immediately gave the woman first aid.

In the mean time, the resort had notified the Phoenix Police that a tiger was loose and had attacked someone. They immediately responded with 15 police cars and a helicopter. There were cops everywhere. Paramedics arrived and took the victim to the hospital. This was about the time Kevin and I arrived.

Kevin and I wisely declined to seize the animal, but cited the trainer for failure to control his tiger. Incredibly, the judge only fined the trainer $250. He was glad to pay and get out of town. The U. S. Department of Agriculture, which regulates animal trainers, later revoked his license.

I interviewed the victim in the hospital two days later. She showed me the bite; the wound was draining, there were two large inch-wide punctures about five inches apart on either side of her calf and various lacerations. The fibula was punctured and broken. The woman told me she had always been proud of the shape of her calves, but was worried one wouldn't be so pretty now. I thought, "What a conversation starter. I'll bet the settlement is substantial."

Several years later a woman called the office requesting a permit to import a tiger cub so she could keep it at her home. I couldn't believe how naive she was. I told her this story. She didn't sound as enthusiastic about owning a tiger when she hung up the phone.

Lucky Day

by Richard Ockenfels

If ever a person had a lucky day in the field, surely it happened on August 20, 1990. As a Research Biologist studying pronghorn mortality in the Dugas area, I had placed a number of radio collars that transmitted a special signal when a pronghorn was still for a few hours. This transmission indicated that the animal had died. We could then locate it using the radio signal and then determine the cause of death. On this day, I was in the Dugas area following a radio signal to investigate a possible pronghorn mortality. Along with me was newly hired Wildlife Assistant, Jim Kirkland, a mid-thirties cowboy type from Arkansas, and new to the wildlife profession. As we hiked on Marlow Mesa toward the rapidly pulsing radio signal, I showed Jim the whys and wheres of radio tracking

As we moved into a brushy area, Jim had the ear phones on and noted the signal was getting louder. Suspecting mountain lion predation, I started to check out thickets of scrub oak and skunk bush . Hearing a twig snap I foolishly stepped into the thicket on my left. Something moved, and behold, I was much closer to a mountain lion than I wanted to be. I jumped one way and the lion the other. Its fluid form loped across the opening less that ten feet from me and past Jim. Our eyes were wide open in amazement. Things happened too fast to get the camera out of the pack.

Surviving our initial meeting, I quickly headed after what I judged to be a female lion. From the rock outcrop ledge, a quick scan of the area revealed nothing until I looked down. Two cold eyes met mine, and the lion leaped straight up, twisted and dropped over some scrub oak and slowly walked away. I got the camera up for two quick, poorly focused shots. Just then, Jim walked up saying he had found the dead pronghorn, an old buck. Trying to show Jim the lion, I pointed toward where it ran, but we saw nothing. Another movement in the canyon below caught my eye.

Using binoculars Jim and I saw a black bear ambling down the drainage among the many rocks. Imagine that, Jim's first day afield on a new job, and he sees a mountain lion and a black bear. And me, twice face to face with a lion over its kill and still in one piece. Just say it was our lucky day!

My Song

by Mary Reed

I remember my retirement party with fond memories. I never had a party like that before and it was very special. It was just for me. A lot of Department employees were there, even the big bosses. It was at Monti's on 19th Avenue. What I remember most was a song that Cheryl Barnes wrote and sang for me. Cheryl worked with me in the Deer Valley South office and she was a very talented lady. I have a tape of the song and it still moves me when I hear it. Because it fits anyone that has retired from Game and Fish, I wanted to share it. It has no title, maybe we could call it . . .

"Hope You Will Miss Us When You're Gone"

Well I hope you're gonna miss us just a little while you're gone
And I trust you've packed good memories of us to take along.
May every mile you travel be a story you can tell
And I hope that your retirement treats you well.

We all agree on one thing and for your happiness we wish
And hope you plan to keep in touch with us at Game and Fish.
You'll always be like family and we all think you're swell
And hope that your retirement treats you well.

No more getting up at dawn
And working til the day is gone.
Sit back, relax, enjoy yourself
Go out and have some fun.

Though someone else will take your job,
they'll never take your place
And we'll have to grow accustomed to somebody else's face.
May time be always on your side — do things
you've always wanted to do
And I hope that your retiring is good for you.

Map of Arizona

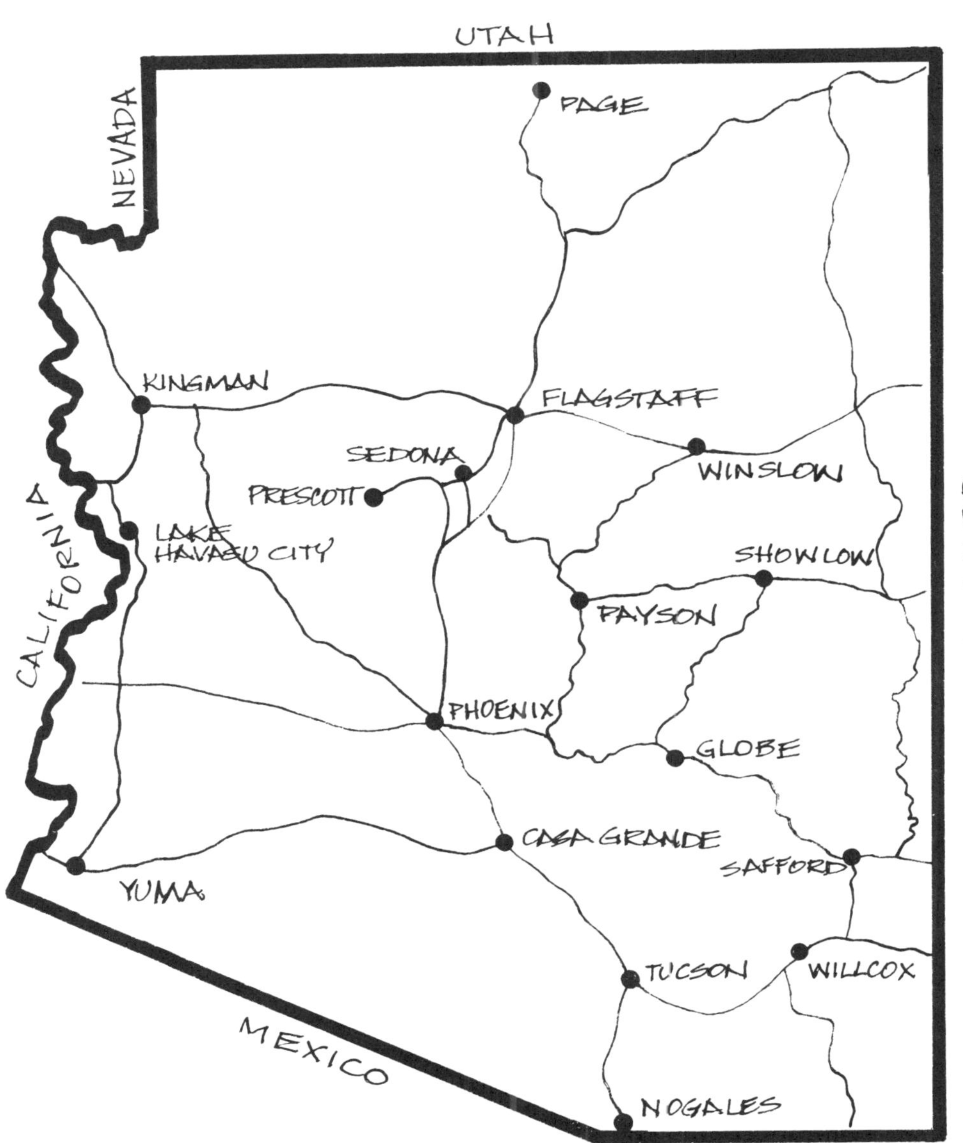

1954
LICENSE AND PERMIT FEES

RESIDENT HUNTING LICENSES

Class	Description	Fee
Class "J"	Combination General Fishing & Hunting	$ 7.00
Class "J"	(Pioneer) General Fishing & Hunting	No. chg.
Class "F"	General Hunting License	4.00
Class "I"	Deer Permit & Seal (Hunting lic. required)	1.00
Class "P"	Turkey Permit & Seal (Hunting lic. required)	.50
Class "T"	Javelina License & Seal	1.00
Class "L"	Elk License & Seal	15.00
Class "N"	Antelope License & Seal	10.00
Class "R"	Bighorn License & Seal	50.00
Class "X"	Guide License	10.00
Class "Z-1"	Trapper's License	1.00

Bear may be taken by any resident possessing a valid hunting license or valid elk license.

NONRESIDENT HUNTING LICENSES

Class	Description	Fee
Class "H"	Small Game Hunting License	20.00
Class "K"	Deer License & Seal	50.00
Class "Q"	Turkey License & Seal	10.00
Class "U"	Javelina License & Seal	5.00
Class "M"	Elk License & Seal	75.00
Class "O"	Antelope License & Seal	50.00
Class "S"	Bighorn License & Seal	150.00
Class "Z-4"	Bear License (No Seal Required)	10.00
Class "Z"	Trapper's License	100.00

MISCELLANEOUS

Class	Description	Fee
Class "Z-2"	Taxidermist License	10.00
Class "Z-3"	Fur Dealer's License	10.00
Class "Z-7"	Alien Big Game Hunting License & Seal (each species)	100.00
Class "Z-8"	Alien Small Game Hunting License	25.00

SERVICE PERSONNEL: (Issued only to service personnel on active duty and stationed in Arizona).
FISH AND SMALL GAME ONLY
CLASS "Z-6" 7.00

Hunting fees in Arizona have gone up just a little in the last forty years! But then, Arizona is not alone in that respect!

1994
LICENSE AND PERMIT FEES

RESIDENT HUNTING LICENSES

License / Permit	Fee
Class F, combination hunt & fish	$34.00
Class F, youth combination hunt & fish	25.00
Class G, general hunting license	18.00
Duplicate Fee	3.00
Deer Permit-tag	17.50
Deer Permit-tag (Kaibab)	22.50
Antelope Permit-tag	53.00
Elk Permit-tag	63.00
Turkey Permit-tag	11.50
Javelina Permit-tag	12.50
Bighorn Sheep Permit-tag	153.00
Buffalo - Bull Permit-tag	753.00
Buffalo - Cow Permit-tag	453.00
Buffalo - Yearling Permit-tag	243.00
Spring Bear Permit-tag	14.00
Bear Tag	11.00
Lion Tag	11.00
Sandhill Crane (2 tags)	13.00

NONRESIDENT HUNTING LICENSES AND FEES

License / Permit	Fee
Class F, combination hunt & fish	$137.50
Class G, general hunting license	85.50
Class H, three day license (small game)	38.00
Deer Permit-tag	78.50
Deer Permit-tag (Kaibab)	83.50
Antelope Permit-tag	253.00
Elk Permit-tag	303.00
Turkey Permit-tag	53.50
Javelina Permit-tag	53.50
Bighorn Sheep Permit-tag	753.00
Buffalo Bull Permit-tag	3,753.00
Buffalo Cow Permit-tag	2,253.00
Buffalo Yearling Permit-tag	1,203.00
Spring Bear Permit-tag	153.00
Bear Tag	150.00
Lion Tag	150.00
Sandhill Crane (2 tags)	13.00

About the Author

John Carr grew up on a ranch near Sonoita, Arizona, and moved to Tucson in 1944. After graduating from high school he spent 16 long months in Korea, compliments of the U. S. Army. Returning to Tucson, he graduated in 1961 from the University of Arizona with a B. S. in Wildlife Management. After graduation, he began his career with Arizona Game and Fish Department as a Wildlife Manager, spending seven years in the Sonoita-Patagonia area. Those years in the field with the wildlife were his most enjoyable. He moved to Phoenix in 1968 and worked as a Game Biologist, a Wildlife Planner, and a Supervisor. The year he spent as Chief of Special Services was his worst and he wouldn't wish that on anyone. He retired from the Department in 1989, but worked part-time for two more years under a special contract.

After retirement he authored the *Arizona Wildlife Viewing Guide*. Today he enjoys traveling, and visiting with his four children and grandchildren. He still enjoys being out of doors, especially during quail season. Woodworking and turning mesquite bowls occupy his spare time.